Santa Claus, Last of the Wild Men

Santa Claus, Last of the Wild Men

*The Origins and Evolution
of Saint Nicholas,
Spanning 50,000 Years*

PHYLLIS SIEFKER

McFarland & Company, Inc., Publishers
Jefferson, North Carolina, and London

LIBRARY OF CONGRESS CATALOGUING-IN-PUBLICATION DATA

Siefker, Phyllis.
    Santa Claus, last of the wild men : the origins and evolution of Saint Nicholas, spanning 50,000 years / Phyllis Siefker.
        p.   cm.
    Includes bibliographical references and index.

    ISBN-13: 978-0-7864-2958-5
    softcover : 50# alk. paper ∞

    1. Santa Claus — History.   2. Nicholas, Saint, Bp. of Myra — History.   3. Wild men — Folklore.   I. Title.
GT4985.S495   2006
398'.352 — dc20   96-38896

British Library cataloguing data are available

Cover art ©2006 Pictures Now

Manufactured in the United States of America

McFarland & Company, Inc., Publishers
  Box 611, Jefferson, North Carolina 28640
  www.mcfarlandpub.com

This book is dedicated to the memory of my parents, Betty and Art Siefker, who showed me the joys of Christmas and of an inquiring mind; and to my present family, Scott, Brandt, and Kurt Nesbitt, who share these treasures with me today.

Contents

Preface

This book started with a child's question: "Who is Santa Claus?"

My first impulse was to inform my sons that Santa was just a man in a costume, but relatives and friends soon set me straight. "You'll deprive your kids of their childhood," they insisted. "It's a child's *right* to believe in Santa Claus."

That strong response provoked a question of my own: "Why does the pudgy gent in a red suit have such a strong hold on our society?"

The pursuit of answers has been a journey of two decades, beginning with standard works in the public library and moving into arcane volumes of myth and scholarship, pursuing a labyrinth of footnotes and casual asides. It involved looking at prehistoric Europe, the oldest written plays, legends, and stories, and even paleolithic evidence and Japan's aborigines. It included reading obtuse treatises and scholarship from diverse countries and fields. I have consolidated this research in a way that I hope will educate, entertain, and sometimes amuse.

This research was conducted mainly through the Buffalo, Chicago, Newberry, University of Illinois, and University of Kansas libraries, and countless libraries accessed through interlibrary loan from books, articles, and theses that spanned almost two centuries—1809 to 1995. I read hundreds of resources and used more than a hundred. Among the most helpful in pointing the way during this long pursuit were numerous articles from *Folklore,* published by the Folklore Society; a wonderful collection of material published in a 1976 edition of *Cultures;* Jacob Grimm's *Teutonic Mythology;* Richard Bernheimer's *Wild Men in the Middle Ages;* E. K. Chambers' *The English Folk Plays;* Samuel Sumberg's *The Nuremberg Schembart Carnival;* Alfred Shoemaker's *Christmas in Pennsylvania: A Folk-Cultural Study;* and, for surviving festivals, Peter Tokofsky's dissertation, *Rules of Fools: Carnival in Southwest Germany.* For the generous use of pictures, my thanks to the Pennsylvania Folklife Society; Michael Mendez, Sydney Hill, and Carlisle Chang of Trinidad; the University of California Press; the Austrian Cultural Institute; the Irish Tourist Board; and Städt. Kurverwaltung of Bad Waldsee.

My hope is that the reader will enjoy Santa and his offshoots' history as much as I enjoyed tracking Santa Claus through the mists of time. I never did answer the question of why Santa has such a hold on our psyches; I'll have to leave that explanation to psychoanalysts or symbolic anthropologists. But I hope the reader will share some of my sense of wonder that a being so ancient and primitive could survive, to remain our symbol of bounty and joy.

A Visit from Saint Nicholas

'Twas the night before Christmas, when all through the house
Not a creature was stirring, not even a mouse;
The stockings were hung by the chimney with care,
In hopes that St. Nicholas soon would be there;
The children were nestled all snug in their beds,
While visions of sugar-plums danced in their heads;
And mama in her 'kerchief, and I in my cap,
Had just settled our brains for a long winter's nap,
When out on the lawn there arose such a clatter,
I sprang from the bed to see what was the matter.
Away to the window I flew like a flash,
Tore open the shutters and threw up the sash.
The moon on the breast of the new-fallen snow
Gave the lustre of mid-day to objects below,
When, what to my wondering eyes should appear,
But a miniature sleigh, and eight tiny reindeer,
With a little old driver so lively and quick,
I knew in a moment it must be St. Nick.
More rapid than eagles his coursers they came,
And he whistled, and shouted, and called them by name:
"Now, Dasher! now, Dancer! now, Prancer and Vixen!
On, Comet! on, Cupid! on, Donder and Blitzen!
To the top of the porch! to the top of the wall!
Now dash away! dash away! dash away all!"
As dry leaves that before the wild hurricane fly,
When they meet with an obstacle, mount to the sky,
So up to the house-top the coursers they flew,
With the sleigh full of toys, and St. Nicholas too.
And then, in a twinkling, I heard on the roof
The prancing and pawing of each little hoof.

As I drew in my head, and was turning around,
Down the chimney St. Nicholas came with a bound.
He was dressed all in fur, from his head to his foot,
And his clothes were all tarnished with ashes and soot;
A bundle of toys he had flung on his back,
And he looked like a peddler just opening his pack.
His eyes — how they twinkled! his dimples how merry!
His cheeks were like roses, his nose like a cherry!
His droll little mouth was drawn up like a bow,
And the beard of his chin was as white as the snow;
The stump of a pipe he held tight in his teeth,
And the smoke it encircled his head like a wreath;
He had a broad face and a little round belly,
That shook, when he laughed, like a bowlful of jelly.
He was chubby and plump, a right jolly old elf,
And I laughed when I saw him, in spite of myself;
A wink of his eye and a twist of his head,
Soon gave me to know I had nothing to dread;
He spoke not a word, but went straight to his work
And filled all the stockings; then turned with a jerk,
And laying his finger aside of his nose,
And giving a nod, up the chimney he rose;
He sprang to his sleigh, to his team gave a whistle,
And away they all flew like the down of a thistle.
But I heard him exclaim ere he drove out of sight,
"Happy Christmas to all, and to all a good-night."

Now popularly attributed to Clement Clarke Moore, this poem was first published anonymously in the Troy Sentinel *on December 23, 1823, and later appeared under Moore's name in his 1844* Poems.

Introduction

It began with a question, a nagging doubt raised by available Santa Claus articles and books that offered only one explanation: Santa Claus is an Americanization of Saint Nicholas, a fourth-century Asian bishop. Somehow, that explanation didn't seem right. One close look at the poem "A Visit from Saint Nicholas," and everything about the enigmatic chimney slider pointed to a different direction. Here was a sooty, bearded man, mounting to the sky like a hurricane, being pulled by exotic arctic stags with names that spoke of the elemental powers of the earth and sky, not the benign, structured world of sainthood.

If Santa Claus really *was* Saint Nicholas, why this shouting, hurricane flying, and storming about? Why did his reindeer have such elemental names as Thunder (Donder), Lightning (Blitzen), and Comet? Why weren't they named Faith, Hope, and Charity? Why wasn't Santa's ride one of righteousness, tranquility, and somber hope, instead of a wild comet ride, an unleashing of powers with undertones of chaos? It was truly an enigma.

Years of research confirmed that initial doubt: Santa Claus is an Americanization, all right, but not of a Catholic saint. Instead, Santa's forefather was the very unsaintlike Furry Nicholas, a major player in winter festivals that have been transplanted from Europe to the rugged backwoods of Pennsylvania. But where did he come from? And why build a festival around a ragged-looking half-wild fellow whose primary activity seemed to be snorting, stomping, and tearing things up?

Our Santa is one of the last descendants of a long line of dark, sooty, hair-covered men, the remnant of a pre–Christian god of awesome power. Our pipe-smoking "jolly old elf" is only one offshoot of this old, old god; throughout the millennia this figure evolved in many ways and in many lands, adapting to new roles as society changed, until today there are remnants of the Wild Man from Russia to Britain to Japan to Greece, in ballet and movies, in Christian churches and in shopping malls. No other being has had such a far-reaching influence on our modern culture. He has shaped our core mythologies in the guise of common legendary characters in mythology, plays, and literature: Santa, Adonis, Harlequin, Robin Hood, Robin Goodfellow, Peter Pan, Satan, the Piped Piper, the court fool, Merlin.

These commonplace figures have a single root in one powerful being — a priest to some, a god to others, and the personification of evil to still others. Originally a beast-god who reminded people of the cyclical nature of the world, of death and rebirth, this Wild Man was part of fertility performances throughout Europe. He was a godhead so strong, so universally worshiped by "pagans," that Christianity found him *the* major impediment to its goal of European salvation. In Europe, Christianity and the old god clashed in anger and violence. To undermine his grip on the people, Christianity labeled his worship evil, and called his followers devilish. In the seventh century, Pope Gregory tapped this creature for the physical form of evil, Satan.

The fact is that Santa and Satan are alter egos, brothers; they have the same origin. In our era, it is difficult to see a relationship between the two. Santa Claus is our Christmas symbol, after all — the representative of generosity, goodwill, and material blessings. And Satan: he may not be an integral part of most Americans' cosmology today, but he definitely is the antithesis of all things bright and beautiful. He is lewdness, temptation, and destruction.

On the surface, the two figures are polar opposites, but underneath they share the same parent, and both retain many of the old symbols associated with their "father." And therein lies the tale. Let us travel back through time and trace the twisted paths taken by an ancient Wild Man as he journeyed from near-forgotten prehistory into the modern world. The following chapters trace how the old god — a fertility deity whose worship covered Europe — traveled two paths into the twentieth century. On one path, he came to personify evil for the growing Christian church. On the other, he became the symbol of holiday, carnival, and new hope. From these two paths, he arrived at both the warmth of our fireplace and in the flames of hell.

Chapter 1

I Knew in a Moment It Must Be Saint Nick

We cannot just summarily dismiss Saint Nicholas. He has been associated with gift-giving for centuries, and his name is, after all, an alias for Santa Claus. Before we see how Saint Nicholas received credit for fathering Santa Claus, let's look at the legend of Saint Nicholas. Certain high points of Nicholas's life are consistently repeated to show the similarity between Nicholas and Santa and to give some substance to the notion that Nicholas became Santa Claus. Conventional explanations also take note of certain items of Saint Nicholas's wardrobe and of his behavior — such as bringing gifts, carrying a sack on his back, and giving sticks to naughty children — to establish him as the figure from which Santa Claus sprang.

The popular explanation for Nicholas's becoming Santa briefly goes like this: Saint Nicholas was a fourth-century Turk who became a bishop. As his popularity spread, the Dutch adopted this Turk as their patron saint. When the Dutch came to America, they brought their beloved saint, and once in America, Saint Nicholas somehow "turned into" Santa Claus. Despite a century of repetition, this story is simply untrue. However, since it is the only "fact" most of us have heard about Santa Claus, the Saint Nicholas legend deserves a closer look.

First, let's look at the ecclesiastical legends about the good saint: St. Nicholas was born in the fourth century in the city of Patras in what is now Turkey. It was apparent he was no ordinary mortal when, as a newborn, he stood upright in his first bath. As soon as he learned to walk, Nicholas toddled off to church and spent all his time there, not bothering with the usual boyhood games.

Nicholas was known in much of Europe as the patron saint of schoolboys, because legend tells us he became a bishop while still a youth. According to the thirteenth-century *Golden Legend*, when the bishop of Myra died, the other bishops gathered to choose a successor. One heard a holy nocturnal voice commanding that the first person named Nicholas who entered the church in the morning be made bishop. Of course Nicholas, skulking about the church as usual, entered before sunrise to fulfill his destiny.

Several tales further explain Saint Nicholas's title as patron saint of schoolboys. In one, a certain schoolboy's father honored Saint Nicholas every day on the saint's feast day. One year, in the middle of the celebration, the devil came to the gates disguised as a begging pilgrim. The father told his son to give the beggar money, which the youth did, only to be strangled by the devious demon. The heartbroken father carried his dead son into the house, crying, "Saint Nicholas, is this my reward for the honors I have given thee so many years?" As he cried out, Saint Nicholas heard and resurrected the lad.

In another of the "schoolboy stories," Nicholas revived three dismembered students. The story relates that an Asian father sent his sons to school in Athens and told them to stop by Myra to receive Nicholas's blessing. At Myra, they stopped at an inn for the night, but their choice of quarters proved unfortunate. The innkeeper and his wife killed the boys, cut up their bodies, and hid the pieces in barrels used for salting meat, intending to sell them as pickled pork. Nicholas sensed evil and arrived at the inn to accuse the couple of their horrid deed. Overcome with awe and remorse, the couple repented. Nicholas forgave them, and the boys subsequently arose, reassembled, from the brine.

George McKnight, in his book *St. Nicholas*, says this well-known Nicholas story is not included in either the *Golden Legend* or the *Roman Breviary*, standard sources for Saint Nicholas legends. McKnight says the odd story may be the result of misinterpreting a painting that illustrates another Nicholas legend. In this legend, three innocent men were condemned to death by the Emperor Constantine because of an enemy's perjured testimony. They were imprisoned in a tower, where Saint Nicholas visited them. In the painting depicting the story, the three captives are drawn smaller than the saint, to emphasize the subordination of the human to the divine. Only the top of the tower is shown, to bring the scene closer to the viewer. In the resulting picture, the imprisoned men look like three boys in a barrel. Later pictures deliberately depict a children-in-barrel scene. According to McKnight, the story and later paintings depicting the slaughtered and salted school boys were attempts to explain the earlier tower painting.

The pack on Santa's back is supposed to represent Nicholas's first gift-giving expedition, when he preserved the chastity of three women. After his rich parents died, Nicholas looked around for some altruistic way to use his wealth. He didn't have to look far, for one of his penurious neighbors was planning to sell three daughters into prostitution and live off their earnings. The man's financial plight and proposed solution horrified Nicholas, who wrapped up a third of his gold and threw it through the man's window, saving the eldest daughter from a life of sin. He did this two more nights, saving her sisters. On

Saint Nicholas resuscitates three dismembered schoolboys in this old Italian print.

the third night, the father followed Nicholas and begged his forgiveness, which the good saint granted.

The birch rod left for naughty children has the following explanation in Holland: The monks of a certain church wanted the responses of Saint Nicholas sung in church. The abbot refused, saying, "I consider this music worldly and profane, and shall never give permission for it to be used in my church." The good saint, long dead and living in heaven, heard these words. Nicholas, who had blithely forgiven human butchery and paternal pimping, was so angered by the abbot's words that he descended from heaven in a rage, dragged the abbot out of bed by the hair, and beat him with a birch rod until he was nearly dead. The point was well taken: from that day, the responses were included in the service.

This is the saint who, according to the oft-repeated story, was so loved by the Dutch that they brought him to America when they emigrated to New Amsterdam, the region that today is New York City and the Hudson River Valley. Nicholas's yearly visits to Dutch-American households were so charming that an entire enchanted America adopted the kindly patriarch. In the process of adoption, Saint Nicholas underwent what can only be called a spontaneous metamorphosis. A typical explanation of this sudden change from saint to Santa is Lillian Eichler's statement in *Customs of Mankind:*

> Santa came to America by way of Holland. The Old Dutch settlers of
> New York brought with them ...San Nicolaas, patron saint of children.
> And San Nicolaas promptly grew a long, white beard, belted his jovial
> stoutness in a red coat, and made his bow to America as Santa Claus.

Saint Nicholas of the Old World had no "jovial stoutness" to belt, however. When the Dutch performed their annual Christmas-season ritual and selected one of their community to play the role of the saint, they could easily have chosen Ebeneezer Scrooge to act out the part. Far from being a fun-loving gift-giver, this seasonal visitor was a stern, dour, judgmental bishop who visited homes in full episcopal attire and demeanor. His purpose was a sober one: to judge good and evil. This grim man's visit was preceded by some anxious hours; to prepare for his visit, children crammed on church lessons, hoping to pass the ecclesiastical quiz that always preceded any candy or gifts ... or sticks or pieces of coal.

Five minutes before the saint's scheduled visit, children in Holland sang a ritual song welcoming him and praising his goodness. A shower of sweets thrown through the doorway signaled Nicholas's presence. Then he entered, somber and straight.

His demeanor and mission were doleful enough, but there was also a note of terror in the person of Black Pete, the hairy, chained, horned, blackened, devilish monster who was Nicholas's servant. Black Pete's job was simple: He glared at the children while the saint drilled the tense youths in Christian verse. As Nicholas rattled off his questions —"What is the first commandment?" "Name the twelve apostles"— and the children struggled with their suddenly faulty memories, Black Pete stared balefully, clutching a gaping sack in his hairy claws. Every now and then he flashed his enormous canines and leaped, growling, toward the frightened children, threatening to beat them with his rod.

The Black Pete figure that accompanied Saint Nicholas on his Christmas expeditions also accompanied women saints on their gift-giving rounds, as shown above. Black Pete's role was to threaten misbehaving children and rattle his chain.

If a child had been appallingly bad, Nicholas warned the youth that Black Pete would stuff transgressors into his yawning sack and carry them to some unknown hell until next Christmas. For the children, the message was clear: Know your scripture or be damned. Saint Nicholas always saved the "bad" children, however, and they received sticks or ashes instead of Black Pete's ultimate vengeance. Far from being a delightful custom, this visit from Saint Nicholas had all the festivity and lightheartedness of the Day of Judgment.

It is easy to understand why the Dutch would soften Saint Nicholas from a grim holiday judge into a jolly gift-bringer, but it's difficult to understand why any nation would bring a forbidding presence like this saint and his now-forgotten companion Black Pete into the celebration of Christmas. The point of the holiday is supposedly to celebrate the birth of Christ. Many Biblical figures would better personify the season of joy and Christ's birth. Why not use the wise men, bearers of gifts, or the shepherds, the humble workers who were first to receive the news? Why not Joseph, the quiet, saintly man who gave unselfishly to make a home and teach a trade to a boy-child who was not his own offspring? Who better than this carpenter to visit children with toys he had made and to share the values of unquestioning love, faith, and charity that he demonstrated so well? And why would those Dutch settlers, or any other community, include a monster like Black Pete in their Christmas traditions?

There are many inconsistencies in the standard stories about the origins of Santa Claus, but our modern Christmas customs begin to make sense when we venture farther back in time, to explore life as it was known in humanity's time-misted past. These were real people, with real lives, traditions, and civilizations. For the most part, they lacked the formalized written language we rely on to tell us of the past, but they left many artifacts and clues to help us glimpse their lives. They also left behind certain remarkable customs, celebrations, and legends that have persisted into the modern era. These traces reveal the true story of the origin of Santa Claus and many other fabled figures, including elves, fairies, dwarves, Pan the forest god, and Robin Hood, who takes from the rich and gives to the poor.

Clearly, the Nicholas legend should be reconsidered. Let us start by taking a good, close look at this saint and at Santa Claus.

Santa wears a shabby hair coat, has an unkempt beard, slides down chimneys, and is covered with ashes and soot. He promises earthly, not heavenly, rewards, and has never been seen in a pulpit. His trademark is a not a cross but a laden sack — hardly the symbol for a saint. He drives a team of reindeer with the exotic names of Dasher, Dancer, Prancer, Vixen, Comet, Cupid, Donder, and Blitzen.

Saint Nicholas, by contrast, is impeccably clean, wears only sanctioned church attire, and travels sedately on a horse or by means of a magical cloak. His sternness, heavenly aspirations, and austerity bear no relation to Santa's carefree abandon and materialism. No prancing or chimney-sliding for Nicholas — just a stately walk and the Holy Writ.

Saint Nicholas and Santa are totally antithetical. A cursory glance alone should clue us that Santa Claus just can't be Saint Nicholas and that the Santa Claus customs have little, if anything, to do with a fictional Asian saint.

There is, however, a better reason for denying that America's Santa Claus descended from Saint Nicholas. It is a simple fact: Saint Nicholas as an amiable gift-giver didn't appear in America until after Santa Claus had become an established figure. The Dutch colonists did not bring Nicholas with them, as is commonly believed. The New Amsterdam Dutch were Reformation Dutch, saint-haters opposed to the Catholic Church; they had no use for Saint Nicholas and other such papist carryings-on. The legend that the Dutch brought Saint Nicholas to America was invented by Washington Irving in an 1809 satire, the fictional *Knickerbocker History*, and has no basis in fact.

This is the conclusion of Charles Jones, who investigates America's Saint Nicholas in "Knickerbocker Santa Claus" and dismisses the notion that Saint Nicholas came to America with the Dutch. Jones says there is no evidence Saint Nicholas existed in New Amsterdam, or for a century after English occupation of New York. Having examined children's books, periodicals, and diaries of the

John Pintard commissioned this drawing of Saint Nicholas in 1810, following the success of Washington Irving's *Knickerbocker History*, but there is little here to suggest a "jolly old elfe" that would capture America's hearts. From the collection of the New-York Historical Society; courtesy of the New-York Historical Society.

eighteenth century, Jones is certain that Saint Nicholas simply didn't make the crossing, and he traces the beginning of America's Santa Claus to the satirical genius of Irving. "Without Irving there would be no Santa Claus," says Jones.

Washington Irving was one of the most popular authors of the early 1800s and is best known to us for his "Legend of Sleepy Hollow" and "Rip Van Winkle." His book *Knickerbocker History* was a huge success when it was published in 1809; it became standard school reading and was recited in homes and taverns throughout the country. In this book, says Jones, the idea of Santa's bringing gifts, parking his wagon on the roof, and sliding down chimneys began.

Jones believes Irving got his ideas about Saint Nicholas from the New-York Historical and Saint Nicholas societies. The Saint Nicholas Society was one of a plethora of ethnic and political saint societies founded after the Revolution-

Later versions of Saint Nicholas showed a diminutive Dutchman, such as this illustration from an 1848 version of the poem "A Visit from St. Nicholas."

ary War. Scots founded Saint Andrew's society; the Welsh, Saint David's; the Irish, Saint Patrick's; and the English, Saint George's. The Saint George Society was an elitist group of pro–English colonists, where fellows of similar ilk could meet. Soon patriots started founding opposing societies. In Pennsylvania, the Delaware Indian chief Tammany was chosen for a symbol; in New York, Saint Nicholas was dusted off and adopted as an anti–British symbol in a society founded by John Pintard.

After the success of Irving's *Knickerbocker History*, Pintard commissioned a picture of Saint Nicholas. Jones says that the volatile combination of Irving's book and Pintard's picture provided the combination for Santa's birth and subsequent success. Thus, according to Jones, Santa's history is startlingly brief: He sprang, fully formed, from the head of Washington Irving in 1809.

Unfortunately, this explanation doesn't hold up on further inspection. *Knickerbocker History* is a broad satire on the New Amsterdam Dutch and their life. They are depicted as a bovine people whose main pastimes are eating and smoking. Saint Nicholas, as their patron saint, dresses in traditional Dutch breeches and reflects their appearance and character. Scattered sparsely through the book are allusions to Nicholas dropping presents from his breech pockets, "rattling down chimneys," and "laying his finger beside his nose," but gift-giving receives little emphasis. Again, there is no physical resemblance, apart from paunchiness and pipe-smoking, to Santa Claus.

The picture commissioned by Pintard can hardly have helped inspire a Santa craze, either. This Saint Nicholas is no Santa Claus prototype, but the Dutch Nicholas resurrected. In fact, Pintard's Saint Nicholas makes the Old World sojourner look absolutely ebullient in contrast. Next to the good bishop is a "good child" with an apron full of gifts, and an unhappy "bad child" who has received a stick as punishment. Below the picture is written:

> SAINT NICHOLAS, good holy man!
> Put on the Tabard, best you can,
> Go, clad therewith, to Amsterdam,
> From Amsterdam to Hispanje,
> Where apples *bright* of Oranje,
> And likewise those *grenate* surnam'd,
> Roll through the streets, all free unclaim'd.
> SAINT NICHOLAS, my dear good friend!
> To serve you ever was my end,
> If you will, now, me something give,
> I'll serve you ever while I live.

The New-York Historical Society did commission a diminutive Dutchman–Saint Nicholas picture in 1837, and similar figures followed, such as the one that illustrated the poem "A Visit from St. Nicholas" in 1848, but these came years after Santa Claus started making a national impact and show little of an elfish nature.

It seems obvious, therefore, that Santa Claus can be neither the alter ego of Saint Nicholas nor the brainchild of Washington Irving. Another visit to that Dutch household at Christmas, however, will give us a clue to the identity of the Santa Claus immortalized in the poem "'Twas the Night Before Christmas." If we peek behind the imposing Saint Nicholas, we see, glowering in the shadows, the saint's reprobate companion, Black Pete. He, like Santa, has a coat of hair, a disheveled beard, a bag, and ashes on his face. He isn't laughing a merry "Ho! Ho! Ho!" but the physical resemblances are definitely promising. In fact, it is this creature, rather than Irving's creation or an Asian saint, who fathered Santa Claus.

Chapter 2

His Clothes Were All Tarnished with Ashes and Soot

Santa's immediate forebear in America came not from New Amsterdam or New York, but from German settlements in Pennsylvania. In fact, Black Pete had already made great strides toward his new identity as the children's friend in Pennsylvania by the time the St. Nicholas Society created its kindlier Saint Nicholas in 1837. In Pennsylvania, as German immigrants celebrated each Yule season, one of their most notable traditions was a character called Pelznichol. The name literally means "Furry Nicholas" *Pelz* in German meaning hide or fur coat — a word that became our *pelt* — and *Nichol* being the character's name, Nicholas. As implied by his name, Pelznichol, or Bellsnickle as he was also called, was "dressed all in fur from his head to his foot"; that is, he was covered with animal skins. This character also was found in America's German communities under the name of Bellschniggle and dozens of other variations of Pelznichol or Bellsnickle.

The reader may be wondering about the existence of so many different names for this character. Later, we will see scores of other names assigned to the wintertime Wild Man that evolved into our modern Santa Claus. The reason for this nominative explosion is simple when we think back to the lifestyle of the people who enacted the Yuletide customs we follow today.

First, it is common in religious or belief systems to avoid calling a god by his or her real name. Even the Old Testament followed this ancient custom. Instead of uttering the name of the all-powerful, worshippers would describe some physical characteristic, or some attribute such as vengefulness or graciousness, for fear of invoking divine wrath or calling undue attention to one's puny self. This same practice exists today in everyday life on a more mundane scale, when employees call the boss "the old man" or some other unflattering nickname rather than his or her given name.

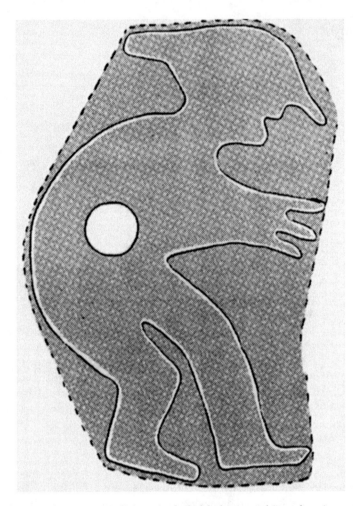

Pennsylvania Christmas traditions included baking cookies of various shapes, including this elfish Pelznichol figure. From *Christmas in Pennsylvania: A Folk-Cultural Study* (1959); courtesy of the Pennsylvania Folklife Society.

Second, in times past, most of humanity lived in rather isolated communities, without benefit of media to tie them together. Customs such as how to celebrate the winter season were passed down by word of mouth. Mass printing didn't even begin until the early 1500s, and the ability to read and write was not a high priority for most of the world's people until recent centuries; instead, it was the privilege of a few. Furthermore, even those who could write were not necessarily interested in recording certain names for the sake of accuracy. People who were averse to uttering a god's real name were even less likely to commit that name to print.

Finally, oral language is a flexible, evolving form of communication. Local dialects naturally develop and persist in isolated communities. Even today, in our mass-media world, people traveling from Boston to Biloxi to Boise may wonder if the residents they meet are all speaking English. This was especially true before television and radio covered the United States and created the non-accented media voice as the norm.

The net result is that the hairy beast-man known as Pelznichol had different nicknames in various communities, even within the same broad language group. The sound of each nickname was further modified by the local dialect, for century upon century. By the time someone wrote down the name, it was different in each locale, with phonetic spelling. (For the sake of consistency and ease of reference, this book will use *Pelznichol* as the generic name for the Pennsylvania gift-giver and *the Wild Man* for the beast-man who fathered both Pelznichol and the modern Santa Claus.)

Along with the different names came many differences in the way various communities rendered the costume worn by the individuals who portrayed the Wild Man in regional festivals. In fact, given the differences in language, dialect, costumes, and behaviors that developed as people carried their Wild Man rituals with them across the Old World and into the New, it is remarkable that so many elements of the celebration remain the same.

The forms in which the Christmas visitor appeared in early Pennsylvania might be lost to us if a man named Albert Shoemaker hadn't combed Pennsylvania's newspapers from the 1800s and brought this character to life again in *Christmas in Pennsylvania: A Folk-Cultural Study*. In this thorough book, we can glimpse the New World Teutonic Christmas climate of more than 150 years ago.

Shoemaker's study tells us that nineteenth-century Pelznichols, whip in hand, went from house to house with cookies and chestnuts, rewarding well-behaved children and frightening and whipping those who had been naughty. Their appearance varied, but they were always black-faced and bell-jingling, dressed in animal skins or patches, and carrying a whip or bag.

The Philadelphia *Gazette* of December 19, 1827, describes Bellschniggle as:

> ebony in appearance, but Topaz in spirit.... He is the precursor of the jolly old elfe "Christkindle" or "St. Nicholas," and makes his personal appearance, dressed in skins or old clothes, his face black, a bell, a whip, and a pocket full of cakes or nuts.... It is no sooner dark than the Bellschniggle's bell is heard flitting from house to house.... He slips down the chimney, at the fairy hour of midnight, and deposits his presents quietly in the prepared stocking.

It becomes apparent that Saint Nicholas as a "jolly old elfe" was well-established in Pennsylvania by 1827, a decade before the New York Historical Society offered its own mellowed version of the saint.

Pelznichol was sometimes silent, and when he did speak, it was usually in gibberish — some unknown, archaic, mystical tongue. The Lancaster *Intelligencer* of December 24, 1881, recalls Christmas in the 1820s, when Bellsnickle appeared with a "hideous visage, his bag of nuts, and his long whip, jingling his bells withal, and speaking in a dialect that seemed to have been brought from the confusion of Babel."

Another old-timer described Bellsnickle, or "the Nicle," as wearing an ugly mask and jabbering in some unknown tongue. He would toss nuts on the floor, and when children tried to pick them up, he would strike their backs or hands with his whip. His appearance through the German-settled colonies ranged from "hideous masks" to blackened faces; his behavior from terrifying to jovial and kindly.

A rather literary description of a kind, mischievous Bellsnickle is found in the following December 21, 1826, Pottstown *Lafayette Aurora* account. The author describes Bellsnickle as

> a mischievous hobgoblin that makes his presence known to the people once a year by his cunning tricks of fairyism. It is reported that he nearly demolished a poor woman's house in one of the back streets a few nights ago. ... He has the appearance of a man of 50, and is about 4 feet high, red round face, curly black hair, with a long beard hanging perpendicular from his chin, and his lip finely graced with a pair of horned mustachios, of which a Turk would be proud; he is remarkable thick being made in a puncheon style, and is constantly laughing, which occasions his chunky frame to be in perpetual shake; he carries a great budget on his back, filled with all the dainties common to the season — he cracks his nuts amongst his people as well as his jokes without their perceiving him.... This genus of the night winds and storms is, when at a distance, entirely a non-descript; but when he approaches his uncouth magnitude diminishes, and you can accurately survey his puncheon frame from top to toe. His cap, a queer one indeed, is made out of a black bearskin fringed round or rather stuck round with porcupine quills painted a fiery red, and having two folds at each side, with which he at pleasure covers his neck and part of his funny face. ... His outer garment, like Joseph's of old, is of many colors ... hanging straight down from the shoulders to his heels, with a tightening belt attached to the waist — the buttons seem to be manufactured entirely in an ancient style — out of the shells of hickory nuts. ... when he runs, the tail of his long coat flies out behind, which gives an opportunity to behold his little short red plush breeches, with brass kneebuckles attached to their extremities, the size of a full moon. His moccasins are the same as those worn by the Chippewa nation. He carries a bow with a sheaf of arrows thrown across his miscellaneous budget, thus equipt, he sallies forth in the dark of night, with a few tinkling bells attached to his bearskin cap and the tail of his long coat, and makes as much noise as mischief through our town.

Artist Ralph Dunkelberger drew this version of Pelznichol for Albert Shoemaker's book *Christmas in Pennsylvania.* Dunkelberger used the description from the Pottstown *Lafayette Aurora* for his model. From *Christmas in Pennsylvania: A Folk-Cultural Study* (1959); courtesy of the Pennsylvania Folklife Society.

In his less kindly atavism, Pelznichol was bestial and alarming, his approach clangorous cacophony. From the *Christian World* of December 23, 1891, we learn that "they could hear his coming, which was terrible in heinous noises, rattling of chains, etc. His appearance was still more frightful, wrapped in furs or skins like a huge animal."

Sometimes the Bellsnickles roamed in groups, and when this happened their purpose was often altruistic as well as awe-inspiring or enjoyable, though inevitably raucous. One former bellsnickler remembered his youth in the early 1800s:

> I went belsnickling several times when I was young. We went to every house in half a township where poor children were. When we had given what we could get from people who could afford it better, we went to some of the big farm houses for fun. ... When we were done visiting the poor children and scared many of them before we did give them the things, we made our headquarters on the farm. We had fiddles and other music.

Of course, Pelznichols weren't active only in small communities. In Philadelphia, the custom combined with other nationalities' Christmas practices to give birth to the Philadelphia Mummers Parade. Mumming, which is an integral part of English Christmases and is responsible for Father Christmas's evolution there, consists of masqueraders going from house to house, where they sing and perform skits, after which they give, or receive gifts from the graced household.

In Pennsylvania, the Pelznichols also were making house visits, and in this melting pot of holiday festivity, English and Teutonic customs met and melded. According to Clement Miles in *Christmas in Ritual and Tradition: Christian and Pagan,* English mummers in Pennsylvania sometimes lost their identity in the process and became known as Bellsnickles in the late eighteenth century. These troupes continued their comic skits of death and resurrection into the twentieth century in some isolated communities.

Yuletide festivals in Philadelphia reached an incredible pitch. From miles around, revellers gathered in the city's center, where they rattled kettles, rang sleigh bells, and blew upon thousands of penny horns. Swedish "shooters" joined them, masquerading with a Pelznichol figure or two in their midst, shouting at the top of their lungs, and shooting guns. Together, the nationalities managed to reign over the city and create ear-shattering chaos, much to the dismay of the staid Quaker City's fathers.

As early as the 1700s the Quakers had tried to subdue the more raucous elements, and grand juries dealt with sentencing those who dared masquerade during the holidays. Outside Philadelphia, the festivities continued, despite the fact that Pennsylvania House of Representatives forbade masquerading in

1801, promising "imprisonment not exceeding three months and a fine of between fifty and a thousand dollars," a monumental fine for those days.

Philadelphia attempted to ban the noisemaking and masking many times. In 1881, a law forbade the "tin horn nuisance" and Christmas Eve masquerading. The mummers, not to be robbed of their fun, moved the celebration to New Year's Eve. Many carried pistols, which they shot off when they reached the center of the city at midnight. Again, city authorities compelled unruly groups to exercise restraint. By 1901, the city council was issuing permits for a grand parade on Broad Street, the first officially sanctioned New Year's Day Philadelphia Mummers Parade.

This parade has never attained the national prominence of the New Orleans Mardi Gras (an extravaganza with similar origins), probably because Mardi Gras in Louisiana is more conducive to festivity than midwinter in Pennsylvania; however, it has received some scholarly attention. Charles Welch, in *The Philadelphia Mummers Parade*, traces the history of the festivity from about the time of its sanctioning.

Welch relates that the favorite costumes of the old mummers and bell-snicklers who comprised the early parades were fur-lined coats turned inside out and beards, "some as large as currant bushes." The fur coverings, along with the blackened faces and beards of the Bellsnickles, were standard attire for the revellers. So common were the blackened faces that the period preceding the Civil War is known as the Lampblack Period in honor of the substance marchers used to achieve the effect.

Even though a blackened face and furs had been two of the most significant traits of the Teutonic gift-givers, by 1905 no one could remember why mummers blackened their faces. Welch quotes a Lebanon County, Pennsylvania, resident who that year tried to explain the origin of bellsnickling:

> I have often heard it said that it was following out a custom established in the south when slaves would appear before their master on Christmas Eve and there dance and sing and play the banjo for the master and guests' entertainment and after each number the slaves would be treated to the best in the house, the one occasion of the year.

This equation of blackened faces with American slavery is echoed in a common misconception that Saint Nicholas acquired his Black Pete servant after coming to America.

Welch himself believed the blackfaced Philadelphia mummers were a caricature of the American minstrel figure, a parody he believed started with the singing and dancing of Thomas "Daddy" Rice in 1828. The National Association for the Advancement of Colored People also misinterpreted the blackface and in the 1960s decried the smearing of burnt cork on faces as presenting the African-American in an unflattering and comic light. Neither Welch nor the

NAACP, of course, could have been aware that this blackness was necessary for the special power and sacredness of an unfathomably ancient godhead.

Boston wrestled with the strident pandemonium as well. There the mummers were offending the more genteel Bostonians as late as 1782, despite a 1753 law banning mummers and pageants in that city's streets. By 1782, mummers, described as the "lowest blackguards" by a literary commentator, took their act to homes, where "there was no refusing admittance. Custom had licensed these vagabonds to enter by force any place they chose." The annalist of these then-fading rituals described the play and its "foolish dialogue":

> One fellow was knocked down and lay sprawling on the carpet, while another bellowed out, "See, there he lies;/but ere he dies/a doctor must be had." The doctor revives the wounded man. In this way they would continue for half an hour, and it happened not infrequently that the house would be filled by another gang when these had departed.

If this scene of annually intruding upon homes and demanding gifts or money seems familiar, it should, as our modern Halloween customs are our last, fading, sanitized remnant of these meandering mummers.

In more isolated New World areas, mumming and bellsnickling continued longer, even until World War II. Reports from such areas as Newfoundland, where various mumming reminiscences were collected in Herbert Halpert and G. M. Story's *Christmas Mumming in Newfoundland*, give us an idea of what the older Pennsylvania Pelznichols were like.

In Newfoundland, Pelznichol appears as the Dark One or *Janney*, a name that was applied to both the Pelznichol figure and the whole throng. These Janneys blackened their faces and added hair, especially whiskers — often whole rabbit skins or a mass of *malldow*, a moss that grows on fir and spruce trees. Sometimes the animal nature of the figure overwhelmed the human, as Janneys donned entire sheep and goat heads, horns and all. To intensify their animal nature, these Janneys walked stooped over, swaying from side to side. They sometimes wore cowbells and chains and, as mentioned in reports from the Straits of Belle Isle, placed pillows over their stomachs and humps on their back. J. D. A. Widdowson and Herbert Halpert, two researchers who interviewed residents about their memories of these bygone festivals, note that the Janneys achieved the hunchback, which was essential to the Janney outfit, by carrying a bag or knapsack on their back. Parents told children the Janneys would put them in the bag and carry them away if they weren't good.

In 1842, Sir Richard Bonnycastle described the mumming activities that marked Christmas in that area:

> There was a sort of saturnalia amongst the lower classes, in St. Johns. The mummers prepare before the New Year dresses of all possible shapes and hues, most something like those of harlequin and the

clown in pantomimes. A huge papercocked hat is one favorite head-
piece, and everyone except the captain is masked. Some of the masks
were very grotesque, and the fools or clowns are furnished with
thongs, and bladders, with which they belabour the exterior mob. They
would perform a play containing a mock sword fight; one is slain and
the doctor is called in to bring him to life again.

In this fashion the Newfoundlanders performed mumming skits, not always to
an appreciative audience. An 1861 statute banned mumming throughout the
colony, but the mummers' home visits continued.

Roger Abrahams and Richard Bauman in "Ranges of Festival Behavior"
discuss Christmas perambulations in the nearby La Have Islands of Nova Scotia, where the visits, called belsnickling, were an annual Christmas event until
they died out in the years after World War II. These activities give us a better
glimpse of the Pennsylvania bellsnickling activities of an earlier time. Residents could hear the groups, each composed of about 12 young, unmarried
men, when they ventured out after dark on Christmas Eve because they blew
horns and clanked bells as they traveled along from house to house. Bauman
tells us the belsnicklers' clothing was of three types: a disheveled figure dressed
in tattered clothing; an animal costume achieved by painting animal features
on the mask and wearing horns; and a woman's outfit. "Those belsnickles
dressed as women use 'squealy' voices and exaggerated feminine movements,
while the others speak with 'coarse' or 'rough' voices and walk hunched over
with a rolling gait," report Abrahams and Bauman.

At each house, they called, "Belsnickles allowed in?" and most houses welcomed them. In the house, they performed clumsy, comic dancing, and the men
dressed as women "minced around the room in an exaggerated caricature of
feminine behavior."

After their performance, the belsnicklers grilled the children on their
behavior during the year, calling each forward and asking if he or she had been
good. The children, terrified of these creatures their parents used as the bogeyman all year, of course answered in the affirmative, and the belsnicklers gave
them candy. After this, the belsnicklers asked their hosts for a "bit of brouse,"
a term for the special treats of cakes, cookies, and apples prepared for these masqueraders.

Thus, across the ocean from Holland, we have Black Pete as the Janney,
Bellsnickle, and Pelznichol, with a bag on his back, in hair or tattered cloth,
blackened, bewhiskered, lumbering, stooped and lunging, as he trod the byways
of Newfoundland, Nova Scotia, and Pennsylvania. And the masqueraders were
noisy — as one witness recalled the Janneys decades later: "When we watched
them comin' down past the cemetery, we could have swored it was the Second
Coming. I can still hear 'em moaning and roaring." When asked where they
came from, the Janneys replied they were from the North Pole, France, or Germany. Because of their alleged and legendary "foreignness," the Nova Scotian

belsnicklers had guides to lead them around the community. Unlike Black Pete, however, these Janneys and belsnicklers didn't have to contend with saints turning them into servants. In this way, they retained more of the original flavor of the Wild Man and his clamorous caravan.

Papa Bois, Caribbean Pelznichol

One more glimpse of this New World Pelznichol and his entourage will show the commonality of activities in this part of the world. In Trinidad, where every year one of the world's most spectacular extravaganzas blazes across the island, we find Pelznichol again, chained, thrashing, behorned, and bestial, in the distant shadows behind the grandeur of today's festival.

The original central figure of the carnival here was called Papa Bois. The word *bois,* meaning either "woods" or "farce," is an appropriate name for a Wild Man who was once a woods-dwelling nature god. We find little written about this ancient beast-man, but a portrait in Errol Hill's *The Trinidad Carnival: Mandate for a National Theatre* shows him as the quintessential Wild Man, horned, bewhiskered, crouching, and wild-eyed, prognathic jaw and all — a true forest creature. In island legend, Papa Bois is the ancient protector of both animals and humans.

According to Hill, in the original processions Papa Bois traveled the nights of Trinidad with a group, a stick-wielding Wild Man. Papa Bois and his companions were true nocturnal creatures because, like vampires, they could not face the light of day. With Papa Bois traveled a witch, and Hill reports the old parade was called the *jouvay,* a name tradition derives from the witch's lament when the sun rose: "*Jouvay, jou paka ouvay?*" ("Daybreak or no daybreak?")

As belief in the power of these creatures of the night dwindled, Papa Bois and the witch altered their forms. What happened next was not so much a disappearance as an evolution. Just as Sir Bonnycastle had described the Newfoundland motley crew as containing fools and clowns in tattered harlequinesque rags, a change from animal skins to tattered rags occurred in Trinidad (and other places as well). As his nature modulated to become more socially acceptable, the man-creature's clothes became less bestial and his behavior less violent.

In Trinidad, Papa Bois evolved into a couple of figures, one being *Pierrot Grenade,* the Grenada Fool. Pierrot wore a grotesque face mask and a costume of rags or paper streamers — simulating the old hair — above his fur garments. Hill explains that this hirsute underwear protected Pierrot Grenade from cuts from whips and sticks, but on a more symbolic level, the tatters were the veneer of civilization overlaying the brute nature of this primal potentate.

Pierrot Grenade was a loquacious masquerader, improvising incessantly as he moved through the streets. Hill relates one of this jester's jabberings

Papa Bois, the Trinidad Wild Man, accompanied by his deer, before civilization transformed him from a forest creature. Artist and folklorist Alfred Codallo collected tales of Papa Bois in Trinidad and drew this rendition of the original folk figure. Courtesy of Michael N. Mendez.

containing the ancient death-and-resurrection theme that echoes throughout Wild Man festivals. In this story, Pierrot relates how he was stabbed by his lover, Constance, taken to the hospital in an ambulance, and healed. Pierrot Grenade is the Wild Man turned fool or jester, whose nonsense talk set the tone of carnival.

The other transmogrification of Papa Bois was a more satanic figure, the *Jab Molasi* or "molasses devil." This devil wore short baggy pants and coated his entire body, face, ears, and hair with stale molasses, tar, creosote, grease, or mud. The Jab Molasi danced quickly through the streets, thrusting his pelvis

Pierrot Grenade, the Grenada Fool, shows a common evolution of the Wild Man's costume, from furs to ragged tatters or streamers. He still retains his ferocious mask, however. Photograph by Sydney Hill; courtesy of Sydney Hill.

One of the Wild Man's offshoots was the Devil, as shown in this 1888 romp on the wild side of Port of Spain, Trinidad. Although most bystanders seem to be enjoying the activity, a gentleman at right — a clergyman, judging by his collar — obviously disapproves. From *The Trinidad Carnival: Mandate for a National Theatre*; courtesy of Errol Hill.

in sexual gestures and threatening to touch others unless they gave him money. Sometimes he wore chains and a wooden lock and carried a pitchfork. He wore horns, a wreath of weeds, or a battered felt hat as he leapt and pranced about.

The devil bands enact the death and resurrection of the beast-man in a skit that depicts his capture. Chained, the beast-man (called the Beast) is led through the streets by inferior devils called imps, while other imps surround and taunt the Beast, who strikes out in lunging movements similar to a bear's. In one playlet, the devil band enacted a struggle between Lucifer, king of the devils, and the beast. The play ended with a victory for the supreme satanic being, who stabbed the beast with his pitchfork and trampled him underfoot, as Hill reports in his book.

An essential part of Trinidad's celebration was *bois,* or stick fighting, the basis of a skillful athletic dance, or *calinda,* that dominated the masquerade in the second half of the nineteenth century. These *boismen,* according to Hill, "took their art seriously...and practiced with the single-mindedness of renowned athletes and artists" as they honed their skills to compete in stick fights that were both battles for status and feats of athleticism and intricate movement. Stick fighters sometimes wore horns, and their costumes were often trimmed with bells. Hill says that nineteenth-century *boismen* were characterized by the following qualities: skill in fighting, sharpness of wit and repartee in conversation and song, talent in dance and music, indifference to authority, and great sexual accomplishments. Carnival songs bragged of the *boismen's* sexual achievements, and it is these songs that gave birth to calypso, popular in America in the 1950s.

Many nationalities and elements blend in Trinidad's carnival — British, French, Spanish, and African. The earliest carnival accounts predate the emancipation of 1834. In those days, white planters dressed in blackface and chains and frolicked through the streets performing the ancient carnival dances and plays. After emancipation, former slaves covered themselves with black varnish and executed the same charade. An account from 1848 tells us a group of blackened Africans traveled through the streets; one of the men had a long chain and padlock attached to his leg, and another man pulled on the chain. The chained man was occasionally thrown on the ground and given a mock beating.

This little playlet often is interpreted as representing the blacks' former slavery, but it has puzzled chroniclers that the white slaveholders performed the same pantomime before emancipation. The rather confused conclusion has been that the black pantomimers were imitating the white pantomimers who were imitating the black slaves. In reality, this capturing and beating of a chained, blackened captive goes beyond the institution of slavery and French and British caste systems into the lifeblood of the carnival itself.

Nineteenth-century Trinidad newspaper accounts referred to the masqueraders as "savage and ferocious hordes," and the ruling classes objected strenuously to the performers' ribaldry and obscenity. Over the years, however, the frolicsome, sexual Carnival has been neutralized, ever gradually neutered, until today it is a copy of the present-day Mardi Gras and Philadelphia Mummers parades — lines of extravagant costumes in a decorous, orchestrated order that would make Papa Bois wince. Papa Bois himself underwent the ultimate transformation in the twentieth century when, as Hill describes the transmogrification, he was given "human dignity and authority," taking him out of the realm of a "weird forest creature." A look at the transmuted Papa Bois reveals a regal gentleman hard to distinguish from a Shakespearean Marc Antony or Henry IV, except for the vestigial horns.

Here Comes Santa Claus

While Papa Bois was evolving into fool and devil, Pelznichol was also changing, to emerge in the early 1800s in America as the personification of Christmas for American children — this time truly an ally to the youth of the land. Pelznichol first appeared as "Santeclaus" in print in an 1821 book called *The Children's Friend*. The first quatrain of the book's poetry reads:

The metamorphosis of Papa Bois was dramatic; he changed from a forest creature into a noble-looking thespian, as shown in this illustration by Carlisle Chang. However, this former Wild Man retains his horns and beard. Courtesy of Carlisle Chang.

> Olde SANTECLAUS with much delight
> His reindeer drives this frosty night,
> O'er chimney-tops, and tracks of snow,
> To bring his yearly gifts to you.

We can see that by 1820, *Santeclaus* had become established as the children's friend. Shortly after this, the most famous of all Christmas poems, "A

Visit from Saint Nicholas" (more familiarly known today as " 'Twas the Night Before Christmas") was published anonymously in the Troy (New York) *Sentinel*, with the German Pelznichol as its model. Although the poem is usually attributed to Clement C. Moore, there is contention about its authorship, an altercation recorded by Henry Litchfield West in an article entitled "Who Wrote 'Twas the Night Before Christmas?' "

Moore, a Hebrew scholar, was reportedly "chagrined" over the publication, "which he apparently considered quite beneath the dignity of a theological professor," according to Charles Jones of Saint Nicholas Society fame. The poem was certainly not in keeping with Moore's character; he was a sober, religious pedant. In his "Knickerbocker Santa Claus," Jones explains Moore's aberration in creating the whimsical poem with these words: "There is a mood of irresponsibility that overwhelms fathers at the Christmas season, and in none is the mood more marked or more catastrophic in its results than in pedants. These sensitive souls, who must always be right as they front the world and consequently succeed in being only stuffy, are at that season caught with their inhibitions down."

Jones, as we have observed, thought Santa was created by Washington Irving and knew nothing of Santa's real history. How he knew Moore was "chagrined" is a mystery, since Moore didn't even claim the poem until 1844, when he published it in a selection of 37 other works — none of which bore any resemblance to this product of his Christmas breakdown, but a few of which were borrowed wholly and unabashedly from classical sources.

The common story of the first publication is that Harriet Butler, daughter of a Troy pastor, was visiting Moore's home when he read the poem to his children. Impressed, she copied it and sent it to her hometown newspaper the next Christmas. According to the descendants of Henry Livingston, Jr., however, their ancestor is the poem's real author. Livingston's daughter, Eliza Thompson, stated in 1879: "I well remember our astonishment when we saw [the poem] — claimed by Clement C. Moore many years after our father's death." Her granddaughter later recited Thompson's story of how the poem originated: Livingston read the poem to his family and a guest at breakfast, after which the guest requested a copy. Later this guest became a governess for Moore's children.

Livingston and Moore were completely opposite personalities. While Moore was a subdued scholar, Livingston was an amateur poet (whose customary verse form was identical to that of "A Visit from Saint Nicholas") as well as a painter and mapmaker. He loved festivity and dancing, adored children and good times, and his favorite expression was "Dunder and Blitzen!"

Whoever wrote it, the poem is important because it features the Germanic Santa Claus figure that would survive, with his troupe of mummers turned into reindeer.

In the 1840s the German gift-giver enjoyed wider exposure when he found

The Children's Friend: A New-Year's Poem to the Little Ones from Five to Twelve, published in New York in 1821, showed an elfish Kriss Kringle with sleigh. From *Christmas in Pennsylvania: A Folk-Cultural Study* (1959); courtesy of the Pennsylvania Folklife Society.

his way into print as Kriss Kringle and Bellsnickle. In 1842, *Kriss Kringle's Book* appeared, followed in 1843 by *Bellsnickle's Gift or a Visit from St. Nicholas.* In 1845, a popular book, *Kriss Kringle's Christmas Tree,* was published. The effect of these publications was that by the mid–1840s the German Christmas man had ventured out from his ethnic community to win the hearts of children everywhere.

In the introduction to *Kriss Kringle's Book,* the editor writes:

Now is not "Kriss Kringle" a nice, fat, good-humored looking man. See how eagerly those little boys embrace him, hoping that he will give them some nice little present or other. Mr. 'Kriss Kingle' [sic] loves good little boys and girls, and if they behave and mind what their parents tell them, they may rest assured that he will pay them a visit, and leave something nice, as a reward for their good behavior.

By the 1840s, Kris Kringle was one of the most common names for the German gift-giver. Folklorist Shoemaker traces the name to *Grisht-kindle,* the word for Bellsnickle's gifts among the Pennsylvania Dutch.

By the mid–1800s, not only had Kriss Kringle become the friend of the little people, he also had made significant inroads into his present role as oiler of the Christmas economy. In 1841, J. W. Parkinson, a Philadelphia department store, hired someone to impersonate Kriss Kringle and billed itself as Kriss Kringle's headquarters. By 1850, the in-store Kriss Kringle had become a common Christmas practice.

The Teutonic gift-giver received even wider exposure courtesy of the artist Thomas Nast, who created a popular series of Christmas drawings for *Harper's Weekly* beginning in 1863. Nast's Santa Claus was the Pelznichol of his Bavarian childhood, a sooty, fur-clad elf. Albert Bigelow Paine, in *Thomas Nast: His Period and His Pictures,* says of Nast's Santa:

> On Christmas Eve came the German Santa Claus, Pelze-Nicol, leading a child dressed as the Christkind and distributing toys and cakes, or switches. It was this Pelze-Nicol — a fat, fur-clad, bearded old fellow, at whose hands he doubtless received many benefits — that the boy in later years was to present to us as his conception of the true Santa Claus — a pictorial type which shall long endure.

Through the years, Nast's figure changed, becoming larger and more grandfatherly. Another depiction that influenced Santa's appearance was J. G. Chapman's 1847 Santa Claus in fur-*trimmed* clothes, with high boots, and a feather in his cap.

From the 1850s on, millions of English-language German Christmas cards were imported to America and sent throughout the land, putting the final feather in Pelznichol's cap and establishing the Teutonic Christmas man as King of Christmas.

In the recent past of the New World, then, we glimpse a common creature and a recurring plot. The being was half man, half beast, behorned and bearded, sometimes with an animal head for a mask. He lumbered and lunged, chained, stick-wielding, unintelligible, bestial, and dangerous. Blackened, humpbacked, and hostile, he invaded the streets at night with his rowdy entourage, crouching, lurching, running, creating havoc. The plot he engaged in was one of capture, chaining, death and resurrection. Companions, including a hag or witch, often accompanied him on his wild, noisy meanderings. But his visit, dangerous and tumultuous as it was, was welcomed as essential to community life.

To make any sense of this strange brute and his companions, it is necessary to descend as far as we can into prehistory as well as to examine the remnant rituals that endured into the twentieth century in many parts of Europe and Russia.

The title page of the popular 1845 children's book *Kriss Kringle's Christmas Tree*, which publicized the Germanic gift-giver. From *Christmas in Pennsylvania: A Folk-Cultural Study* (1959); courtesy of the Pennsylvania Folklife Society.

Top: Nast's Early Santa was not as people-oriented as the modern Santa. *Bottom:* Nast's famous Santa Claus first appeared as a furry, disheveled elf.

Later, Nast depicted a larger, more kindly gent attired in cloth instead of fur.

Chapter 3
He Was
Dressed All in Fur
from His Head to His Foot

The beast-man that made the crossing to America as Pelznichol was generally known in European folklore as the Wild Man, and we find him and his bestial relatives dominating village festivals in the Middle Ages — that broad span of time from about 450 to 1450, between the fall of the Roman Empire and the beginning of the Renaissance. Richard Bernheimer gives a detailed view of this creature in his comprehensive *Wild Men of the Middle Ages.*

According to Bernheimer, the Wild Man was an awesome creature — hair-covered, humpbacked, and bestial. A belief from the Tyrol, an Austrian province in the Alps, held that the Wild Man sat shivering and morose when the sun shone, but when rain, hail, and sleet blessed the land, he smiled and ecstatically exposed his body to the elements. As the storm raged, the Wild Man added to the fury by shaking and uprooting trees. As a creature of storm and fury, he loved thunderstorms, and thunder (Donder) and lightning (Blitzen) were his trademarks.

Most of the time he lived peacefully in the woods among his beloved animals, but when his anger was aroused, he was fierce, his wrath terrifying. Bernheimer says the Wild Man's adherents believed he could make lakes disappear and towns sink into the ground when moved to revenge. The Wild Man was so jealous of his solitude that his first impulse was to tear any trespassers to pieces.

The Wild Man was more than a demon of storm, fury, and destruction; he also was responsible for birth, growth, and fecundity. He was an intimate of the universe's deepest secrets, and his goodwill was invaluable. He cared for the forest animals hunted by humanity and was willing to advise and help humans. Peasants could learn about harvest prospects, herbs, and dairy

39

procedures from him, and he advised them about the weather, when to sow and when to reap. Possessing superhuman knowledge, the Wild Man also could prophesy the future.

But he was more than a soothsayer, for upon his life and death the whole cycle of life depended. His people believed that the Wild Man was a divine being and if he were not killed periodically, the earth would stop yielding its fruits, animals would die, and humanity itself would cease to exist. Each year the people held a ritual renewing the earth, and periodically they sacrificed this god in his prime. Usually, this ritual included a mating between the Wild Man and a woman, bringing into play the fertility aspect of the god while setting the conditions for the renewal of life through new birth.

Renewal or year-end festivals of this type are usually explained as follows: Ancient people thought of life not as a continuous cycle, but as a series of short-term leases that fell due annually. The year was based on the vegetation cycle, and end-of-year occurred when the vegetation died, the soil was depleted, and the earth turned brown and cold. Without proper supernatural assistance, the earth might not revive to support the people and the animals that sustained them.

The Wild Man was the link to the unknown and uncontrollable. He was the vessel through which life flowed to the people and the land; he was the conduit of divine power, the god-humanity connection. As such, if he became frail or infirm, his power would diminish; as a result, crops would wither, animals would cease to produce offspring, and human fertility would suffer. In many communities, the human leader of the group claimed these same powers, as though he himself were the Wild Man. The phenomenon of a political-social leader claiming to be a god is common throughout the annals of recorded human history. The pharaohs of ancient Egypt and the kings of France did it; even modern leaders of religious cults often claim to be the physical embodiment of god.

There are many obvious advantages in claiming to be both king and god. For one thing, your slightest wish would be absolute law. But there is a very crucial drawback: The god-king must die at regular intervals to keep the cycles of nature in balance.

It is apparent that in the very earliest Wild Man rituals, people believed that their god of nature embodied the mysterious forces that kept nature in balance and maintained the cycle of the seasons. It's easy to understand that an ancient person would be terrified at the thought of spring arriving and staying forever; the scenery might be beautiful all the time, but fruit might never ripen, because there would never be a summer for maturation and a fall for harvest. In our modern era, worries about global warming still generate primal fear, but we have satellites and space shuttles to keep constant watch over the earth, and a vast pool of scientific knowledge holding out the hope that humankind can do something to head off a disastrous alteration in the balance of nature. The ancients, however, had no science to rely on for understanding and action. Instead, they watched the sky by day and the stars at night, studied closely the behavior of plants and animals, and turned to the realm of mystery in search of guidance, looking for something they could do to keep the natural order orderly.

It was especially critical for the ancients that the seasons keep changing, and in their proper order. What might happen if the god of nature got senile or forgetful and didn't keep things in place? A late spring or an early fall brings hardship aplenty to people whose lives are dependent on the bounty of nature. The mere thought of winter arriving and lasting forever would send chills to the very core of one's being — it could mean the end of all life.

So while the ancients might have accepted the authority of some person who claimed to be both king and god, they were not willing to accept that this leader, no matter how powerful, could overturn the very rules of nature itself. It would be unnatural if the being who embodied all the forces of nature did not go through the same death-and-rebirth cycle as the earth. Therefore, to make life happen, to assure the continuation of vegetation and human and animal life, the god must die. And if he also happened to be the king, then the king must die. To assure that the leader would not weaken and bring devastation to everything, he was executed in his prime and consumed by his worshippers — apparently every seven years in places such as Ireland; every nine years in France and Scandinavia.

In ceremonies, the beast-god was impersonated by the tribal shaman, who was in contact with both universal and human powers. In some communities and some ages, it is apparent that he was actually deprived of life as part of the ritual. But this execution became increasingly impractical as the leader advanced beyond shaman to become the judge, the planner in war, the uniting force of a nation, the giver of both social and divine law. Some societies had two separate individuals as king and shaman (an early separation of church and state), but some of the most advanced early civilizations combined the mystical and civil powers in one individual. It's a very efficient way to govern, but it gets tricky toward the end of the year.

The king might be all-powerful, but the king must die; it was an unalterable law. To get around this dilemma, many a leader adopted the simple strategy of replacing himself with a substitute king for this unpalatable part of his role. This mock king who assumed the king's role for a short time at year's end was executed in his place, and the naive gods didn't notice. In some rituals, an animal took the leader's place. The reasoning behind such a strategy was simple: The king-god derived his divinity from the natural world, and in fact the Wild Man was as much animal as man, so he could be slaughtered and consumed symbolically in his animal atavism. Then the king would be ritually renewed and resume his high office for another year. The word "scapegoat" lingers on in the English language as a remnant of this ancient practice.

After the sacrifice, the body of the animal was consumed as the god, and people absorbed his life-giving qualities to assure their own fertility. Then the worshippers paraded around the countryside, spreading the fertility to the land.

The execution of the divine connection — the god-on-earth or his substitute — was an important part of the year-end festival performed to renew the world. The time was one of hope and renewal; work was laid aside, official business suspended, and wars outlawed. People tied to the plow and anvil were free, and peasants and princes were equal. The structure that bound society all year was turned upside down, and chaos was the order of the day. These social practices continued in many advanced civilizations, and they linger in our custom of April Fool's Day, when society grants permission to turn things topsy-turvy with pranks.

The Saturnalia and Kalends of ancient Rome were two such festivals that carried on the old customs. Masqueraders crowded the streets dressed in animal skins, no business was allowed, drinking and gaming were everyone's vocation, and class distinctions were abolished or reversed. An important part of this universal holiday was choosing a mock king, who dressed in royal robes and whose duty it was to perpetrate and perpetuate mockery of the normal. By the time we have accounts of the Saturnalia and Kalends, the mock king was no longer slain. In festivals we can trace, the god-human connection eventually was slain only symbolically in such activities as the Wild Man rituals.

The most comprehensive account of ritual god-killing and its remnant rituals is found in Sir James Frazer's *The Golden Bough*. Although scholars today question many of his conclusions, Frazer's prodigious scholarship laid the groundwork for untold scholarly treatises as well as plots for fiction as diverse as Mary Renault's *The King Must Die* and Tom Robbins' *Jitterbug Perfume.*

Capturing the Wild Man

Bernheimer has studied the Wild Man rituals of death and renewal extensively. His synopsis of the basic elements states that in the oldest recorded rituals, worshippers penetrated the forest and captured the beast-god, or else he appeared suddenly outside the village, roaring and snorting, becoming increasingly frenzied as men with chains and ropes captured him. Bound to humanity by massive chains, the Wild Man glowered and fumed. His face, with its matted beard, was grotesque. Horns projected from his head or from the sides of his mouth, like a boar's. Hunched, he shambled along, ape-like, glowering and swaying, leaping, and threatening humans foolish enough to approach him. The Wild Man often carried some symbol of his superhuman strength. In some ceremonies, this was a tree torn out by its roots, which eventually became the Yule Log and May Pole. Sometimes he carried a club or mace of twisted and roughly shaped wood. This was often shaped like a phallus, a symbol of his fertility powers. The Wild Man rattled and clanked wildly in his chains as he was dragged into the village, where he was mated with an earth goddess, killed by an archer, then resurrected or replaced by his son.

The plot sounds simple, but it is like no play we see today. The main actor was considered a nature god, untamed by humanity's laws. His ritual capture reflected his role as a god of fury, elemental power, and life and death. The Wild Man was just that — wild; insane, frenzied, possessed. The person chosen to wear the costume was possessed by the spirit of life itself, by the godhead. He was the god on earth. Catching, chaining, and eventually killing this formidable creature was no small undertaking and would be ventured only for the most profound reason, namely the continuation of life itself.

Folklorist Violet Alford gives an idea of the flavor of the festivals even today, centuries after they have lost their original significance. Alford, who observed remnants of these plays in the 1950s in the Pyrenees Mountains (between Spain and France), recorded them in "The Springtime Bear in the Pyrenees" in the journal *Folklore*. As an objective, seasoned, sophisticated observer of folk festivals, she offers this reaction to one of the plays:

> The Bears break away, and, to give an impression of the general atmosphere, I may say that I found myself in company with several men fleeing into a cafe. Together we broke the glass door, and together we rushed out again, without dreaming of offering to make good the damage and without a word of apology. ... The whole affair, from its anticipation to that last, glorious terrifying scream, is a true folk orgy.

The shaman or priest "playing" the Wild Man was transformed psychologically. Joseph Campbell explains this phenomenon in *The Masks of God*: "When the sacred regalia has been assumed the individual has become an epiphany of the divine being itself. He is taboo. He is the conduit of divine power. He does not merely represent the god, he *is* the god; he is a manifestation of the god, not a representation."

Researching the twentieth-century Trinidad carnival, Errol Hill spoke to the man who played the main devil, Lucifer. In *Trinidad Carnival*, Hill quotes that man's description of the transformation that came over him when he assumed this ancient disguise: "When the moment comes for me to take up that mask, and I take the mask and put it on, I become a different being entirely. I never feel as if I'm human at all. All I see in front of me is devils! Real! Until a long time while after before I get myself to knowledge again."

For a modern man donning a costume once a year to play a part in a festival, the disguise of the Wild Man turned devil had that complete an effect. How much more total the absorption of the priest of that god's religion — the god on earth — that represented him in these plays. The effect was total metamorphosis into the godhead, a metamorphosis that was accepted by all

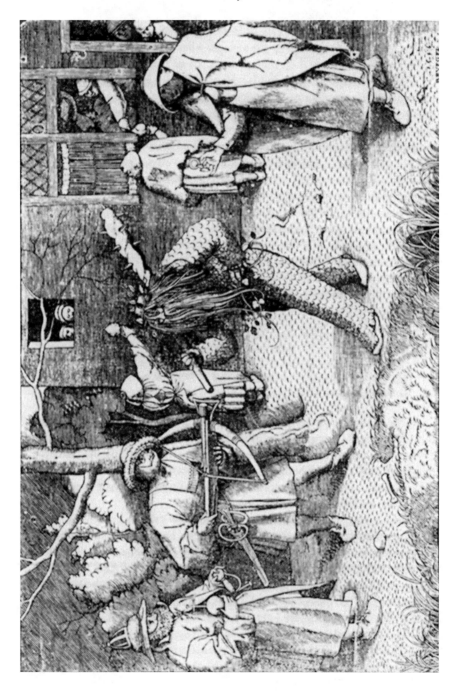

members of the community. Maximilian Rudwin in *The Origin of German Carnival Comedy* says: "There is not the slightest doubt that the masked men delegated to perform the ritual acts were regarded by the rest of the community as the demons they represented. To the primitive mind the actor is, for the time being, the god or demon whom he indicates."

Rudwin relates a 1499 incident in Leipzig where a girl was accused of stabbing a masked young man to death during Carnival because he had teased her. She declared she had not killed a human being, but a demon, and was found innocent.

A Remnant of Pre-Civilization

We don't know how long the Wild Man has been part of our world's rituals, but he has been around at least since the beginning of writing. We find this beast-god as the Wild Man Enkidu in the oldest known text, the *Epic of Gilgamesh,* which was written around 1750 B.C., perhaps as early as the third millennium B.C., and lost to the world until the late nineteenth century. The Wild Man is the remnant of a religious frame of mind that preceded cities and civilization, so by the time we have Assyrian writing, he has had untold centuries to begin to change into a cleaner, more humanoid form, seen in this story as Gilgamesh, king of Uruk in Mesopotamia. But the metamorphosis is not complete, for gods of the old and new societies, the agricultural and state, both exist in this tale.

As anthropologist Claude Levi-Strauss notes, myths often arise in an attempt to reconcile two vastly different cosmologies, often when a people find their old deities or worldview out of step with newer realities. The *Gilgamesh* epic reflects a time of social transition: the Wild Man, Enkidu, is the remnant of godhead from a more primitive time; as an alter ego to the city-dwelling King Gilgamesh, Enkidu still has a hold on the people.

In this story, the people of Uruk were disgusted with their leader Gilgamesh, whose "arrogance knows no bounds." The gods heard the people's lament and went to Aruru, the goddess of creation, saying: "You made him O Aruru, now create his equal; let it be as like him as his own reflection, his second self." So the goddess created Gilgamesh's brother and double, except this doppelgänger was a classic Wild Man: "His body was rough, he had long hair like a woman's; it waved like the hair of Nisaba, the goddess of corn. His body was covered with matted hair like Samuquan's, the god of cattle. He was innocent of mankind; he knew nothing of the cultivated land."

Opposite: This 1566 woodcut showing the play of the wild man is patterned after a painting by Pieter Brueghel the Elder. Here the archer aims at the Wild Man, while the maiden, at the right, holds a ring to lure the creature. Other participants ask for donations at the house.

A local hunter saw Enkidu and, terrified, reported the sighting to his father, describing the creature as "the strongest in the world, he is like an immortal from heaven," and telling how Enkidu had torn up his traps, filled in the pits, and helped the captured creatures escape. The father told the hunter to go to Uruk, tell Gilgamesh about the creature, and ask him for a temple harlot to overpower the beast-man.

The plot worked; after six days and seven nights of lovemaking with the priestess, Enkidu turned toward his beloved beasts, but they ran away. The priestess persuaded Enkidu to return with her and led the former forest-dweller into the city, where Enkidu and Gilgamesh met and grappled, "holding each other like bulls. They broke the doorposts and the walls shook, they snorted like bulls locked together." After Gilgamesh threw Enkidu, the two embraced and became friends. As a Wild Man, Enkidu could interpret dreams, and he served his more refined brother in that capacity and guided him through his journeys.

The Wild Man motif seen in the Gilgamesh story has been around at least 4,000 years in recorded literature, yet the origins of the tradition remain a debated mystery. In tracing the history of the Wild Man/beast-god, most scholars have focused on his horns as the dominant characteristic, since two of his most common animal forms are a goat and a stag. The horned beast-god dominated religion from at least the Paleolithic era, when humans were first gathering into communities that laid the foundations for civilization. One of the earliest pictures of the horned god is the famous Sorcerer of Trois-Frères found in the Caverne des Trois-Frères (Cave of Three Brothers) in France. Deep in the cave is an engraving of a man dressed in animal skins, a figure that dominates the other cave engravings. Joseph Campbell gives this description of the 30,000-year-old painting:

> The pricked ears are those of a stag; the round eyes suggest an owl; the full beard descending to the deep animal chest is that of a man, as are likewise the dancing legs; the apparition has the bushy tail of a wolf or wild horse, and the position of the prominent sexual organ, placed beneath the tail, is that of a feline species — perhaps a lion. The hands are the paws of a bear. Moreover, it is the only picture in the whole sanctuary bearing paint — black paint — which gives it an accent stronger than all the rest.

After the Paleolithic era, we lose track of the horned beast-god until the Bronze Age and the development of written records, when he reappears in Egypt, Mesopotamia, and India. Many of the gods that dotted religions are considered descendants of the Wild Man, the horned half-man, half-beast. By the time we meet him in written literature, in the *Epic of Gilgamesh,* he is being supplanted by a god more appropriate for a literate, sophisticated society, but this horned beast-god lies at the beginning of the Egyptian, Babylonian, Greek, and Roman pantheons.

The Sorcerer of the Caverne des Trois-Frères in France is a 30,000-year-old etching of a priest dressed in animal skins found deep in the cave.

Frederick Elworthy in *Horns of Honor and Other Studies in the By-Ways of Archaeology* says Mesopotamian gods were horned, and gods' prominence in the Babylonian hierarchy could be told by their number of horns. The great deities had seven horns, while inferior gods had to be content with one pair. When the Egyptian king or priest appeared as the god Asshur with his queen Ishtar, the Earth Goddess, he wore the maximum number of horns.

The Egyptian god Amon wears ram's horns, and Herodotus tells us that at the great festival of Thebes, Amon's figure was wrapped in ram skins. Since horns were synonymous with godhead, Alexander the Great donned them when he declared himself a god, and was called *Dhu'l Karnain,* Two-Horned. The profound significance of this goat-god through history persists in our language today; some etymologists trace the word *god* to the German word for goat, *Gott.*

Maximilian Rudwin says: "Goat formed deities and sprites of the wood existed in the religions of India, Egypt, Assyria and Greece. The Assyrian god was often associated with the goat, which was supposed to possess the qualities for which he was worshiped. This animal was also connected with the worship of Priapus, the Greek god of vegetal and animal fertility. The goat was similarly sacred to the Northern god Donar or Thor." The Germanic god Odin also wears horns on his helmet.

The horned god tradition was even retained in Judaism. Tradition gives Moses horns; Elworthy says one authority gives a long list of sources showing Moses as actually horned, and he adds that people believed in Moses' horns into the Middle Ages. Elworthy says, "The Israelites were familiar with horns upon the heads of the gods of Egypt and fresh from bondage they would readily believe that their great law-giver had become deified."

Many scholars have looked to Greece for the beginning of Wild Man rituals, especially to Dionysus and Adonis, both goat-gods. These two deities, who were later cleaned up to the degree that Adonis has become a metaphor for extreme masculine beauty, were actually offshoots of the one god Pan, according to the Greek historian Herodotus. *Pan* means "all," and is a common prefix in such words as *panorama,* meaning a wide or complete view. The name Pan indicates this goat-god was originally the supreme, or only, all-encompassing deity.

Herodotus, world traveler and Greek historian of the fourth century B.C., attempted the promethean task of writing a history of humanity, including their deities. As we have already noted, in ancient times people did not speak the name of their god; it was sacred or didn't exist, so they referred to the god by some attribute or characteristic — "kind," "beneficent," "horned" — in their songs of praise or obeisance. Herodotus says that as poets and others talked about Pan in terms of his different aspects, the qualities became personifications or names, which later were interpreted as individual gods — beginning what Herodotus calls the "mischief of polytheism."

Two men with beards and tails carry worshippers in this depiction of a Dionysian rite. One of the women carries a fawn, which will be torn apart in the ritual. MacCulloch says the ivy leaves around the women's heads and the stem dividing the figures are emblems of Dionysus.

Herodotus blames the Greek poets Homer and Hesoid for this polytheism, the endless Greek pantheon of gods and goddesses. Until their time, says Herodotus, there was but Pan, the All. These and later poets, blind to their own theology, made a god out of every title or characteristic of the All. Soon the intellectual, poetical, and musical personifications of the All sat above Pan in the Greek hierarchy of gods, and Pan found himself slipping among Greek intellectuals. He was considered a lecherous, subhuman creature not fit for the company of more refined deities.

Pictures of Pan are late, after 500 B.C., and show a standard goat-man with a beard, small horns, and goat legs. Under the name Dionysus, Pan continued his sway over the Greeks, at least for a time. Dionysian or Bacchanalian revels are synonyms for wild, drunken orgies, where worship took the form of drinking, copulation, dancing, and ripping a goat or a sacrificial victim apart, eating the victim, and spreading some of the remnant on the land to make it fertile. Dionysus was sometimes associated with a bull, sometimes with a goat, and Frazer says he was worshiped as "the one of the Black Goatskin."

Dionysus was central to Greek religion. Aristotle states that tragedy itself evolved from festivals honoring Dionysus; in fact, the word *tragedy* means "goat-song," and Euripides' tragedy *Bacchae* centers on Dionysus, who has returned from establishing his rites throughout Asia. Michael Grant in *Myths of the Greeks and Romans* says Greek tragedy began when "a goat, the animal sacred to Dionysus and held to represent him is ritually torn to pieces in imitation of the rending of animals which formed part of the Dionysian orgies." After the tragedy form expanded to encompass other themes, however, "satyr plays" became comic interludes for the more sophisticated Athenian tragedies. These rough-humored, earthy side-plays served as humorous foils to the nobler works as Athens moved beyond its agrarian roots.

As in Greece, the horned fertility god is found in Western Europe in Celtic remains. In Paris, an old altar stone shows a bearded god with two antlers growing from his head. The name *Cernunnos* is inscribed above the figure, from the Latin word for *horn*. A monument at Rheims shows this horned god as the supreme god, squatting between Apollo and Mercury who, because of their subservient position, have to stand. Cernunnos holds a bag that pours out acorns and beech nuts, the fruits of the earth, which fall in a stream between an ox and a stag. Another altar stone from France shows Cernunnos with a sack in his lap and two small people, less significant gods, by each horn. A statuette from Autun identifies Cernunnos with the Celtic god Dis, god of the underworld. Alexander McBain in *Celtic Mythology and Religion* says it is this Dis that the Celts worshiped at the end-of-year festival Samhain, in which beast-men stormed the byways and ruler's palace. McBain says the October 31 Samhain celebrations were the remnants of a seven-year king-killing expedition.

In England, Cernunnos the horned god lives on as the Cerne Giant, cut into the chalk of Dorset in England. The huge figure lies above the ruins of a monastic shrine that was built over a shrine of Cernunnos. Although it has lost its horns over the centuries, the figure retains its club and phallus. Cernunnos also survived on as Herne, or, more colloquially, Old Hornie. Herne eventually found himself a character in Shakespeare's *The Merry Wives of Windsor*. In this play, Falstaff disguises himself as Herne the Hunter, "with great horns on his head," horns he offers to the merry wives' husbands. In the play we learn of Herne the Hunter, a Wild Man still carrying the pesky chains that bind him to humans, and of how the old people brought his tale to new generations:

> There is an old tale goes that Herne the hunter,
> Sometime a keeper here in Windsor forest,
> Doth all the wintertime, at still midnight,

The Celt's horned god is preserved on this second-century Gundestrup Bowl from Denmark. Inside the bowl is a sacrificial scene.

This horned deity with torques on his antlers is from an altar stone found at Notre Dame, Paris. MacCulloch says the writing above the head reads *Cernunnos*, from the Latin for horn.

The horned god, possibly Cernunnos, sits between two less important gods (whom John MacCulloch identifies as Apollo and Mercury), as grain spills from his lap to fall between the bull and the deer. The stonework is from an altar found in France.

Walk round about an oak, with great ragg'd horns;
And there he blasts the tree, and takes the cattle,
And makes milch kine yield blood, and shakes a chain
In a most hideous and dreadful manner.
You have heard of such a spirit, and well you know
The superstitious idle-headed eld
Received and did deliver to our age
This tale of Herne the hunter for a truth.

Although Dionysus had evolved into a clown and was now relegated to romping on the periphery of the Greek stage or giving Falstaff an opportunity for bombast, outside the centers of civilization the goat-man ritual persisted remarkably intact into the twentieth century. In 1906, traveler and Renaissance man R. M. Dawkins recorded one of the "purest" modern forms of the goat-man ritual in the Balkans, a rugged, mountainous region in southeast Europe that comprises all or part of six modern nations — Albania, Bulgaria, Greece, Romania, Turkey, and what until recent years was called Yugoslavia. In this festival the Wild Man, a goat-god, was brought into the village, executed, and revived.

The festival Dawkins witnessed began with a parade, led by two goat-men. They shambled through the village with bells around their waists and ankles. Their blackened faces grimaced, and padding gave them humped backs. One goat-man carried a huge phallus; the other carried a crossbow, the execution weapon. An "old woman" carrying a doll in a basket paraded with them, as did blackened "gypsies" and an array of other characters. As they paraded from house to house, the phallic goat-man pounded the phallus on doors and demanded money from the residents, as the old woman and gypsies performed what Dawkins calls "obscene acts" of copulation outside each house.

A play of death and renewal was basic to the ritual. In the play, the old woman and gypsies forged a mock plowshare. Then the old woman took the baby from its basket, declaring it was too large for the basket. The baby instantly grew into the phallic goat-man, who demanded food and a bride. The archer goat-man brought the bride, and the phallic goat-man and his bride copulated. The marriage was cut short, however, when the archer shot the groom. The bride then grieved, and the phallic goat-man revived. Celebrating his resurrection, the characters pulled a plow into a circle and danced a round dance with the plow in the center. Seeds were scattered, the plow was drawn through the village, and the people wished for good crops.

The play Dawkins witnessed had changed little from its original form in both attire and action, but just a few years later it had altered significantly when another traveler, A. J. B. Wace, traveled Thessaly and South Macedonia for three years, looking for other surviving Balkan rituals, which he reported in "North Greek Festivals and the Worship of Dionysos" in 1910.

In some of the plays Wace reported, two new characters had been added. One of them was a doctor, who resuscitated the fallen groom. This doctor character entered the plays throughout Europe as spontaneous regeneration lost its credibility, and his was inevitably a comic role. The second addition to the cast, the Arab, was not so much a new character as an alteration of the archer goat, the executioner. The archer as Arab had become a villain figure who retained the black goat mask, goat skin, lust, and sometimes a tail. The bridegroom in some plays had become a conventional human with a rusty sword instead of a phallic stick, although he retained a goat's beard and the essential bells on his waist and elbows.

In a representative play, the Arab "got fresh with" the bride, and the groom

R. M. Dawkins observed this 1906 Greek goat-man, who wore a sheepskin mask and shirt and numerous bells as he paraded through the streets of Skyros, Greece, with his wife.

Top: A. J. B. Wace looked for other Balkan survivals of the goat-man plays and reported this bride and bridegroom in 1910. The groom, a boy now instead of the man of old, had a goat's mask, bell, and sword. *Bottom:* Wace also found this version of the goat-man. Although his face was no longer covered completely with a goat's head, this bridegroom retained a goat's beard and long hair. His horns have altered to become floppy "ass ears."

fought him, defending his lady's honor. The Arab killed the groom, and the bride flung herself on the dead body, weeping violently. She then hurried to get a doctor, who put a piece of soap into the groom's mouth or resuscitated him in some other humorous manner. The groom revived, danced, and simulated intercourse with the bride.

In this altered form, the old amorality of the fertility rite had disappeared, and the drama had become a spectators' play, a confrontation between "good guys" and "bad guys," with the Arab assuming all the bad guy traits, including animal licentiousness, hairiness, and murder. The goat-man had been trifurcated — different elements of his character spread among three personas. The doctor assumed the ability to resurrect the dead, but since modern audiences knew this was impossible, he was a comic character. The groom retained his prerogative of mating with the woman, but his role as a fertility god was slipping fast. The Arab assumed the bestial aspects of the god, including his lechery.

In the other areas Wace traveled, the play and masqueraders had disappeared, sometimes because they were banned by the police. In Halmyros, despite a police ban, Wace and his traveling companion, M. S. Thompson, saw several bands of young men going house to house, "but even here they were pursued by the police to stop chicken stealing, and to prevent their creating a disturbance with their songs." On Epiphany, says Wace, the village was filled with bands of these youths, one of them dressed as a bride. As they passed through the streets, they stopped villagers; the bride offered an orange or apple, and the groom threatened the waylaid citizen with his sword until the person paid. The bridegrooms wore goatskin masks, and one had a pair of goat's horns tied to his hat. Generally the groom had blackened his face and carried an old sword or bayonet. Always, he wore bells.

From Lore to Literature

The Wild Man or goat-man persisted in places other than the Balkan hinterlands. In fact, he prospered in popular literature, as shown in an eighteenth century chapbook that relates a story almost identical to Gilgamesh — strikingly so, considering the Assyrian epic wasn't deciphered until the 1900s. *The History of Valentine and Orson* relates how the pregnant wife of the emperor of Greece, banished from her husband's empire, gave birth to twin sons in the forest of Orleans in France. A she-bear carried off one of the babes, and the weakened queen pursued the bear on her hands and knees, leaving the other babe behind. Meanwhile, her brother, King Pepin of France, found the the first child and raised it as his own. The bear-raised child grew up to be a "wild hairy man, doing great mischief to all that passed through the forest." Valentine, the king-adopted babe, became a knight, and when he heard about a Wild Man

Woodcuts in the eighteenth-century *History of Valentine and Orson*. Top left: The mother helplessly pursues a she-bear who has taken one of her twin sons. This son will be raised by the bear to become the Wild Man Orson. Top right: The court-raised twin, Valentine, hides in a tree before he confronts Orson. Bottom left: Valentine captures Orson and leads him back to the court. Bottom right: At court, Orson finds his trusty club an adequate weapon against standard swords.

no knight could defeat, Valentine offered to conquer the beastly creature. The two battled to a standstill, at which time Valentine told the Wild Man that if he would yield, Valentine would help Wild Man become a "rational creature."

The Wild Man accepted Valentine's offer and accompanied him to court, where he was baptized Orson, meaning "bear." Orson turned out to be a superb knight, but couldn't talk until Valentine cut a thread under his tongue. When the king of France died, the pair took turns governing the empire until Valentine died seven years later. Orson then ruled for seven years, after which he abdicated, turning over his kingdom, wife, and children to the Green Knight, and returned to the woods. The length Valentine and Orson reign — seven years — is significant because it corresponds to the time span for ritual killings of Wild Man priests, and later kings, in France. As a play, the story of Orson and Valentine was part of Christmas festivities in Nova Scotia, the Canadian province settled by the French in 1605.

Just as a woman conquered Enkidu, a woman was responsible for capturing another character known to most of us, though few are aware of his Wild Man heritage. King Arthur's prized mentor and magician, Merlin, derived his wondrous powers from his Wild Man father, according to Geoffrey of

Monmouth's twelfth-century *Life of Merlin* and the thirteenth-century *Story of Merlin.* Merlin's maiden mother lost her way home and, as she slept under a tree, a Wild Man mated with her, resulting in Merlin. Merlin lived half of his life normally, but he was seized by fits of wildness that drove him into the woods, where he became a "sylvan man" and lived "like a beast."

Merlin arranged his own capture so he could put the Wild Man's prophetic abilities to the king's use. Disguised as a stag, Merlin revealed that only a Wild Man could explain some dreams troubling the emperor. He also obligingly gave instructions on how to capture the Wild Man (with a woman). In this tale, Merlin continues the Wild Man's exclusive ability to tap into the divine to benefit humanity.

Twentieth-Century Survivals

The Wild Man's ancient ritual of death and rebirth also continued throughout parts of Europe other than Greece. In the 1950s Violet Alford recorded many of the surviving festivals in the Pyrenees Mountains. In these festivals, the Wild Man is almost always called the bear. Rhys Carpenter says the Wild Man and bear figures are interchangeable, as shown in the linguistic connection of *Orcus* (Wild Man) and *Ursus* (Bear). Bernheimer agrees the distinction between man and beast is not always "rigorously maintained," and that both can be seen as essentially the same fertility god.

Just as she did in *Gilgamesh,* a human maiden lures the Wild Man from his forest in Alford's report from Arles-sur-Tech in Southeast France, where the nubile human Rosetta enters the woods to lure the ferocious Wild Man into the hunters' trap. Unsuspecting, the hairy creature approaches the maiden. He sees the trap too late, and the hunters surround him quickly, placing the growling, protesting bear in massive chains. The hunters lead the creature back to the town square, where the people have constructed a plaster cave for him. Here he takes Rosetta — to mate with this woman, to imbue her with his ancient life force. A shot rings out, and the god lies dead. But it is too soon; the marriage has not been consummated, and the groom revives. After the sex act, the Wild Man is shot again, this time to remain dead as the community celebrates.

The other festivals Alford witnessed retained bits and pieces of this ritual. In the Valley of Luz, the bear is a shambling man in goatskins and a bear's head. He is led by a "trainer," who carries a pole with bells and a cow horn. Three armed men accompany the pair, and a peasant woman carries a basket. Natives told Alford the bear used to be "married" to the woman, but in Alford's twentieth-century version the bear was merely shot, then resurrected when the trainer blew a horn in his ear.

The Wild Man/bear festivals took place in the spring, the time of rebirth. Costumed players appeared in the traditional hairy garb, and a hug from one of them assured fertility. Often springtime parades throughout Europe featured the Wild Man and his spouse, accompanied by newly married couples, whose fertility was assured by their march with this symbol of fecundity. Wild Man dances emphasizing fertility were often included in plays celebrating weddings, known as *charivari,* which often served up rough, sexual humor to the betrothed pair and continued in some American communities as chivarees to newlyweds.

In France, Charles VI, who reigned from 1380 to 1422, participated in these charivari at least twice; in fact, it was this pastime that proved too much for his unstable sanity. In a long line of kings bearing the name Charles, he is distinguished as "Charles the Mad." Bernheimer describes the mad king's experience:

> Charles VI of France, at best not a man of too well-posed equilibrium, could not deny himself the pleasure of participating in charivaris when the opportunity arose; and that he did so in 1389, on occasion of the marriage of one of the ladies in waiting, he found himself attacked by the officers of the queen, who, not recognizing him under his mask, treated him to a sound thrashing.

This experience was bad enough, but the king and five nobles fared even worse when they dressed like Wild Men for a 1392 charivari. Chained together, the Wild Men cavorted, but the Duke of Orleans wanted a closer look at the dancers. Unfortunately, this involved holding his torch closer, and the revellers' hairy costumes caught fire. Bernheimer continues, "Chained as they were to each other, the revelers had no means of disengaging themselves and four of them perished miserably. The king was saved only because his quick-witted aunt, the Duchess of Berry, threw the train of her robe over him in time and smothered the flames. The king's precarious sanity broke in consequence of the shock."

Other remnants from the original Wild Man–priestess marriage live on in other ways. The motif of the marriage of a woman and a beast-man is common in the Germanic folklore collected by the Grimm Brothers in the 1880s. The best known modern survival of these is "Beauty and the Beast," which was made into a successful Walt Disney movie in 1993.

The Wild Man hunt also endured in some areas. Frazer's *Golden Bough* relates numerous Wild Man rituals such as one in Bohemia, where a Wild Man was chased through the streets until he stumbled over a rope. Hunters caught the creature, and an executioner stabbed the blood-filled bladder on his body. The next day a straw figure representing the Wild Man was carried to a pond and thrown in by the executioner.

Jennifer Russ in *German Festivals and Customs* relates some of the Wild Man activities that took place in Germany at Whitsuntide, the fiftieth day after Easter. Russ reports that children in Swabia, in southwest Germany, blackened their faces and went around the village with buckets, wearing hats of green

The Wild Man lived on in his original hairy form in some parts of Germany, as shown in this picture from an unidentified location in Bavaria.

wheat and begging for food. In Thuringia, a boy camouflaged himself with leaves and moss, wore a tree-bark mask, and hid in the wood while other children searched for him. This custom, says Russ, is known as hunting the Wild Man, Green Man, Grass King, or Leaf Dwarf.

   Charles Billson in a 1908 *Folklore* publication shows us an old Jass or "jester" of Thun, Switzerland. The Jass was the central figure in a three-day Shooting Feast. In a calfskin coat and horns, the Jass walked around the town

This picture of the Jass or Jester of Thun, Switzerland, is from about 1870. The Jass walked around town in calfskin coat, horn, and baton.

and beat youth with his sizeable baton. In his bells and animal mask, the Jass was naturally the local bogeyman, and parents threatened their children with the Jass if they didn't behave.

In 1936 the *Illustrated London News* reported Wild Man activities in Bavaria:

> On the eve of St. Nicholas Day certain masked men come out of the snowy woods on skis and approach a village. An atmosphere reigns

over the houses. The older, more experienced inhabitants and the children remain indoors, and peer through the windows into the night not without apprehension for what they will see. Horns of elfland blow. The "wild men" wear voluminous distorting costumes of animal skins and heavy concealing headdresses with horns or antlers. They knock at doors and windows and claim kisses of the girls or catch them in the street and rub them with snow. The reign of the Wild Men lasts till daybreak.

In parts of Greece, the goat-men persisted as well. James William Brown describes twentieth-century goat masquerades on a small Greek island in his novel *Blood Dance.* At carnival time, says Brown, "young men turn themselves into beasts" once a year and dance through the streets. Although there were many kinds of costumes, the most important ones, "the ones that mattered," were the goat dancers, says Brown: "They were fearsome things, covered in shaggy pelts from head to waist, the face of a goat, the harness of clanking bells."

As in most festivals where the ancient festival persisted into modern, Christianized times, a legend "explained" why young men would wrap themselves in goatskins annually and frolic through the streets, hopping and jumping, under a harness of heavy bells until they were exhausted. On this island, the explanatory tale goes, a shepherd's flock was killed by wolves. In anguish over the loss of his livelihood, the shepherd skinned the sheep, wrapped the skins around himself, covered his face with a sheep's head, and fastened their neck bells into a harness. After that, he went to the village and clanked and banged from cafe to cafe, drinking, his dance becoming more and more frenzied, until at last he threw himself into the sea. This was the supposed origin of the goat-men's clangorous dancing, and each year the village priest blessed the goat dancers before they began their ancient frolic.

What we have here is the basic Wild Man — a hairy, blackened, humpbacked, stick-carrying beast-man. It is rare for the Wild Man to have survived in that form; he usually had changed quite a bit by the time we have good historical accounts of this figure and his rituals. Of course, people in whose lives the Wild Man plays were a normal ritual seldom stopped to record the goings-on, just as moderns don't record the church rituals or Fourth of July parades they include in their normal existence; they are simply a part of one's life. They are recorded only when outsiders, folklorists, anthropologists, and curiosity-seekers happen upon them. Generally the Wild Man celebrations continued unrecorded, vitally integrated in the villagers' yearly pattern.

Thus, we have Wild Men and goat-men central to the great civilizations' religions, although by the time we meet them in writings, they have become peripheral characters, cavorting on the sidelines in the centers of learning. In more remote areas of Europe, however, the Wild Man continued to frolic among his people, working his ancient magic, oblivious to the higher, more aesthetic gods, or blending comfortably into the community church ritual.

We know that by the Middle Ages the Wild Man and his festivals had become central to village rituals throughout Europe. The Wild Man, under scores of identities, held unparalleled power. At the same time, however, the Holy Roman Empire, which also stood at the apex of the feudal pyramid, was spreading its influence, bent on unifying Europe under the church's political power. Under the circumstances, it was inevitable that the Church and the Wild Man would clash, and when they did, something had to give.

Chapter 4

Satan Dons Furs

As the Wild Man romped and reigned in splendor and terror in European villages, new forces were spreading through Europe, changing people's lives. Christianity was one of these, spreading northward into Europe and western Asia from the Mediterranean region and challenging the old gods' power.

The Wild Man's festival was a fertility rite and included all the necessary elements, from carrying huge phalluses to having intercourse on the public plaza — an action people hoped would inspire the animals to copulate as well as aid human fertility. As god of such a festival, the Wild Man's activities were flagrantly erotic. To the Christian fathers, who promoted monogamous sex for followers, celibacy and ascetic living for religious leaders, the Wild Man became more and more the personification of lust and debauchery. It is not surprising that this heathen god became the model for Pope Gregory I's picture of the devil — a goat-skinned man with cloven hooves, beard, horns, humpback, and stick.

Before Pope Gregory's reign, from 590 to 604, the Christian devil had been considered angelic-looking, when he was considered to have a physical form at all; he was, after all, an upper-caste angel prior to his rebellion and dismissal from heaven. In the Old Testament, there is little mention of Satan, because the Yahweh of old encompassed all the savagery that some peoples might attribute to an anti-god. Satan is mentioned only about a half-dozen times in the New Testament, and in those instances he has no specific look.

In early Christianity, Satan still hadn't achieved much of a physical identity. He might be a formless tempter, a teaser — sometimes identified as a serpent, a dragon, a leviathan, or a flash of lightning. Mostly he is Lucifer, the angel who fell from heaven. The earliest church pictures of Satan occur in the sixth century in miniatures and frescoes, where he can be distinguished from the other beautiful angels only by the fact that he is falling; there is none of the animal nature, physical deformity, and licentiousness of later depictions. That didn't officially start until the seventh century, when Gregory the Great described Satan as having horns and hooves, a black color, weather-controlling powers, and — to top it all off — a terrible stench. Gregory himself continued to think of evil as a psychological concept, the spirit of temptation; he tapped the Wild Man as Satan to show heathens the error of their ways and the identity of their god.

It is common practice for the god of one religion to become the Devil of the religion that replaces it, and Pope Gregory's depiction of the Wild Man as devil formalized an association clerics had made for centuries. In the fifth century, St. Peter Chrysologus urged Christians to convert those who "have masqueraded in the likeness of animals, who have assumed the shape of herd animals, who have turned themselves into devils." In the sixth century, St. Caesarius of Arles exclaimed:

> Is there any sensible man, who could ever believe that there are actually rational individuals willing to put on the appearance of a stag and transform themselves into wild beasts? Some dress themselves in the skins of herd animals. Others put on the heads of horned beasts, swelling and wildly exulting if only they can so completely metamorphose themselves into the animal kinds that they seem to have entirely abandoned the human shape.

In France, the Council of Auxerre in the 570s forbade masquerading as a calf or stag on January 1 and banned distribution of "devilish charms." The earliest ecclesiastical laws of England, the seventh-century *Liber Poenitentialis,* prohibited disguise as wild animals. The law includes penances for "those who in such wise transform themselves in the appearance of a wild animal, penance for three years because this is devilish."

Jeffrey Russell in *Witchcraft in the Middle Ages* says the church condemned beast-masking, with its belief in shape-shifting, more than any other pagan event. The ancient festival was held to increase the number of animals for the hunt and called for wearing animal skins, horns, and beast masks. Scholars agree myths of werewolves, or man-wolves, are the result of stories of priests "changing into" a deer or wolf. Instead of actual transformations from human to animal, they were based on accounts of persons taking off and putting on animal skins; they "changed into" the animal in the sense that we "change into" something more comfortable. This analogy is a little simplified, however, because we don't psychologically identify with our clothing in the way the person dressed as the Wild Man identified with the creature.

In "Romanian Werewolves, Seasons, Ritual, Cycles" in the journal *Folklore,* Harry Senn traces the Romanian werewolves that form part of the Christmas tradition in northeast Romania and northern Transylvania to the Lupercalia of ancient Rome, when members of wolf and goat fraternities took to the streets to honor Dionysus. Says Senn: "Mumming and processions did not cease with the disappearance of the ancient gods in Greece. ... Modern-day Greek celebrants blacken their faces and cover themselves and features. They are covered with shaggy hair, heads and sexual organs out of proportion to the rest of their bodies, and legs, ears, and horns borrowed from the goat."

These festivals of hunting magic were resistant to change, because people's lives were bound directly into the earth and its produce. While Greek and Roman philosophers and poets rhapsodized about gods of poetry, music, and inspiration, the peasant was concerned with the yield of the field and the number of calves born. In the same way, Christianity, with its esoteric doctrines and concern with heavenly abodes, had little impact on these people. In addition, Christianity was an alien, imported religion at first; early missionaries seldom mixed with the populace they were sent to convert, and reformers were considered foreigners who lived apart from the natives. For example, Theodore of Taurus nominally organized the English church in the seventh century, but the Christians were considered an odd, unpopular group. The later Augustine mission and its successors took the short cut to power by concentrating on the rulers. The result was that, although the rulers professed Christianity and the nations were nominally converted, the masses followed the old gods.

The old gods were being publicly worshiped as late as the sixteenth century in the British Isles. As Lewis Spence relates in *The Mysteries of Britain*, an idol was brought to the attention of Cromwell, secretary to Henry VII. A letter to Cromwell states people flocked to a statue of Darvell Gadarn with oxen, horses, and money. The idol was taken to Smithfield and burned, along with a priest of the same name as the idol. Spence equates Darvell Gadarn with the Celtic god Hu Gadarn, who appeared in the shape of an ox. It was this kind of god, not a remote, heavenly one, whose favor people sought to preserve their harvest and well-being.

In addition to Christianity's being perceived as an alien, somewhat irrelevant religion, a significant part of the church's "conversion problem" was its selection of earthly personnel. In its haste to set up churches, the Catholic Church often recruited its priests from the ranks of the old priesthoods. This led to ancient heathen rites being celebrated alongside the new, and often at the same worship service. As late as the 1600s in some areas, while a thin veneer of Christianity covered Europe, beneath this veneer priests and peasants frolicked in ancient worship. European Christianity was a combination of the earthy nature-based heathenism and the newer, more esoteric heavenly Trinity-based religion coexisting in the same rites.

The church accommodated this beast-masking and wild reveling to some degree by allowing it on certain days. In many European areas the three days following Christmas were given over to three different groups for unchristian mockery. The deacons had the 26th; the priests the 27th, and the students and choir boys took over the church on the 28th of December. Laws were relaxed and morality reversed under a "bishop of fools" or a "bishop of bon accord," as clerics subverted church sacredness to the old heathen customs. This development brought horror and outcry from higher church officials, and in 1198 the bishop of Paris demanded the shocking feast be abolished, but 150 years later it was still going strong, as George McKnight notes in a similar protest of 1445:

> Priests and clerks may be seen wearing masks and monstrous visages at the hours of office. They sing wanton songs. They eat black puddings at the horn of the altar while the celebrant is saying mass. They play at dice there. They cense with stinking smoke from the soles of old shoes. They run and leap through the church, without a blush at their own shame. Finally, they drive about the town and its theatres in shabby traps and carts; and rouse the laughter of their fellows and bystanders in infamous performances, with indecent gestures and verses scurrilous and unchaste.

It was in this era that Saint Nicholas entered the Christmas scene, according to McKnight. The students' festival, called the "boy bishop" or "boy Nicholas" festival, was one of the most popular of these feasts of fools. Medieval schools were run by monasteries, which encouraged students to act out plays about their patron saint Nicholas, the original boy bishop. On December 6, students chose a boy bishop, who ruled until December 28. These boy bishop or boy Nicholas holidays often fell short of the dignity the church intended to promote. A typical boy bishop parade was one in thirteenth-century Aberdeen, Scotland, where the boy bishop and his fellow students paraded the streets with "imps and satyrs and devils"—Wild Men—in unrestrained, "obscene" festivity. The old god, the Wild Man, was an essential part of the boy bishop parade that McKnight says "once prevailed throughout the length and breadth of the land in every parish church as well as in cathedrals, collegiate churches and schools." Church and state officials fumed against the Feast of Fools until the Wild Man finally found himself eased out the church door, along with his feasts. In the British Isles, says McKnight, the festival lasted until the sixteenth century; in France it died in the 1720s, and in Germany it lasted until 1779.

Ironically, as the Wild Man's rituals were subverting church doctrine in the Feast of Fools or boy Nicholas festivals, the reverse was taking place in village festivals, where strange, new, white-clad saints minced alongside the traditional raucous troupers. Often the Wild Man found his chain held by a saint, and his role relegated to that of a clumsy servant or, as shown in Holland, Black Pete—the scourge that awaits evildoers. Usually the substitution was unsuccessful; these staid figures hardly personified the holiday spirit people expected and wanted. As a consequence, the saints often found themselves devolving into their heathen predecessors.

Jacob Grimm in *Teutonic Mythology* says:

> In Christian times they [the church] would choose some saint to accompany Christ or the Mother of God in their distribution of boons,

but the saint would imperceptibly degenerate into the old goblin again, but now a coarser one. The Christmas plays sometimes present the Saviour with His usual attendant Peter or else with Niclas. At other times however Mary with Gabriel, or with her aged Joseph, who, disguised as a peasant, acts the part of Knecht Ruprecht [the German Wild Man]. Nicholas again has converted himself into a "man Clobes" or Rupert; as a rule there is still a Niclas, a saintly bishop and benevolent being distinct from the "man" who scares children; but the characters get mixed, and Clobes himself acts the "man."

Grimm's observation shows what happened in Germany when the church tried to supplant the Wild Man and his entourage with saints. The saint would inevitably degenerate and take on some aspects of the Wild Man, and the festival's central character remained the old god.

The church had a similar problem in the plays it enacted. The Wild Man as devil was reinforced in Church plays that sprung up in the 1100s as an alternative to village plays. Church patriarchs, seeing their flocks' love of the village performances, decided to put on their own dramas. Instead of the gross, animalistic obscenities of festival plays, however, these plays featured the moral tribulations and triumphs of saints and biblical characters.

The church hoped its plays would draw the people's minds from the profane buffooneries; however, these miracle and morality plays were dull and sanctimonious, and fell far short of the hoped-for success. The church fathers introduced the devil and various vices for comic relief, and Truth, Beauty, and Mercy found themselves playing alongside the Seven Deadly Sins. The Wild Man, as vice or devil, helped popularize these plays, giving the people a sensuous, uncouth comic character they could identify with, feel superior to, or cringe before.

Paul Carus in *The History of the Devil and the Idea of Evil* says the devil's role was one of a buffoon, and his part soon dominated the previously sanctimonious productions: "In Mediaeval mysteries God the Father, God the Son, and Satan appear on the stage, and the last one is practically the main actor in the whole drama." In these plays, the devil's common entry line, known as the "devil's bluster," was "Ho! Ho! Hoh!" Of course, the stage devil was inevitably black, hairy, and often endowed with the traditional oversized phallus, either as a bodily attachment or in the form of a club. These plays ended in the sixteenth century under pressure from Puritan and other anti–Papal elements that protested showing sacred events on stage.

Grimm mentions the "man Claus (Clobes)" as opposed to the Bishop Nicholas. This "man Claus" or servant Claus was the Wild Man, for the Wild Man was called Nicholas or Claus in Germany in many areas; in fact, Nicholas is one of the most common devil's names in German, a name that remains today when Satan is referred to as Old Nick. Margaret Murray suggests Saint Nicholas was invented to take the place of the old Claus, the Wild Man. Thus the usual

As a comic figure, Satan inevitably upstaged his more prestigious fellow actors in medieval mysteries, as in this German example.

explanation that Santa Claus "came from" Saint Nicholas seems to be backward: Saint Nicholas was created to take the place of the heathen god, the Furry Claus. This complete reversal did not take every place in Europe, although the boy bishop aged considerably as he tried to assimilate Furry Claus's luck-bringing and gift-giving into his repertoire.

As Christianity strove to make its political and religious mark on Europe it assimilated the old Wild Man customs, and many Christian rituals today, such as the communion speech, "Take, eat, this is my body which is broken for you," reflect Christianity's absorption of old rites.

This assimilation was acceptable to a point, but the Wild Man's hold on the continent was impeding the church's domination, and the church reacted. In the thirteenth century the church declared worshiping the old gods a heresy, but purging them was a problem because so many priests were recruited from members of old religions. In 1282 the priest of Inverkeithing was accused of leading an Easter fertility dance around the phallic god. He pleaded "common usage" of the custom and was allowed to keep his post. In 1303 the bishop of Coventry himself was accused before the Pope of doing homage to the devil.

After centuries of protest, the church gained enough earthly power to persecute the devil worshippers. After the Black Plague and social upheavals that rocked Europe in the 1400s, a spiritual pessimism lay over the land. As Gillian Tindall in *A Handbook on Witches* phrased it, "Surely God had sent the plague in terrible retribution for heresy? Mankind seemed helpless in His avenging yet capricious power."

Plague occasionally had attacked humanity, but the outbreak of plague that swept through Europe and parts of Asia in the fourteenth century was beyond imagination; it is estimated to have killed up to three-quarters of the populace during a twenty-year period. Modern science tells us the infection results from bacteria, but the people suffering and dying had no microscopes, only mysticism, to explain the calamity. Churches, as centers of learning and community organization that dealt in the issue of death and afterlife, took the lead in trying to counteract this wholesale slaughter by some unknown agent of doom. Lacking tetracycline, they looked to the Trinity for relief. The church believed and preached that this Black Death was sent by God to punish humanity for pagan ways and heathen worship, among other transgressions.

It was the perfect opportunity for the church to expand its influence among the masses and fight against followers of the old ways. Many people were put on trial for engaging in the ancient rites, and many died as punishment. The bishop of Coventry was tried, but let free because of his prominence. A lady of rank, Dame Alice Kyterler, was tried for witchcraft in Scotland but freed because of her rank; her less prestigious followers died at the stake. Trials in Berne, Switzerland, followed, and again those of high rank went free while the poorer members burned.

After these skirmishes, the church in 1484 unleashed its armies against the recalcitrant heathens. In that year Pope Innocent VIII issued a papal letter, or bull, that is usually considered the beginning of the all-out war against heathenism, which by this time was being called "witchcraft." The bull relates:

> It has come to our ears that numbers of both sexes do not avoid to have intercourse with demons Incubi, Succubi; and that by their sorceries, and by their incantations, charms, and conjurations, they suffocate, extinguish, and cause to perish the births of women, the increase of animals, the corn of the ground, the grapes of the vineyard and the fruit of the trees, as well as men, women, flocks, herds, and other various kinds of animals, vines and apple trees, grass, corn and other fruits of the earth; making and procuring that men and women, flocks and herds and other animals shall suffer and be tormented both from within and without, so that men beget not, nor women conceive; and they impede the conjugal action of men and women.

So that there would be no mistake when Christians met him, the devil was described in detail. That description should be familiar by now. The devil is humpbacked, black, and hairy; he wears goat skins, has horns, carries a club, and is a sex fiend. This papal bull of 1484, imposed on a world still reeling from the Black Plague, reinforced and gave new impetus to an orgy of persecution and extermination that would have done Hitler proud. In Bamberg, Germany, between 1609 and 1633, 900 persons were burned, including the burgermeister. The bishop of Geneva burned 500 persons in three months; the bishop of Wirzburg exterminated 900. The Savoy Senate condemned 800 *en masse*. In a century and a half, from 1404 to 1554, the church's earthly armies of God reportedly burned at least 30,000 persons as witches.

Among those executed were members of the Goats, a secret society that terrorized the territory of Limburg in the 1770s. R. Lowe Thompson in *The History of the Devil: The Horned God of the West* relates:

> These wretches met at night in a secret chapel, and after the most hideous orgies, which included the paying of divine honours to Satan and other foul blasphemies of the Sabbat, they donned masks fashioned to imitate goats' heads and sallied forth in bands to plunder and destroy. From 1772 to 1774 alone the tribunal of Foquemont condemned four hundred goats to the gallows. But the organization was not wholly exterminated until about the year 1780, after a regime of the most repressive measures and unrelaxing vigilance.

This systematic extinction of opposition stretched into the eighteenth century and finally resulted in the forced eradication of any viable popular opposition to the Christian Church.

Scholars who have studied witchcraft from an anthropological, social viewpoint disagree on the nature of the evil the church targeted. Margaret

Murray in *The God of the Witches* contends the old religion was highly organized from earliest times and refers to a comment by Cotton Mather that the witches "form themselves after the manner of Congregational Churches" to support her view that "the cult was organized in as careful a manner as any other religious community; each district, however was independent."

Murray, an Egyptologist by training, created quite a furor with her books about witchcraft in the 1920s and 1930s. In fact, the modern Wicca movement is based on her findings, and many scholars followed her lead. But, although Murray brought witchcraft into the light as part of an integrated folk worldview rather than a Christian bane wrapped in mysticism, her broad conclusions and scholarship have been roundly criticized by folklorists, who are appalled at Murray's influence.

The Folklore Society, of which she was president in 1953 at the age of 91, even published a 1994 article, "Margaret Murray: Who Believed Her, and Why?" attempting 40 years later to distance itself from what it considered her reckless and unwarranted conclusions. The article begins, "No British folklorist can remember Dr Margaret Murray without embarrassment and a sense of paradox." Their primary objections are her contention that the old ways were a unified religion, on an organizational par with the Catholic Church; her desire to find a single horned god behind every deity; and her forcing data into the stunningly influential views of Frazer's *Golden Bough*. Unfortunately, Murray's zeal probably inhibited the serious study of old folkways as folklorists began to avoid the now-tainted study of witchcraft.

Jeffrey Russell in *Witchcraft in the Middle Ages* disagrees with Murray's conclusion, contending that the folk festivals were unselfconscious traditions. The Catholic Church's target, says Russell, wasn't peasants romping through the streets with their old beast-god; after the 700s, and particularly after 1100, a new religion emerged, based on Christianity and worshiping its devil *as* the Christian devil. The great witch hunts that began in the 1300s, says Russell, were directed mainly against heresy *within* the church, more than the old habitual peasant rites. The heathen religion first confronted by the church, he says, was "unselfconscious, being without organization, institutions, or dogmas. Its elements were a magical world view, the practice of sorcery, folk traditions, especially relating to agriculture and the hunt, and a willingness to ignore or oppose authority and public opinion by consorting with supernatural powers described by the Church as evil."

Russell says the same disasters that prompted Catholicism to consolidate its earthly domain — the plague, economic chaos, the fall of feudalism — also precipitated this conscious insurrection. Since ancient times, the god of any religion has been associated with order and continuity; the "evil" spirits have been synonymous with chaos, the rending of social and religious ties, and death. Christianity was no exception, and the chaos of the Middle Ages seemed to be the power of evil taking over the world. This chaos included a restlessness in the eleventh and twelfth centuries, followed by plagues and famines in the fourteenth. Wars and social rebellion characterized the fifteenth century, as well as rapid changes in political, social, and religious institutions.

Thompson said the devil reached his zenith of power in the thirteenth century, and that the "witch cult and its devil are the lineal descendants of the Old Stone Age Magic. The old magician is the true ancestor of this witch god … who gave reality as well as an outward form for the popular conception of the evil that was an all-powerful obsession in the Middle Ages." Elworthy, ruminating on the fate of Pan and his European counterpart Cernunnos, concludes, "That a divinity like Cernunnos should end his career by being absorbed into the incongruous character of the devil seems just what one might have expected."

Russell says, "With the increasing disintegration of mediaeval society, the prince of disorder, the Devil, haunted the popular and artistic imagination ever more darkly." It was in this crushing disorder, says Russell, that the heretics were born and flourished. One, Catharism, began in the 1100s. Catharists taught that the Devil ruled the world, that God was alive and well but unavailable in heaven. If the devil is in charge here, they reasoned pragmatically, it makes sense to propitiate this infernal deity rather than hopelessly struggle against him. Another cult, the Luciferians, which appeared in Germany around 1220, believed all things are God and therefore the devil is God. Lucifer was unjustly cast down from heaven and would be restored to his rightful place some day; on earth, meanwhile, he should be worshiped. Catharism was very popular with Germans, French, and northern Italians — all areas where witchcraft persecutions were among the most vicious. Russell says that in Spain, Scandinavia, and southern Italy, where Catharism was weak, witchcraft persecutions were relatively mild.

This ongoing pogrom definitely affected people's allegiances. Many embraced Christianity, for saints and Jesus provided heavenly intervention. Others stayed with the old god as a conscious religious, or anti–Christian, decision. Thompson says, "In many areas only fanatics and the most extreme types of perverted or ambitious men and women dared to incur the terrible penalties to which they were exposed. The Church also had long offered a rival field in which the born magician could employ his talents with greater honor and safety." Thus the old religion changed, for some, from a folk affair rooted in the life of the community into what Thompson calls a "secret cult … a meeting of sorcerers mainly given over to the black magic of hate."

Generally, the old religious observances were abandoned, not under the threat of some abstract eternal damnation, but under the quotidian reality of torture on earth. For the most part, the old peasant rites were modified by Christianity, absorbed into its walls, and given new life through a dying and resurrecting Jesus Christ. One of these modifications resulted in Christ's birth taking place about the time of the old Winter Solstice ceremonies. Although history seems to indicate Jesus would have been born in the spring, the Christian church moved the celebration of his birth into late December, conveniently overlapping and eventually pushing out the old ceremonies that centered on the Wild Man's orgiastic capture, mating, death, and resurrection. At the same time, the new birthday conveniently replaced the annual rebirth of Mithra, the Roman god who was reborn every December 25. If the people could continue their old festivals, highlighted by two weeks of holiday at year's end, they gradually ceased to care whether this was done in the name of a saint, a Christian god, or a heathen deity.

Village festivals changed radically as well, as we'll see in the next chapter, but a look at the old rites now under the rubric "witchcraft" sheds light on some of the Wild Man's actions in village plays as he adapted to a changing world. Two types of dances were central to the rites, according to Murray — processional and ring (or round) dances. The processional dance was a follow-the-leader type, with the devil leading the revelers in a fast-paced run. The meeting ground was sacred, and sometimes the dancers assembled in the village and danced to the sacred place, often a churchyard or sacred grove. The processional dance itself could be the act of worship, or a means of getting to a holy place, where a ring or circle dance was performed.

We see this processional dance in Wace's Greek sample of the Wild Man festival, where the goat-men came into the community loudly, ringing bells and slapping the ground with whips, while villagers followed them throughout the village as they traveled about, blessing houses and beating the land and people with goatskin strips to stimulate fertility. We also saw groups of Pelznichols in America running loudly through the streets, following Pelznichol, ringing bells and shouting at the top of their lungs.

The ring or round dance lived on in traditions about fairy rings as well as in Wild Man dances throughout Europe. This round dance is ancient; a drawing from the upper Paleolithic shows women with peaked hoods dancing around a central phallic male figure. The practice continued into modern times, reflected in May Pole dances and in morris and sword dances that marked historical European festivals. Grimm comments that the witch dances reported in the Hessian trial of 1631 were "like that of the sword dancers. When the ring dance was over they beat each other with single-staves and mangle-bats."

The ceremonies included rainmaking and activities intended to stimulate the growth of animals and crops. Dancers disguised in animal skins cavorted on "holy days," the most important being the last of October and the first of May, the mating and birthing times of animals. In their animal guises, the people had intercourse, hoping the fertility would rub off on the animals they imitated. Often the devil or Wild Man provided music on a flute, pipe, or violin, with the tradition of the piping Wild Man going back at least as far as Pan and his fellow satyrs. (Pan had such confidence in his beautiful tones that he

This sixteenth-century picture of an Elves Dance by Olaus Magnus shows cavorting goat-men, the larger, and therefore more important, figures supplying the music.

challenged the great god Apollo to a musical contest. But Apollo's lilting lyre won, just as the great god triumphed over Pan in the Greek pantheon.)

Murray envisioned the old religion, which she considered an organized pagan group, as "a joyous religion which must have been quite incomprehensible to gloomy Inquisitors and Reformers who suppressed it." But the Wild Men and their descendants, such as Black Pete, brought not only luck and fertility, but terror as well. Justifiably or not, the Wild Men and his descendants were associated with child-snatching and child sacrifice; they were the *bogeymen* (*boggons* being one name for the Wild Man celebrants).

R. Lowe Thompson includes child sacrifice in a list of rites performed by witches: "The special rite included blood sacrifices, such as a cat, a dog, a hen, a red cock, or an unbaptized child." Although the child follows the cat, dog, and poultry on Thompson's list, it was probably this sacrifice that removed the old religion from the "wholesome" category and made misbehaving children quake at certain times of the year. Murray says that as Christianity gained more converts, child sacrifices, formerly offered by their parents, became more difficult to obtain. This began the child-snatching that reinforced parental threats of the Wild Man or bogeyman.

Incest, cannibalism, child sacrifice, and wild sex orgies permeate accounts of witch activities, but most of the accounts are written by horrified Christians; in addition, these are standard charges against any insurrectionist religion, and in fact were standard accusations against Christianity in its early years. Around 190 A.D., Theophilus wrote vigorously against the widespread idea that Christians ate humans and had orgies. Thus the charges were hardly unique during the witchcraft mania; they had been dragged out of mothballs each time a new group disagreed with the dominant religion of the time.

Whether witches made a practice of child-stealing or not, people were convinced they did, which is why the Wild Man in his role as Black Pete or Pelznichol was universally feared by children. He allegedly stuffed malefactors into his bag, and his cannibalistic tendencies were graphically represented by such frightful creatures as the Kinderfresser (child-eater) of the Nuremberg Carnival, whom we'll meet in Chapter 7.

Christianity eventually made more inroads in people's lives, and as other influences came into play, the Wild Man lost his hold on his worshipers. Christ was becoming the nominal center of the people's religion, and the Wild Man an archaic holdover, an anachronistic grotesque. Bernheimer says: "As man learned to increase his inner distance and to look upon the wild man from the vantage point of his own superiority [his] fear turned into a laughter and a mockery, as it always does when a demon loses the terror which previously surrounded him. What had been formidable, now becomes grotesque."

The Wild Man became a curiosity, an object of ridicule, and consequently he mutated into a fool character who leapt about and sputtered gibberish, formerly a sign of divine possession. His leaping, growling, and clumsy sex play became just that — play. The Wild Man became a buffoon character, coarse and lusty, and the "man who scares children," in Grimm's words.

After the church institutionalized him as the devil, the future didn't look promising for the Wild Man and his supporters. So, while one incarnation of the Wild Man went on to dubious notoriety as stoker of the eternal inferno, his descendants also branched off into more legitimate, less malevolent directions, paths that ultimately led to Robin Goodfellow and Robin Hood, Harlequin, the fool, Pelznichol, and Santa Claus.

Chapter 5
Merrie Olde England: From Pagan to Puck

The growing dominance of Christianity wasn't the only change sweeping through Europe. The feudal system collapsed; a strong middle class arose, including influential trade guilds; and education spread. These all affected people, as well as the primitive god that had served them. The Wild Man remained the central holiday figure, but under fire from the Christian religion, one part of his lineage seemed stuck supervising an eternal fiery furnace. Another part of the Wild Man managed to adapt more successfully to the changing times, as he assumed roles that personified cynicism, merriment, and holiday. In England, this path led him to become Robin Goodfellow, Robin Hood, and Father Christmas.

This transition from Wild Man to revered outlaw and Christmas symbol wasn't automatic, and the Wild Man had to start over with a rather menial part in the festivals he had once owned. One of the earliest roles assigned the Wild Man in urban areas was that of order-keeper or policeman, who cleared the way for other more comely paraders. Because of his aggressive, antisocial behavior and habit of attacking bystanders, he was a natural for the part.

To clear the parade route for the more civilized revelers, the Wild Man brought out the fireworks that had symbolized his power over thunder and lightning and used them to help scatter spectators. The Wild Man assumed this crowd-control role in most large festivals, such as a 1610 St. George procession in Chester. Robert Withington's *English Pageantry: An Historical Outline* notes that parade "was headed by two men 'in green evies [ivy] ... with black heare and black beards, very owgly to behould, and garlands upon their heads, with great clubbs in their hands, with firr works to scatter abroad, to maintain way the rest of the showe.'"

As order keeper, the Wild Man remained leader of the pack and eventually turned this role into a more auspicious part, the master of ceremonies. Scholars say the original plays were carried out with no explanation because they were communal actions understood by everyone. As they lost their common significance, and as the people became spectators instead of celebrants, a need to "explain" or justify the strange actions arose. The Wild Man, traditional leader, became the presenter, the leader who took the acting troupe from house to house, asked permission to perform, and introduced the characters.

This presenter role was usually a comic one; as ex-god, the Wild Man remained at the festivals' center, but as his worshipers' awe and terror disappeared, he became a buffoon, the holiday fool. There are a few extant documents noting the transition from Wild Man to fool, as in the town records of Norwich, England. When the Company of St. George ceased in 1732, it gave the town its property, including "two habits, one for the club bearer, another for his man, who are now called fools." Usually the transition took place unnoted in convenient town records, however.

Surviving texts give the British fool-presenter scores of names — Tommy, Jack, Nicholas, Robin, the Clown — but generally folklorists call him, simply, the fool. The fool, as a former god, is not really a part of the new civilized society; he is an outsider, a critic of the world's ways, a character whose unique position gives him license to lampoon subjects others wouldn't dare approach. He is the clown who thumbs his nose at society's mores and refuses to cower to its conventions. His unrestricted, unruly behavior and mocking, obscene tongue gave voice to the people's most hidden thoughts — thoughts only this strange creature could cry aloud in the town square.

The Wild Man's erratic, often destructive, behavior was "licensed" — a permission granted thousands of years ago when he was regarded as sacred and his strange gibberish and maniacal behavior were signs that he was possessed by the godhead. No matter how the Wild Man changed over the centuries, how his fur might give way to other garments, he kept this freedom of speech jealously guarded. Stand-up comics of today, who retain this same freedom to mock people and social conventions, can thank the Wild Man for their privileged immunity.

Puck the Good Fellow

In Elizabethan England, one of the best known Wild Men turned jokesters was Robin Goodfellow, known to us today through Shakespeare's *A Midsummer Night's Dream* as the leaf-clad Puck, leaves being a common covering for the Wild Man in his role as god of vegetation. Robin Goodfellow was a very popular literary and folk prankster, and a 1628 book about him, *The Mad Pranks and Merry Jests of Robin Goodfellow,* was a bestseller in its day.

Robin, like Merlin, was the son of a Wild Man and a "mortal" woman. His father, Oberon, and his friends would dance at this mortal woman's house, and one day she discovered she was pregnant. She told her neighbors the child's father was some man that came at night but was always gone by daylight. Far from being shocked, the older women envied her, for "so noble a father as a fairy was."

Robin turned out to be quite a handful. He was a terrible brat, and ran away from home at the age of six when his mother finally threatened to spank him. When Robin grew a little older, Oberon appeared and told him about his lineage. Robin also learned from his father that he could change his shape at will. The merry fellow used this shapeshifting in his new role as a jokester.

In spite of his reputation as a practical joker, Robin didn't care for it when the tables were turned. A representative story relates that Robin asked a man, "What is a clock?" The man replied, "A thing that shows the time of day." "Why then," said Robin, "Be thou a clock and tell me what time of day it is." The other fellow bantered, "It is the same time of day as it was yesterday at this time." Now, in the context of this conversation, the man's reply seems appropriate, but Robin was highly insulted. The man had been chasing a horse, so Robin changed into the horse and stood so the man could mount him. He then hurled the "churlish clown" to the ground and almost broke his neck. Again posing as the horse, Robin allowed himself to be mounted, then rode into deep water. There he changed into a fish and swam away, laughing, "Ho! Ho! Hoh!" as the man almost drowned.

Another prank Robin would play was to walk in the night with a broom on his shoulder and cry, "Chimney sweep!" If anyone called for him, he ran away laughing, "Ho! Ho! Hoh!" In his chimney sweep disguise, Robin chanted:

> Black as I am from head to foot
> And all doth come by chimney soot.

This sort of humor may not strike us as particularly funny, but Robin's pranks were very popular in the 1600s; however, we can see from his charade as a chimney sweep that he had lost his religious hold on the cities at least. Why, indeed, would a hairy man be wandering around in the middle of the night, smeared black from head to foot and carrying a broom, unless he were a chimney sweep?

The same line of thinking has made May Day the chimney sweeps' holiday in England. In fact, a chimney sweep often was chosen in England to be Jack-in-the-Green, the ivy-covered Wild Man who headed the May Day parade, encased in a wickerwork pyramid. Apparently the old revelers, "all covered with ashes and soot," became confused with the soot-covered boys that cleaned London's chimneys. Chimney sweeps, despite their short life span, youthful servitude, and hazardous work, were considered lucky — an association for which they can thank the Wild Man. Americans are familiar with this association of luck with chimney sweeps through the movie *Mary Poppins,* in which Dick Van Dyke declares in song that good luck comes from shaking hands with a sweep.

Robin is a buffoon in *The Mad Pranks and Merry Jests of Robin Goodfellow*, but he is also next in line to kingship, for he is son of Oberon, king of the
fairies. This association with the fairies is clear in Shakespeare's play when one
of the fairies addresses Robin Goodfellow:

> Either I mistake your shape and making quite,
> Or else you are that shrewd and knavish sprite
> Called Robin Goodfellow. Are not you he
> That frights the maidens of the villagery,
> Skim milk, and sometimes labor in the quern,
> And bootless make the breathless housewife churn;
> And sometimes makes the drink to bear no barm;
> Mislead night-wanderers, laughing at their harm?
> Those that Hobgoblin call you, and sweet Puck,
> You do their work, and they shall have good luck.
> Are not you he?

In that passage Robin Goodfellow is called Puck and Hobgoblin, names
that clearly put him in a religiously suspect category for Shakespeare's con-
temporaries. Gillian Edwards, Murray, Grimm, and T. F. Dyer have studied the
names of fools, jokesters, devils, and Wild Men and show that Puck and Robin
are old English names for the devil. Robin's surname puts him squarely in the
heathen camp as well, as Goodfellow was a euphemism for witches or followers of the old gods; these faithful were often called fairies, elves, or Good People. Grimm equates Robin with the devil and with the German gift-giver
Knecht Ruprecht, noting that Robin and Ruprecht were common names for the
devil in England and Germany, respectively. Grimm says: "Robin fellow is the
same home-sprite whom we in Germany call Knecht Ruprecht and exhibit to
children at Christmas, [and] who in comedies of the 16th-17th centuries
becomes a Raepel, a merry fool in general."

Thus Robin Goodfellow, despite his confusion with chimney sweeps, is the
old fertility god, the Wild Man turned prankster. In *The Mad Pranks* Robin
clearly has his fertility god status in mind as he brags:

> Hornes have I store, but all at my back;
> My head no ornament doth lack.
> I give my horns to other men,
> And neer require them againe.
> Then come away, you wanton wives,
> That love your pleasure as your lives:
> To each good woman Ile give two,
> Or more, if she thinke them too few.

Robin's willingness to service all women as often as they wish does require
some superhuman power. His comment about giving his horns to other men

Robin Goodfellow as shown in *The Mad Pranks and Merry Jests of Robin Goodfellow* is the definitive Wild Man.

refers to the common symbol of being cuckolded. The cuckolded, or betrayed, husband sprouted imaginary horns on his head, a common literary occurrence in medieval literature. The symbol is not particularly well known today, but those familiar with James Joyce's *Ulysses* may remember Bloom sprouted imaginary horns when Molly was unfaithful.

At the same time Robin was making a hit as a street satirist in the cities, he still was regarded as the devil in other areas. Murray cites a seventeenth-century prayer which equates him with Satan or the bogey man who will "get you if you don't watch out":

> Saint Frances and Saint Benedight,
> Bless this house from the wicked wight
> From the nightmare and goblin
> That is hight Goodfellow Robin;
> Keep it from all evil spirits,
> Fairies, weasels, rats, and ferrets;
> From curfew time
> To the next prime.

The woodcuts of Robin Goodfellow in *The Mad Pranks* show not a bogus chimney sweep but a Wild Man as well as a god, the central figure in a fertility dance. A hairy goat-man, he is shown dancing as the central figure, surrounded by his smaller, therefore less significant, worshipers. That Robin, Oberon, and their ilk were responsible for fertility and the normal progression of seasons is seen in *A Midsummer Night's Dream,* for Oberon, the fairy king, and Titania, the fairy queen, have quarreled, and the results are disastrous for humanity:

> ...the winds, piping to us in vain,
> As in revenge, have sucked up from the sea
> Contagious fogs; which falling in the land
> Hath every pelting river made so proud
> That they have overborne their continents.
> The ox hath therefore stretched his yoke in vain,
> The ploughman lost his sweat, and the green corn
> Hath rotted ere his youth attained a beard;
> The fold stands empty in the drownèd field,
> And crows are fatted with the murrion flock[.]
> .   .   .   .
> And thorough this distemperature we see
> The seasons alter: hoary-headed frosts
> Fall in the fresh lap of the crimson rose[.]
> .   .   .   .
> ...The spring, the summer
> The childing autumn, angry winter change
> Their wonted liveries; and the mazèd world,
> By their increase, now knows not which is which.
> And this same progeny of evils comes
> From our debate, from our dissension;
> We are their parents and original.

Oberon and Titania, the goddess and god of fertility, are responsible for this chaos. Vegetation has stopped growing, the seasons are askew, and the ox

In this picture of Robin Goodfellow from *The Mad Pranks*, we see Puck as the central figure of a dance, not a bogus chimney sweep.

has "stretched his yoke in vain." Only by patching up their differences can Oberon and Titania ensure the survival of humanity.

In their Shakespearean role as fertility gods, Oberon and Titania bless the marriage of Theseus and the Amazon Queen by sending their fairies through Theseus' home, thereby assuring healthful and abundant progeny. The association with fertility was strong in Shakespeare's mind as well, for the play was composed for a 1595 wedding festival, possibly the Earl of Derby's.

In Robin Goodfellow, we see one fate of the Wild Man. He remains outside society, a commentator and jokester, and lives on today as a character in Shakespeare's play. Despite his popularity in his time, however, Robin Goodfellow never garnered the fame that his alter ego Robin Hood received as a social rebel.

Robin Hood

Grimm equates Robin Hood with Robin Goodfellow, who Murray says was alternatively called "Robin the Devil." We first find Robin Hood romping around the May Pole in Olde England and leading spring celebrants into villages. The May Pole is a vestige of the tree the Wild Man dragged into the village piazza. Robin Hood dresses in green, the color of his original leaf-covered garments; the Wild Man's fur often was replaced by leaves, in ceremonies where the old god was honored as the deity for agriculturalists as well as hunters.

E. O. James in *Seasonal Feasts and Festivals* sees Robin Hood as the garden-variety man in green or Jack-in-the-Green, the leaf-covered Wild Man of spring festivals, the annual fertility victim. Robin Hood often appeared in mumming plays as Robin Wood, Robin Wode, or simply Wode or Wood, and his appearance at one time clearly showed him as a leaf-covered man in greens. Robert Withington traces his Robin Wode name to the Anglo-Saxon word *wudewasa,* meaning "man of the woods, a faun or satyr," and the *Old English Dictionary* says *Wode* also means "madness." This madness is the same insanity found in the German word *Wut,* which Jan De Vries says originally meant godly possession, "high mental excitement ... being possessed by a spiritual force." We found this same double-meaning for a name in Papa Bois, where *Bois* means both "woods"and "madness."

The festival of the leafy Wild Man is the same as that of his hairy counterpart, and Frazer's 1922 *Golden Bough* relates some of the leaf-clad Wild Man plays. In the German areas of Saxony and Thüringen a leaf- or moss-covered man hid in the woods while the other village youths sought him. After they found the Wild Man, they chained him, led him from the woods, and fired blank muskets at him. The Wild Man then fell to the ground, after which a "doctor" bled him and he revived. "At this they rejoice, and, binding him fast on a waggon, take him to the village, where they tell all the people how they have caught the Wild Man. At every house they receive a gift."

Frazer also relates a Bohemian festivity in which a man dressed up as a Wild Man was chased through village streets until he fell over a cord stretched across a lane. An executioner then stabbed a blood-filled bladder the Wild Man wore around his body. "So the Wild Man dies, while a stream of blood reddens the ground. Next day a straw-man, made up to look like the Wild Man, is placed on a litter and, accompanied by a great crowd, is taken to a pool into which it is thrown by the executioner," says Frazer.

With his background as a leaf-covered Wild Man leading May Day festivities and his identity with Robin Goodfellow, it shouldn't be too much of a surprise to find Robin Hood as a priest in non–Christian religious rites. Murray cites the amazing devotion to Robin Hood throughout the British Isles as evidence he was more than a local Sherwood Forest rebel.

In *The Vision of Piers Plowman,* written in the late 1300s, Sloth, one of the

The Wild Man was often called Hood or Wood in England, as in this depiction of a Holwell, England, Wood, who led the parade with his club. This Wood found fame and fortune as Robin Hood.

Seven Deadly Sins, says: "I know not my paternoster perfectly as the priest singeth it, but I know rimes of Robin Hood ... I would rather hear of harlotry or the cobblers' summer games [May Day games arranged by the Shoemakers' Guild] or lying tales to laugh at and belie my neighbour, than all that Mark and Mathew, John and Luke ever wrote." Ironically Sloth, whose sin was that he preferred the old festivals to the newer religion, had been a Christian priest for more than 30 years. This was a common headache for the Christian Church, for if the pastors weren't following the heavenly lamb, the sheep would certainly stray from the fold.

In the 1400s Robin Hood was still a spectacularly favored folk figure. E.K. Chambers says Robin Hood's fame spread far and wide, and the Scottish chronicler Bower tells us in 1447 that "whether for comedy or tragedy no other subject of romance and minstrelsy had such a hold upon the common folk." Robin began to lose stature in the 1500s, however, as the church became more powerful and the old heathen figure fell into disrepute. For example, in 1508 it was compulsory for the people of Aberdeen, Scotland, to ride with Robin Hoode [sic] and Little John to honor St. Nicholas, but by 1580 Robin's old supporters shunned him. He was denounced as a harbinger of evil, and his May games were labeled "lewde sports, tending to no other end but to stir up our frail natures to wantonness."

Murray sees Robin's death as that of a priest-god dying for his people, for the oldest ballads tell how Robin Hood went to his cousin, a convent prioress, for a bloodletting. The prioress left his wound unbound, and Robin bled to death. His death was not much of a shock for his public, however, for as he went to the priory for his "cure," the route was lined with people lamenting his approaching death. That would happen only if his death was expected, predestined because of his role as the fertility god. In mumming plays that contained his death and resurrection, Robin was most often shot with an arrow.

British Mumming Plays

We've seen the fate of the Wild Man in England as Robin Goodfellow, a displaced fertility god trying to survive on the London streets, and as Robin Hood, a woods-dwelling redistributor of wealth whose fellow paraders have become Maid Marian and a bunch of "merry men." Both had left their community festival and struck out on their own with differing degrees of success.

The Wild Man festivals themselves continued throughout the British Isles on such days as May Day and Plough Monday, the Monday after Twelfth Night, when farm work resumed. These British community festivals that evolved from the Wild Man festivals are known collectively as mumming plays. Gareth Morgan in "Mummers and Momoeri" (*Folklore*) says the word *mumming* comes

The Plough Monday fool dances with a comely maiden in this nineteenth-century woodcut.

from the Greek word for mask, which also developed connotations of "abuse and scurrilous language," the same type of language that marked the Wild Man turned Fool in mumming plays.

Our best reports of the old Wild Man fertility rituals and their surviving remnants come from the British Isles, where a concerted effort was made in the early and mid–1900s to collect these plays before they disappeared from memory. Reginald Tiddy and E. K. Chambers did the cornerstone work on English mumming plays in the early 1900s, and Alan Brody in *English Mummers and Their Plays* added hundreds of plays to Tiddy and Chamber's compendium in the late 1960s.

Brody has categorized British mumming plays into three broad types: the wooing ceremony, sword play, and hero combat play. Although each of these plays has a different emphasis, and the characters vary, Brody concludes that all the hundreds of collected plays have two elements in common: "they all contain a death and resurrection somewhere in the course of their action."

Brody says the wooing ceremony, which emphasizes the mating of the Wild Man/fool and the woman or "Bessy," is the most "basic" type — that is, the closest to the original Wild Man festival. The wooing ceremony's plot is simple and familiar: the fool woos the woman, often called Bessy. A fight breaks out over the woman, and the fool is killed. A comic doctor revives the slain fool, the pair marries, and the town rejoices. The villagers pull a plow through the village and community, an ancient effort to stimulate the earth's fertility. The

Beelzebub as the comic devil was a favorite character in British mumming plays. Katherine Miller says the first requirement for the costume is a "fearful-looking black mask, preferably one with horns." From *Saint George: A Christmas Mummers' Play* by Katherine Miller. Illustration ©1967, renewed 1995 by Wallace Tripp. Reprinted by permission of Houghton Mifflin Company. All rights reserved.

fool is always blackfaced or wears a beast mask and invariably wears skins or dresses in tatters with at least one bell attached.

    The plows used for the ceremonies were not for everyday work. Charles Kightly in *The Customs and Ceremonies of Britain* says that in medieval times, old, one-horse plows, reserved for this annual ceremony, were blessed by parish priests, with some plows kept in the church all year. These symbols of fertility, endorsed both by the Christian Church and tradition, were not for mundane use.

Although the Plough Monday plays were banished by the Protestant Reformation, they have been revived in many areas of England. Kightly notes this resurrection has not been universally welcomed:

> [F]olklore enthusiasts have revived a less hallowed but perhaps still more ancient Plough Monday custom, which was once widespread throughout the corn-growing eastern English counties from Essex to Northumberland. There, bands of young farm labourers, fantastically dressed in tatters or ribboned and rosetted shirts, would haul a decorated plough about their villages, demanding largesse from all they met; and, in many cases, ploughing up the pavements, dunghills or gardens outside houses which declined to pay up.

In these British Isles wooing ceremonies, we see the same activities as in the ceremonies involving the Grecian goat man — a hairy, ambling beast-man mating, dying, and reviving, after which the villagers pull a plow through the village for luck. The Wild Man's role, however, is no longer that of a god, but the fool, a clown who spouts gibberish and acts in silly, sexual ways. His movements once assured the earth's life; now they are described as "comic" or "antic."

Just as happened in Greece in the early 1900s, the executioner assumes the devilish attributes of the Wild Man in England. In a Nottinghamshire play, for example, the fool presents the play, but when the old woman claims the fool is her child's father, Beelzebub enters, knocks her down and kills her. The fool here is busy shedding his devilish attributes and giving them to the blackened Beelzebub, who cavorts merrily, despite being saddled with a club and chains, hairy clothing, and a humpback. This Beelzebub is far from a terrifying character, however, for with the hair came the humor; he is the clown. When he entered the playing arena, his common introductory speech was:

> In comes I, Beelzebub
> On my shoulder I carry a club,
> In my hand a frying-pan;
> Don't you think I'm a jolly old man?

And he was. Beelzebub often carried the really earthy comedy routines the people loved.

Brody's second mumming category is the sword play, but another activity, the morris dance, existed. This round or ring dance often took place around a May Pole. Enid Welsford in *The Court Masque* says the morris dance was both a village folk dance and a favorite court performance through the seventeenth century in all of Europe. Although the characters and action showed minor deviations, the basic features were the same: The dancers danced and leaped acrobatically, clashed sticks or wooden swords together rhythmically, wore bells on their knees or ankles and ribbons or tattered cloth on their bodies, and blackened their faces. A hairy fool and Bessy always accompanied these spritely, athletic dancers. The morris dance preserves the original perambulation of the worshipers and the round dance, but there is no play of death and resurrection. The fool has been ousted as a central character; he cavorts on the sidelines, making bawdy comments and simulating intercourse with Bessy. Emphasis is on the dancing and the dancers' dexterity with their wooden staves.

A representative British example comes from the 1814 *History of Yorkshire*, where the dancers — young men whose shirts were decorated with ribbons — "exhibited various feats of activity, attended by 'Bessy,' in the grotesque habit of an old woman, and by the Fool, almost covered with skins, a hairy cap on his head, and the tail of a fox hanging from his head. These led the festive throng, and diverted the crowd with their droll antic buffoonery." The woman in the morris dance is often called Maid Marian; the fool, of course, is Robin or Hob.

Hone's *Every Day Book, or a Guide to the Year*, published in 1827, says in Wales the fool is "always the most active person in the company," for he is parade marshal, orator, buffoon, and money collector. His "countenance is also particularly distinguished by a hideous mask, or is blackened entirely over." In Ireland, says Hone, "a clown, of course, is in attendance: he wears a frightful mask, and bears a long pole with shreds of cloth nailed to the end of it, like a mop." These paraders are called the "good people" in Ireland and can do "all sorts of mischief without the slightest restraint." This "mischievism" persists in all Wild Man parades, and as we saw in the Plough Monday revivalists, lives on today for people who don't contribute to the celebrants. Our Halloween customs of mischief and vandalism get their diminishing license from this same heritage.

The morris dance was waning even before the Protestant Reformation prohibited the dance in 1654 and failed to spring back after the ban was lifted. During the late nineteenth century, however, the British developed an interest in folklore and folkways. In 1899, Cecil Sharp, a folk song collector, chanced upon a dance in the Cotswald region. Not only did Sharp add morris dances to his repertoire of folk collectibles, he taught the dance to folklore enthusiasts, beginning a full-scale revival. Kightly reports that hundreds of revivalist dances exist today throughout Britain because of Sharp's efforts.

In the sword play, the second of Brody's categories, the staves and sticks that Wild Men parried and morris dancers clashed rhythmically are replaced by swords. The sword play shows a shift in the mumming plays, from dancing to fighting, from fertility and life to destruction. This shift in emphasis reflects the growing influence of chivalry and warfare.

In Balkan, Teutonic, and English festivals, men had romped with sticks, bashing them together rhythmically, sometimes forming a design above a dancer's head, sometimes linking them together. In earlier times, the sticks had been branches that were used to beat people and the earth to stimulate fertility. But with that original meaning forgotten, the activity was interpreted as fighting rather than a sacred act of blessing. Rods that were once branches of the god's sacred tree became symbols of human destruction.

In this way the sword dance was born. As Chambers notes, words in the sword dance serve only to introduce the dancers. The main concern is to exhibit the intricate skills of accomplished acrobat dancers, much like the consummate stickmen of Trinidad. In Germany at least, the sword dance is at least 2,000 years old. Roman historian Tacitus in *Germania* wrote that the Germans "have but one kind of public show: in every gathering it is the same. Naked youths, who profess this sport, fling themselves in dance among swords and levelled lances."

A few British sword dances also retained the fool's mating activities. One example is a 1779 Lincolnshire play, which includes both an elaborate sword dance and a marriage celebration, and the fool remains the central character. In this play, the six sword dancers are the fool's sons. They announce they are going to decapitate their father who, although reluctant to die, declares he will do so for the common good, echoing the ancient unsavory obligations of kingship. But, willing or not, the fool plays for time by consigning a lengthy, comical will. The sons lose patience, place their swords around the fool's neck, withdraw them quickly, and the fool falls "dead." He is self-resurrecting, however, and arises, declaring he was not dead at all. A love scene follows, as the fool and his eldest son vie for the woman, and the fool wins her.

In most sword dances, the fool was excluded, for his clumsiness detracted from the skillful display of grace and agility. He did remain the leader and presenter, however, and contributed the earthy humor the people loved. An example of this humor, which reflects his heritage as a fertility god, comes from a Gretham, England, sword dance. The fool says in his introductory speech:

> So all you young lasses stand straight and stand firm,
> Keep everything tight and close down,
> For if anything happens in forty weeks' time,
> The blame will be laid on the clown.

In this play, the fool talks disrespectfully to the king, who tells the dancers to "try your rapiers on the villain." With their swords, the dancers form a hexagon around the fool's neck, withdraw the swords quickly, and the fool "dies." A doctor enters to revive the slain fool with medicine he calls "white drops of life," which he offers to any young woman. The doctor claims he gave two spoonfuls to his grandmother, "which caused her to have two boys and three girls." In this play, the doctor assumes some of the Wild Man's prerogative of producing life.

The valiant knight fighting the Wild Man was a favorite medieval theme. The Wild Man already has bested two knights in this German picture by Hans Burgkmair from about 1503.

The sword dance was an extremely popular form of mumming in Scandinavia, the Netherlands, Switzerland, England, Germany, and Austria, but died out under strong religious opposition in the seventeenth century. We see the German Pelznichol's association with the sword dance at Lübeck, Germany, where the fool was named Klas Rugebart (Claus Roughbeard), one of the many Wild Man–Clauses who symbolized festivity in German communities. The sword dance has been revived in many European communities, as has the May Pole, in the form of highly choreographed, somewhat romanticized resurrections of Thinges Olde.

Brody's third category demonstrates that knighthood and chivalry did more than change clubs to swords in many areas; in some parts of Britain, they altered old festivals almost beyond recognition, and the sword dance became a drama folklorists call the hero combat play. The influence between village and court worked both ways: While chivalry was changing the Wild Man festival, the Wild Man was becoming a central character in chivalric romances of the 1300s and 1400s. In these romances the Wild Man personified the bestial, untamed nature of the male sex and became the stock enemy of the heroic, idealistic, ascetic, godly knight.

A very popular motif was hunters or knights venturing into uncharted forests, discovering a Wild Man, and dragging him back to the local castle as a conversation piece. Sometimes the Wild Man panicked and escaped; sometimes he fought the knights. A third alternative was that the Wild Man was tamed and became a superior knight, at ease in courtly company. We saw this theme in *Valentine and Orson,* and as we saw in *Gilgamesh,* it is an ancient one.

The Wild Man gave the knights a villain to slay or best in battle. A typical plot cast the Wild Man as a lecherous beast with no regard for the virtue of the female, who had to be rescued by the proverbial knight in shining armor. In these stories, the Wild Man abducted a lady and dragged her into his woods or cave. The dauntless knight followed the creature, battled him, and rescued the lady.

These tales were spread from town to town by chapbooks and itinerant entertainers who brought news of the outer world and its ways to isolated villages. By the 1300s, in many areas the original Wild Man festivals were continued more from an ill-defined sense of "luck" than for any religious reason, so they were were easily influenced by forces such as knighthood, an institution which captured the people's imagination.

The village fair, an annual or semi-annual gathering, was an important occasion.These gatherings probably started for convenience; they gave people from outlying areas a chance to trade produce for manufactured goods. Peddlers could find their customers at the fairgrounds, instead of having to trek from farm to farm. Entertainers came to offer up their plays and performances for cash or merchandise. As royalty emerged atop the feudal system, kings and princes displayed their wealth and power by adding displays of jousting and dueling and other tournaments to the entertainment.

There was a lot of cross-fertilization between the village festival and the court. Enid Welsford in *The Court Masque* says "common people" attended these courtly tournaments and imitated the pageantry and themes they witnessed there. From their beginning as simple combats, the courtly tournaments became elaborate, ostentatious productions which sometimes incorporated Wild Man activities from village festivals. Welsford says, "The tournament, in particular, was turned into a grand public mummery; knights came to the lists in all kinds of fantastic disguises; the challenges were couched in terms of romantic gallantry, which furnished suggestions for the plots of many later French and English masquerades." In one 1438 French tournament, the jousters from Valenciennes came disguised as Wild Men, a costume that appeared periodically in fifteenth-century jousts.

Under the influence of knighthood, the sword dance became the hero combat play, which had a structured plot. With this transformation the emphasis shifts from intricate sword play by nameless dancers to bombastic contests between identified protagonists. The structure revolves around the chivalric Rules of Battle for knightly conduct, which Dorothy Sayers enumerates in her introduction to *The Song of Roland,* an epic poem of the eleventh century. *The*

Two Wild Men joust with saplings, one with radishes on his head, the other with onions or garlic. This fifteenth-century German engraving illustrates the interaction of chivalry and Wild Man plays.

Song of Roland is the most famous of about 80 mediaeval French epics, the *Chansons de Geste,* which extolled the legendary exploits of the Emperor Charlemagne and his knights, the Paladins. The tale of Roland's death in battle in 778 influenced European epics in regions as far-flung as Iceland. These epics not only shaped the literary version of knighthood, they also influenced the village plays.

Brody says these same Rules of Battle shaped the hero combat play, changing it from a communal enterprise to a spectator drama. In the Rules of Battle, the *defiance* comes first, as the challengers meet and threaten or insult each other. Then follows the combat; in a prolonged single combat, this is interrupted by a pause, when each combatant calls on the other to surrender. If both refuse, the battle continues until one is beaten. Then comes the *death blow,* followed by the *victor's boast.*

In these plays the executioner character of village festivals became the infamous Turk or Saracen from the Crusades, while the Wild Man himself, ironically, became a heroic knight. Sometimes this knight is a comic character, often called Bold Slasher or Captain Bluster. Although Chambers sees Bold Slasher as an extension of the dragon of St. George legends, Alex Helm points out that "examination of the traditional [Bold Slasher] costumes shows the general effect is more of a leaf-clad person." Bold Slasher's lineage, like that of most mumming players, goes back to the Wild Man.

The village hero combat in England is often called the St. George play, since that character was the most common protagonist. Saint George, who became patron saint of England in 1349, was considerably more successful than Saint Nicholas in depaganizing the play. As warrior saint and patron saint of England, George was a perfect candidate for the hero role.

George achieved fame at the Lydian city Sylene, where a venomous dragon terrified and poisoned the countryside. To placate the monster, the people offered him two sheep a day. As the sheep supply waned, they cut back to one sheep a day. Soon the sheep were gone, and they resorted to sacrificing a person a day to the dragon.

The sacrificial victims were chosen by lot from all the inhabitants, and eventually the king's daughter drew the lot. Resigned to her fate, she dressed as a bride and went to meet the dragon — echoing the beast-maiden mating theme — but on the way met Saint George, dressed in full knightly panoply and mounted on a great white charger. George wounded the dragon and led it to the city. Instead of slaying the beast, however, he used it to strike a bargain in the name of God: He would slay the dragon if the king and 14,000 citizens would convert to Christianity. If they refused, George would unleash the dragon. Under the circumstances, the people chose to convert. Having saved a virtuous lady from "marriage" with a beast made George a good candidate for the knight's role, and his big score for the Christian Church tended to counter the possible objections of religious leaders to the play's more pagan elements.

George also fit in beautifully as a character in an old death-resurrection drama. According to legend, the Christian George opposed the heathen king of Persia. The king commanded George to perform a sacrifice to Apollo, but George refused and was imprisoned and tortured. God visited George in prison with the bad news that he would not only suffer seven years, but be killed three times as well. The good news was that, as a reward for holding to his faith, George would ascend to heaven after his fourth and final death. In his first death, George was decimated, but after the Archangel Michael collected his parts, God touched the pieces and reconstituted George. George's final death was by decapitation, when milk and honey instead of mortal blood flowed from his body. With three deaths and resurrections, plus a decapitation, to his credit, George was a natural for a major role in the old Wild Man festivals.

A representative text of the hero combat play, offered by E. K. Chambers in his 1933 collection *The English Folk Play,* shows the Wild Man in many guises. This play apparently made it relatively intact to the United States and was being performed in Kentucky Christmas celebrations in the 1930s. In the play, the Wild Man as presenter has become Father Christmas. He also exists as three extra characters, often called "supernumeraries," a word dramatists use for characters with no actual part in the drama and no apparent reason for being there. But it is in his role as Father Christmas that we see how the fool

Saint George brings the dragon home as a bargaining chip in this picture from Hone's nineteenth-century *Every Day Book*. Under the influence of knighthood and chivalry, Britain's mumming plays often became St. George plays.

as presenter and master of ceremonies has retained his position as leader of the revels and holiday symbol.

The play begins with a grand, rhyming introduction by Father Christmas, "come to show you pleasure, and pass the time away." He has also come for a drink of beer, and he warns that unless it is the best in the house, "we cannot show you no Christmas at all." He promises "activity" of unprecedented scope and excellence, and finally calls for the entrance of St. George.

St. George enters and chants of his exploits against the dragon. He calls for a challenge, and Father Christmas obligingly summons the Bold Slasher. He enters — "In come I, the Turkish Knight" — issuing his challenge to St. George. They exchange insults and boasts:

> St. George:
> Thou speakest very bold
> To such a man as I;
> I'll cut thee into eyelet holes,
> And make thy buttons fly.

> Bold Slasher:
> My head is made of iron,
> My body is made of steel,
> My arms and legs of beaten brass;
> No man can make me feel.

After each boasts at some length of his superior fighting prowess and the other's imminent death, they do battle. Bold Slasher falls, and Father Christmas cries out:

> O cruel Christian, what hast thou done?
> Thou hast wounded and slain my only son.

He calls for a doctor, who enters. Father Christmas asks for some credentials: Where has he been, and what has he done? The doctor responds, "Italy, Sicily, Germany, France, and Spain, / Three times round the world and back again." What can he cure? "All sorts of diseases," the doctor responds:

> The itch, the palsey and the gout,
> Pains within and pains without;
> If the devil is in, I can fetch him out.

The doctor then ministers to Bold Slasher with the liquid in his little bottle, for "the stuff therein is elecampane; / It will bring the dead to life again."

Sure enough, Bold Slasher revives. At this point Beelzebub enters, with club and dripping pan — "Don't you think I'm a jolly old man?" He is followed by Johnny Jack, "with my wife and family at my back" (a bag of dolls he carries in a sack). At last little Devil Dout enters, closing the play with a request for money and a threat:

> Money I want and money I crave;
> If you don't give me money, I'll sweep you to the grave.

All exit, with Father Christmas in the lead.

In the hero combat play, chivalric rules of battle have restructured the plot: the contestants meet, challenge and boast, then fight. Here also is the ultimate decimation of the Wild Man. He appears as five separate characters, each reflecting one of the many roles he assumed when he lost his godhead: Father Christmas, the doctor, Beelzebub, Johnny Jack, and Devil Dout.

The doctor here assumes the supernatural power of life and death the Wild Man once held in his furry palm, but the doctor's foreignness is always emphasized by his looks or a recitation of the places he has traveled. He is the only modern character who might be a logical "curer," but, again, since doctors can't bring back the dead, the role is a comic one.

Beelzebub, Johnny Jack, and Devil Dout rarely all appear together, but at least one was always present as the last vestige of the Wild Man's original physical appearance. These figures all are comic "devils" — that is, they retain the original appearance of the Wild Man, hairy, blackened, club-carrying, and humpbacked. Little Devil Dout also is a blackened, hairy character, who is sometimes called the Sweeper. He carries a primitive broom or besom, a bunch of leaves or sticks, like Robin Goodfellow's and the brooms witches ride in stereotypical depictions.

Father Christmas carried a frying pan and a dead rabbit. Little Devil Dout had a blackened face, humpback, and streamers simulating hair across his arms and neck.

Johnny Jack's distinctive characteristic is his humpback. Sometimes he is not a humpback at all, but carries a bag with his "family" — a group of dolls — on his back. The humpback is an essential attribute of the Wild Man; the goat men had padded humpbacks, and the Gilles of Switzerland retain these humps as their only remnant of the Wild Man attributes. Chambers is intrigued by the hump and wonders why it exists: Was the hump originally a bag, or the bag a way to simulate a hump? One very practical explanation is that this padding protected the actor from the many beatings laid on his back by frenzied worshipers. These beatings were supposed to awaken the life-force within and were considered beneficial, just as the beatings the Wild Man gave bystanders were supposed to promote fertility.

The act of hitting people, notably children, with sticks was once a common practice during holiday celebrations. In Poland on Dingus Day, the day after Easter, adults beat their children with twigs to aid growth and health. This practice persisted in the Polish community in Chicago during the 1950s and 1960s, when schoolboys would pull off their belts and swat each other on the first school day after Easter recess.

Beating people for luck was common in Germany and the Netherlands. In Swedish homes, the first person to rise from bed on a holiday gave other family members twigs, whereupon they set to beating each other — a holdover, not of sadism, but of the idea that beating awakens fertility and growth. The birch twigs left by Santa Claus and Saint Nicholas were originally a wish for fertility and life — not a judgment of "bad" behavior. Ancient Greeks beat the image of their beast-god Pan when food became scarce, in hopes of awakening his fertility-giving powers, and wassailers in England to this day beat trees at Christmas to promote a bountiful crop. In America, this custom of stimulating growth and assuring luck through hitting survives as the ever-popular birthday spanking.

At one time the children in Johnny Jack's bag were the children the Wild Man snatched when they were naughty; in a kinder age, they were explained as dolls for the children. Samuel Sumberg says: "A more enlightened age has filled the bags of this ogre's descendants, ugly Knecht Ruprecht or genial Santa Claus, with rewards for deserving children, while the bad boys are merely ignored."

A third possibility is that the humpback was real — that the original Wild Man was really humpbacked, and that this humpback part of his sacredness. As we will see later, the "dwarfs" of Germany are described as humpbacked. A good luck charm on a necklace the author owns is a Bona or "good person," an elfish figure with a pointed hat and a large hump on the back; the charm is an obvious phallic symbol. The Pennsylvania cookie cutter showed a humpbacked Bellsnickle. It is considered good luck to touch a humpback's hump — an odd custom, unless the humpback had some profound significance at one time. The devil is supposed to be humpbacked, as are the Wild Man and Fool.

Father Christmas

Father Christmas, of course, is the most important offshoot of the fool in the quest for Santa's background because that role allowed the Wild Man to survive as the symbol of festivity. The fool had long been the symbol of holiday and loose living that characterized year-end festivals, so it was natural that he came to personify Christmas under the names of "Christmas" or "Yule." One of the first written accounts of the Wild Man in this role occurs in 1572 in York, when the archbishop wrote in a letter to York's mayor that "this rude and barbarous custom [is] maintained in this city and in no other city or town of this realm to our knowledge." The parade was led by Yule and Yule's wife, who, according to the letter, rode "through the city very undecently and uncomely."

The figure of Father Christmas gained legitimacy and wide popularity as the symbol of holiday when he appeared in the work of Ben Jonson, one of the most influential British dramatists of the early seventeenth century and scriptwriter for Charles I's masques after 1625. Jonson christened this character Father Christmas in his 1616 *Christmas Masque,* dressing him in a high-crowned hat and long beard and equipping him with a short thick club and a drum.

Renaissance writers like Jonson loved to personify everything, so Father Christmas came to court with his family of ten children, led on a string by Cupid. The children were personifications of the main elements of British

Christmas celebrations: Misrule, Carol, Minced Pie, Gambol, Post and Pair, New Year's Gift, Mumming, Wassail, and Baby Cake. Most of the attributes of the Wild Man festivals are represented in these children. The archer has become Cupid; Carol is the singing that accompanied the troupe; Gambol is the dancing; Mumming is the play itself. The Lord of Misrule is the spirit of topsy-turveydom that marks year-end festivals.

Opposite: Father Christmas presents his mumming troupe at a home. Included in his cast of characters are the Turkish Knight and Saint George, whose outfit is covered with ribbons. From Thomas Hervey's 1888 *Book of Christmas.*

   Above: Old Christmas, his head entwined in holly leaves, rides a goat in to end the year, carrying a wassail bowl and his replacement in his arms. From the 1888 *Book of Christmas.*

By the mid–1600s, Christmas had not only been personified, he had been imprisoned. During the Puritan regime, Christmas festivities were outlawed, and a 1645 pamphlet, *A Hue and a Cry After Christmas*, lamented his loss. Actually the pamphlet's full title is almost as lengthy as the publication itself: *The Arraignment, Conviction and Imprisonment of CHRISTMAS on St. Thomas Day last. And How he broke out of Prison in the Holidayes and got away, only Left his hoary hair, and gray beard, sticking between two Iron Bars of a Window. With an Hue and Cry after CHRISTMAS, and a Letter from Mr. Woodcock, a Fellow in Oxford, to a Malignant Lady in LONDON. And Divers passages between the Lady and The Cryer, about Old Christmas: And what shift he was fain to make to save his life, and great stir to fetch him back again. With divers other Witty Passages.*
The pamphlet describes how Christmas broke out of his prison and

> only left his hoary hair, and gray beard, sticking between two Iron Bars of a Window ... For his age, this hoarie headed man was of great years, and as white as snow he was full and fat ... but since the catholike [Catholic] liquor is taken from him, he is much wasted, so that he hath looked very thin and ill of late; but the wanton women that are so mad after him, do not know how he is metamorphosed, so that he is not now like himselfe, but rather like Jack-a-lent.

When Christmas reappeared during Queen Victoria's reign, he had aged considerably from his experience and become more of an ancient than the virile man "wanton women" had once been so mad for. Thomas K. Hervey in the 1888 *Book of Christmas* laments the aging of Father Christmas and the passing of the festive spirit that used to accompany Yuletide in England.
Hervey writes that in Jonson's days "the old man [Father Christmas] was, for the most part, well received and liberally feasted. He fed, with his laughing children, at the tables of princes and took tribute at the hands of kings." Although he showed

> beneath the snows of his revered head, a portly countenance (the result of much reveling), and eye in which the fire was unquenched, and frame from which little of the lustihood had yet departed ... in these days the patriarch exhibits undeniable signs of a failing nature.... It is but too obvious that, one by one, this once numerous and pleasant family are falling away, and as the old man will assuredly not survive his children, we may yet, in our day, have to join in the heavy lamentation of the lady, at the sad result of the "Hue and Cry."

Hervey's concern about Father Christmas's imminent demise was premature; he has managed to outlive his numerous children, though he has indeed lost a great deal of his machismo in the process. No one today thinks of Father Christmas-Santa Claus as a virile symbol. Nevertheless, while royal families, reformationists, governments, and churches rise and fall, this Wild Man somehow lives on.

The German Pelznichol influenced England's Father Christmas even before citizens of both countries emigrated to the colonies. In the eighteenth century George I, Elector of Hanover, Germany, became king of Britain and Ireland. Until Victoria, the British monarchs were German, which, as Harrison phrases it, "had the effect of introducing into English life more than a trivial element of German taste." However, it was Victoria's consort, Prince Albert, who was most influential in bringing German customs to the British court.

The German influences show, as do the effects of a nineteenth-century rage for personification and the international influence of Ben Jonson, in the Father Christmas character who appeared in the poem "A Visit from Saint Nicholas." Father Christmas had new "children" in America, for it was a new country incorporating influences from myriad nations. Now the old man had reindeer instead of offspring to symbolize elements of the old celebrations. Gambol became Dancer and Prancer; the drumbeats and fireworks that signaled the actors remained as Donder and Blitzen (Thunder and Lightning); Bessy survived as Vixen; Cupid is the modern archer/executioner. The running pace at which the maskers entered town is immortalized in Dasher. Comet is the ride of the Wild Man through the skies, as we'll see in the next chapter. In the melting pot of America, it is not surprising that the German Pelznichol and the British Father Christmas traditions blended in the most famous Christmas poem of all time, giving the Wild Man festivals new life.

Chapter 6

When Out on the Lawn There Arose Such a Clatter

The Wild Man proved infinitely adaptable in his quest for survival. He took on different forms in different places, changing to suit the society and the times. He became a symbol of merriment in most countries, but one of the Wild Man's more remarkable transformations was his evolution into a slender, agile dancer whose name has come to symbolize romance and wit: Harlequin. In Italy, Harlequin became the symbol of a comedy genre that encompassed wit, acrobatic and verbal ability, disguise, love, improvised dialogue, and stock characters — the *commedia dell'arte,* the comedy of skill, the comedy of the people.

Although today he has faded as a stage figure, Harlequin was instantly recognizable until just a few decades ago. His was an exceptionally long life on the public stage, for Harlequin and his troupe found themselves in print in 1611, when Flaminio Scala published 50 dramatic pieces, many of them harlequinades or comedies. As Allardyce Nicoll points out in *The World of Harlequin,* Scala's collection, Shakespeare's *First Folio,* and Ben Jonson's *Workes* all appeared within 12 years of each other.

The harlequinades differed from other plays in that they recorded activities that were part of the culture already. Because of this, the same characters, under dozens of different names, appeared in all the plays. These stock characters are familiar adaptations of Wild Man festival characters. One of these was Pantaloon, an elderly merchant, whom David Madden in *Harlequin's Stick, Charlie's Cane* describes as a "miserly, overreaching, credulous, talkative, sententious old fool," deceived in these plays by either a wayward wife or an eager virginal daughter. This character is the Italian cousin of the English fool, who vies with his son for the Bessy, for Pantaloon often competes with his son for a woman's attentions. Pantaloon wore a dark brown mask with a hooked nose, forward-pointed beard, and sword. The doctor, of course, is another stock character that lived on in these Italian comedies, but this doctor was an astrologer or lawyer as often as a physician. As in the British and Greek plays, the doctor is a farcical character and an opportunity to poke fun at men of learning; he pretentiously spouts gibberish and ridiculously jumbled bits of knowledge.

Resembling Britain's Bold Slasher and knightly St. George was a third stock character, the military man or captain. As Madden describes the captain, "When he enters in his flamboyant outfit, including a plumed hat, wearing a flesh-colored mask with a Cyrano nose and a fierce mustache, carrying a hideous sword, he creates terror for the moment, swaggering, parading, blustering, threatening, bragging of his feats in love and war, but he dodges if someone sneezes, he flees if someone makes the faintest aggressive gesture."

Other characters include the Lovers, often with Columbine as the woman, and the plot usually revolves around the wooing and winning of a woman, often with sword play and mock deaths.

Harlequin is a comic servant; waiting on the elderly Pantaloon just as he waited on an aged Saint Nicholas in Holland. In these plays, Harlequin often keeps the action moving as an adviser and instigator, but he is outside the world of right and wrong; according to Nicoll, "Harlequin exists in a mental world wherein concepts of morality have no being." His character combines simplicity and wit, credulity and wisdom, but always contains a generous dose of lechery.

These Italian comedies were improvisations, skeleton outlines and stock characters fleshed out by verbal and mental agility. Harlequin's plays were popular in Italy from the sixteenth through the eighteenth century and were carried to Paris and Madrid, where they became part of these countries' theatrical repertoires. In England, Harlequin was a standard character in Christmas pantomimes. Today few people are familiar with Harlequin, except as a synonym for a certain breed of romantic fiction, although he was universally known and a favorite subject for Pablo Picasso and Cézanne. Modern Americans are, however, familiar with the legacy Harlequin's comedies left in the form of Charlie Chaplin and the early silent film comedies, as Madden illustrates in his book *Harlequin's Stick, Charlie's Cane*. Punch and Judy shows, popular in Europe and on American children's television before the Sesame Street era, also stem from the Harlequin tradition. Punch, in his diamond-patterned outfit and pointed elf cap, was a hand-puppet character whose attire and behavior reflected the role of Harlequin.

One of the earliest written records of Harlequin appearing in this role as a romantic fool, and in something like his modern attire, appears in 1600, when a Harlequin play was performed at King Henry IV's marriage to Marie de Medici. By that time, Harlequin had shed the Wild Man's hairy covering but kept his beastly black mask, fringed to suggest a moustache and whiskers. His outfit consisted of a jacket and trousers covered with irregular patches, a derivation of the Wild Man's furs, and he carried the Wild Man's traditional club.

In the next centuries, the patches became symmetrical triangles; the crude bows that had tied his coat were replaced with civilized buttons; his old pants leg tightened and rose to accommodate fashionable white stockings. Harlequin was on his way to respectability, but still clung to his bewhiskered mask. By the early nineteenth century almost all vestiges of the Wild Man had been discarded. Beautiful multi-colored diamonds were topped by a conventional black cloth mask. Besides the mask, the only clue to Harlequin's origin remained in his acrobatic leaping. Harlequin had shed his devilish costume and flourished.

Harlequin's formalized stage role evolved out of the traditional festivals, in which newlyweds often paraded. Harlequin, like the other Wild Man, was a fertility god, and his presence was a standard part of many wedding festivals, like the one that helped push King Charles VI over the edge of sanity. A key role for Harlequin and his cousins in villages was to bless the bride and groom at weddings and lead the celebratory charivari romps.

Harlequin's image was not always so benign and welcome, however. According to Otto Dreisen: "Harlequin of modern times is the medieval devil Herlekin become a human clown." R. Lowe Thompson in *The History of the Devil: The Horned God of the West* states simply: "Harlequin was employed as a synonym for Satan." Bernheimer says, "It is in the Harlequin's disguise of our ballets and carnival entertainments that a last fleeting visual memory of the wild man and the Wild Horde survives into the cultural milieu of the present day."

Harlequin's transmutation from Wild Man to respected stage performer illustrates how civilizing influences could produce a total turnabout in the Wild Man's image. Before he took up the comparatively respectable life of the stage, Harlequin was a hell-raiser, leader of the Wild Man's celebrants, who were often called the Wild Horde. As Wild Man, he also was the fairy king, and he occupies both roles in a thirteenth-century French play by Adam de la Halle. In the play, a character remarks: "I hear the Hellequin troupe approaching. I hear many little bells ringing"—the same clue that tells us Santa Claus is coming to town. Hellequin's bearded, elflike servant enters to woo the fairy queen on behalf of his mighty master Harlequin, continuing the theme of mating of the god and goddess of fertility.

Folk tales of the "wild horde" and "wild hunt" abound in Europe, but written accounts that use those names appear only after the 1100s, and then only in the writings of literate, awestruck Christians. By this time, the original festival had become equated with a devil's romp, which seems to become more destructive each time we read of it. One early written account of the wild horde comes from the *Anglo-Saxon Chronicle* of 1127 and is quoted in *The Lost Gods of England*:

> Let no one be surprised at what we are about to relate, for it was common gossip up and down the countryside that after February 6th many people both saw and heard a whole pack of huntsmen in full cry.

Pictures of Harlequin from the sixteenth century show a blackened, bearded mask, irregular patches for clothing and a club in his hand.

By the seventeenth century, Harlequin's patches had become more symmetrical designs, but the animal-like mask remained intact.

Classical gods and themes began to influence the Harlequin plays; as he became less central to the plot, Harlequin's outfit became more lavish, and beautiful patterns replaced the early patches. This early nineteenth-century Harlequin shows no trace of the early Wild Man, with the exception of the black mask and the (considerably prettified) club.

This interesting sixteenth-century woodcut has been described as "Harlequin bring-ing the children home to their real father," but a closer look shows these mannikins are hardly children. The "father" is Pantaloon of the commedia dell'arte, in which children are conspicuously absent. This probably is based on a carnival scene in which the fools lead a large Harlequin through the streets. The fools in the basket were a common carnival motif, and Harlequin appeared in some fourteenth-century German carnivals with these "children" on his back.

> They straddled black horses and black bucks while their hounds were
> pitch black and staring with hideous eyes. This was seen in the very
> deer park of Peterburgh town, and in all the woods stretching from the
> same spot as far as Stamford. Reliable witnesses who kept watch in the
> night declared that there might have been twenty or even thirty of
> them ... as far as they could tell.

In the earliest references to Harlequin, he is the Wild Man or Wild Hunter leading this wild horde. As such, he became a demon-god in the eleventh and twelfth centuries in the British Isles as well as in France. The archdeacon of Oxford reported a Harlequin horde sighted at the border of Hereford and Wales in 1154, and described it as "night wandering troops which were called Her-lethings ... which circled round madly and wandered endlessly."

These parades of masked and raving men often went unnoted in writ-ing during Christian times, especially since adherents to the old religions weren't prone to publicize their activities, but sometimes they were recorded by horrified Christian clerics. The *Ecclesiastical History* by Ordericus Vitalis

(1075–1143) tells about a French priest traveling in the country on New Year's Night, 1091. On his way back home, still far from civilization, he heard a loud noise like an army approaching. Terrified, he was about to hide when the moonlight revealed a gigantic person, who raised a huge club and ordered the priest to stand still. A procession of men and women, half hidden by flames, swept by. The astonished priest declared: "It is no doubt Herlechin's troupe. I have heard say that many have seen it formerly, but rejected the report with incredulity and ridiculed it."

After the actual parade had ceased to exist, or evolved into a civilized per-ambulation, the wild horde persisted as a myth concerning an invisible evil horde that circled the earth during the twelve days of Christmas. Clement Miles writes, "Throughout the Teutonic world one finds the belief of a 'raging host' or a 'wild hunt' of spirits, rushing howling through the air on stormy nights." In some Germanic countries, people believed in the wild horde into the twen-tieth century.

When an ancient practice continues after its meaning has been forgotten, stories are created to explain it, and Harlequin and his wrecking crew had roamed the British Isles long enough to undergo this transformation. Accord-ing to one such explanatory legend, a king named Herla and the king of the elves were both planning to be married. The elf king attended Herla's wedding, and the next night Herla attended the elf's wedding. Herla stayed with the elves all night — or so it seemed; however, when he returned to his own land, he discovered he had been absent for generations instead of one night, and Saxon invaders had ravaged his kingdom while he sported in Elfland. After that, shamed, he wandered, a homeless vagrant ambling about the countryside as Harlequin.

Just as King Herla was created to explain Harlequin's night wanderings in Britain, Charles the Great took over Harlequin's Wild Horde leadership in France. Likewise, the Danes placed King Waldemar at the head. According to legend, Waldemar loved hunting so much he declared, "God may keep his heaven, so long as I can hunt for evermore!" God punished Waldemar's blas-phemy by taking him at his word, so Waldemar rides nightly and is especially active during the Twelves, that is, the twelve days of Christmas. As soon as one hears his "Ho! Ho! Hoh!" and the crack of his whip, it is wise to hide, especially if one is a Christian. Coal-black hounds lead Waldemar's train of blackened demons, and he always follows a specific route. If he meets any men, Waldemar will give them his hounds to hold; in return he gives them apparent trifles, which later turn into gold. Both Charles and Waldemar report-edly found themselves leading the wild horde after a maiden with a magic ring irresistibly drew them into a woodland, where they now hunt night and day.

From Germany comes another wild horde leader, Hackeleberend, report-edly chief master of the Duke of Brunswick's hounds until he died in 1521.

While hunting, Hackeleberend defeated a boar after a long battle. Overcome with the flush of victory, he kicked at the animal, shouting, "Now slash if you can!" But the hapless Hackeleberend kicked so hard the boar's tusk stabbed his foot, which swelled so much his boot had to be cut off. He later died from the wound. Before he died, a minister urged him to repent, but Hackeleberend (like Waldemar) cried out: "The Lord may keep his heaven, so he leave me my hunting!" The accommodating parson replied, "Hunt, then, till the Day of Judgment." So Hackeleberend hunts, in storm and rain, with carriage, horses, and hounds. Naturally he is noisiest during the Twelves.

The Dutch may not have brought Saint Nicholas to the New World, but they did import the wild horde, according to Esther Singleton in *Dutch New York*. On St. Martin's Eve, "no one could be induced to stay near a crossroads. Terrible things were heard and seen there, for it was as if Hell had let loose its occupants. Evil spirits roamed around in company of those who had sold their soul to Satan for money or other gifts, on condition of wearing a werewolf shirt on St. John's or St. Martin's Eve." The horn blast of the wild hunter marked these evil spirits' approach, says Singleton.

Before becoming mythologized to include kings, the wild horde traveled on foot, accompanied by the sounds of thunder and lightning, bells, and whips. In other words, the wild horde was the Wild Man's troupe of raucous revelers. Grimm relates that the wild horde in Mansfield County, Germany, appeared at Shrovetide, the same time as the "wild man run" that fathered the Nuremberg carnival. People lined the route to watch this parade, which was led by Eckhart, a bearded man with a staff who warned the people to move out of the way and told some to go home. Behind him came people riding and walking, some allegedly with no heads or carrying their legs across their shoulders, according to Grimm's report.

Instead of the Wild Man or his replacements, sometimes the Wild Woman or fertility goddess led these mobs, often enough that the term "wild horde" sometimes is a synonym for "witches' revels." Grimm reports that Holda and her train of "elves" openly wandered through Germany as late as the fourteenth century. She led a ring of dancers in what Grimm calls "witch" dances, and local women joined in her retinue. The terms "Holle-riding" or "Holda-riding" were synonymous with witches' riding as late as the nineteenth century in Germany.

Although Holda's retinue often was considered a destructive run, some stories of her wild horde show not terror, but tenderness. In a story about Holda's counterpart Berchta, a young woman's only child had died, and the mother wept constantly and inconsolably on the child's grave. The night before Twelfth Night she saw Berchta sweep past, leading a pack of children. Last in line was a little child carrying a jug of water that kept splashing on its shirt. The child was so weary from its load it could not keep up with the others, and when it came to a fence the others had climbed easily, it stood still, unable to climb. The woman recognized the child as her own and ran to lift it over the fence. The child said, "Oh, how warm a mother's hands are! But do not cry so much. You know that every tear you weep I have to gather in my jug." From that night forward the mother ceased to weep.

This female leader of the wild hunt was called Frau Gauden in some parts of Germany. Frau Gauden, a rich lady who loved hunting more than anything else, rashly uttered the same words that doomed Waldemar: "Could she but always hunt, she cared not to win Heaven." Frau Gauden had been blessed with 24 daughters, all with their mother's passion for hunting, and one day as the group hunted in abandoned delight, their lips again muttered that blasphemous wish. Before their mother's amazed eyes, the daughters' dresses turned into tufts of fur, their arms into hairy legs, and soon 24 bitches barked around their mother's hunting wagon. The whole party rose into the clouds, where they are condemned to hunt until the Day of Judgment.

Frau Gauden, Holda, and Berchta avoided crossroads, for there some part of their carriage would inevitably break. Once Gauden's carriage broke and, unable to fix it, she awoke a laborer for help. The man fixed the wagon, and Frau Gauden gave him her dogs' droppings for a reward, assuring him they were not so worthless as they seemed. At daybreak, the droppings had turned into gold. Frau Gauden also loved young children and brought them gifts at Christmas time.

In Norway, women called Lucci and Gurorysse led the wild horde in a procession known as the Asgard march, which Grimm sees as a corruption of *asgard-reida*, meaning thunder and lightning, elements that were standard accompaniments to the wild horde. The horde's approach could be heard from far away, for they laughed hilariously and rattled iron rods when a crime or blasphemy was committed. Since they journeyed among humanity only during the loose-living Twelves, they were kept laughing all the way. Lucci today is best-known as the angelic Saint Lucci, the benign Norwegian Christmas gift-giver who fulfills the role taken by the American Santa Claus, and Berchta has become an angelic gift-giver in parts of Austria.

Dealing with the Deceased

The Wild Man fertility parades have become confused with stories of the annual return of the dead, which lives on as All Souls Day. Clement Miles says: "It is difficult to say how far ... supernatural beings — their name is legion — who in Norway, Sweden, Denmark, and Iceland are believed to come out of their underground hiding-places during the long dark Christmas nights, were originally ghosts of the dead."

Rituals that surround the return of dead spirits abound in many cultures. Three thousand years ago the Babylonians set out food for the returning dead at their New Year festival. In ancient Egypt, the living lit lamps so the dead could find their way. In Greece a festival, Anthesteria, was held during the first month of the year and attended by ancestral spirits. The Romans held a nine-day Paternalia to honor the deceased before the new year began. In the British Isles and northern Europe the dead also returned at the beginning of the year, at Samhain or Halloween. In Sweden, food and drink is still set out for the ancestors. Frazer tells us the Lett of Latvia used to entertain the dead for four weeks at year's end, from September 29 to October 28. The "quick," or living, prepared every kind of food and placed it on a well-heated, clean floor for the revered ancestors. Late in the evening, the man of the house called upon his departed ancestors by name to come and partake.

This ancient custom of receiving and honoring dead ancestors at year's end is found throughout the world, from Mexico to Burma, Germany, and Africa, and was continued by the Catholic Church in All Souls Day. The ancestors' return was accepted with mixed anxiety and anticipation. As long as the souls were convinced they were being honored, the family was assured of good fortune, and the ancestors returned peacefully to their graves, but if they were offended, they might curse the household and bring disaster.

This universal honoring of ancestors was so important that some scholars believe the origin of mumming, and of religion itself, is found in ancestor worship. Some support for the connection with mumming comes from Sicily, where the dead were considered the Christmas gift-givers. On the night of November 1, old year's end, the dead supposedly left their graves, stole gifts from the rich shopkeepers, and distributed them to their relatives.

The confusing relationship of the wild horde, the dead, and Santa's night-riding sleigh is shown in a Slovakian tradition where the winter solstice is called St. Thomas Eve. Like Halloween, it is a night of supernatural events, and St. Thomas himself is supposed to drive about in a chariot of fire. After arising from his grave on this shortest day of the year, St. Thomas is assisted by all the dead men named Thomas, who also rise for the occasion. They help him to his chariot and walk with him to the churchyard cross, which glows as St. Thomas kneels before it, then rises to bless his namesakes. Michael Harrison in *The Story of Christmas: Its Growth and Development from the Earliest Times* notes the saintly substitution didn't make this wild hunter any more welcome than his heathen counterparts: "In the houses people listen with awe for the sound of his chariot, and when it is heard, make anxious prayer to him for protection from ill."

When the wild hunter ascended to the heavens, as in the St. Thomas legend, the sleigh he drove appeared as a comet — hence the name of one of Santa's reindeer. It also is noteworthy that the wild hunter's "Ho! Ho! Ho!" is also Robin Goodfellow's signature call, the medieval devil's bluster, and Santa Claus's laugh as he races through the skies.

In Pursuit of Prey and Reprisal

Sometimes the wild hunt or wild horde was interpreted not as general mischief-making, but a hunting party, and often the wild hunter pursued a woman, with ancient animal lust or murder in mind. In the folklore of regions as widespread as the Austrian Alps, Sweden, Denmark, and England, Bernheimer cites stories of riding demons who chase wild women through the countryside to tear them apart. Even if the Wild Woman escaped death when she was captured, she was thrown over the demon's steed — a horse, a unicorn, or a stag — tied down by her own hair, and carried away. In most of these stories, the wild hunter is known simply as the Wild Man.

In one French tale the hunter's death was caused by his false mistress, and so he chases her through the woods every Friday, the witches' sabbath, and has her torn to pieces by his hounds. Each time she arises again, and the gruesome hunt resumes. Grimm says that the Bavarian wild hunter pursued little woodwives or mossfolk. The hunt could not be seen by mortal eyes, but people could hear him blustering in the air so that the air "crickled and crackled."

In Yugoslavia the Wild Woman, with long filthy hair and ugly face, is pursued by the sorcerer Villa, which is also the name of the German god Odin's archer at Asgard, and the local fairies. As she flees, this woman changes into an animal or rides away on one, her favorite steed being the stag, one of the animals most commonly associated with traditional wild people.

Bernheimer says medieval writers romanticized the Wild Man's murderous pursuit and transmuted it into an abduction to fairyland. The Wild Woman, now a well-bred lady, was often rescued by a knight, who saved her from sexual violation. The scale of romance began to tip in favor of the Wild Man, however, in the middle fourteenth century, as the institution of knighthood began to lose its glamour. At the same time chivalry's image was becoming tarnished, people were becoming enamored with the romanticized noble savage living at one with nature. At this time of plague and chaos in Europe, the idea of unspoiled humans living in a beneficent environment had a special appeal. As a result of the changing state of the world, the Wild Man sometimes won the damsel in these forays; instead of taking her off to certain death or defilement, however, the Wild Man escorted her back to nature, where they lived an idyllic life.

A more popular prey was the wild boar, and Grimm finds remnants of Freyr worship in such Christmas festivities as bringing in the boar's head. Grimm sees the Germanic wild hunter Dietrich von Bern as an offshoot of the Germanic fertility god Freyr, whose worship included sacrificing a boar, an animal considered so holy people swore by its bristles. Freyr rode a golden-bristled boar through the night sky and was the god of sowing, reaping, and harvesting as well as the god of peace. As a fertility deity, Freyr's most prominent attribute was an enormous phallus. Sexual activity formed an important part of his worship, and "swarthy" victims were sacrificed to him at Upsala, Sweden. Because he rode comet-like on his golden boar in the night sky and was responsible for the earth's bounty, Freyr, who was described as dark-skinned himself, is sometimes nominated as a likely predecessor for Santa Claus.

The Saxons hunted the wild boar at Christmas time, and even today the boar's head forms part of elaborate traditional Christmas feasts in Britain. Bringing in the boar's head was once a necessary ritual in British Yuletide: Trumpets blew, the door to the great dining hall swung open, and a platform with a steaming boar's head was carried in. Spectators posed as if to attack it, laughing and cheering, recalling the days when the beast was actually hunted.

R. J. Campbell in *The Story of Christmas* says the Celts hunted and slew the "sinister" boar at year's end as symbolic warfare against the powers of darkness and chaos. The Teutonic gods lived on wild boar, and in the Germanic heaven Valhalla the boar hunt was a daily ritual. Each day a colossal boar appeared at the edge of Valhalla's forest. The dead heroes and Thor, Vali the archer god, or Tyr hunted the beast, roasted it, and ate it. All in all, life in Valhalla was very redundant, because the next day, the same boar reappeared, and the hunt took place again. This Valhalla legend echoes the original fertility ritual, as the archer god Vali hunts and slays the representative of the god of fecundity.

The boar is both a symbol of fertility and an agent of death and resurrection in many mythologies. Adonis, one of the plethora of dying and reviving Greek Dionysian gods whose death is necessary for life on earth, was killed by a boar in Greek mythology. Adonis was later interpreted as a sun god, and the fourth-century writer-philosopher Macrobius saw his death as the sun being "defeated" by winter, "for the boar is an unkempt and rude creature delighting in damp, muddy, and frost-covered places and feeding on the acorn, which is especially a winter fruit. And so winter, as it were, inflicts a wound on the sun." Adonis, who was worshiped in Egypt, Greece, and Rome, may live on in Christian religious practices, for he died, descended into hell, and rose again on the third day. In festivals, Adonis often appeared as a goat-man.

In Ireland, the hero-god Dermot O'Dyna, whom T. W. Rolleston in *Myths and Legends of the Celtic Race* calls a "Gaelic Adonis," is killed by a wild boar containing the avenging spirit of his half-brother. In this strange legend, Dermot's brother ran between his knees, and Dermot squeezed his knees together, killing the child. He then flung the body to hounds from which the child had been fleeing. When the dead child's father saw what had happened, he hit the dead body with a "Druid rod." A huge earless, tailless boar arose, and the father commanded it: "I charge you to bring Dermot O'Dyna to his death." The boar then rushed from the hall and roamed the forests until Dermot became a man.

After a life of love and outlawry, Dermot met the earless boar again when he saw his old lord and enemy Finn running from this boar with his hunting party. Dermot exclaimed to Finn: "By my word, it is to slay me that thou hast made this hunt, O Finn; and if it be here that I am fated to die, I have no power to shun it." His weapons were powerless against the giant boar. The boar ripped out Dermot's bowels as Dermot dashed out the beast's brains, and they died together. This legend,with a hunting party allegedly formed to hunt and kill this Adonis figure, preserves at its core the preordained hunting and killing of the god of life, death, and fertility.

As if confusion of festivals of the dead and the Wild Man festivals weren't enough, still another post–Christian motif interweaves with Harlequin and the wild hunt — that of the vengeful heathen gods who, deposed by their former worshipers, swear retribution. When the people discarded their old deities for the Christian god, they did so with great trepidation, for they believed the old gods would not be shunted aside so easily. Grimm tells us the Germans believed the old gods lived in enchanted mountains, where people would hear drumming and fighting as the old gods prepared their revenge for the humans who had discarded them.

As late as the twentieth century some Norwegians believed the gods would rouse themselves to battle Christians, says Michael Harrison in *The Story of Christmas*. Inevitably the gods chose the mystical Yuletide season, when they would come shrieking down the mountains in a howl of wind and carry off any Christian foolish enough to be outdoors. Harrison cites an 1896 Norwegian book relating how one village heard the warning sounds as they prepared to celebrate Christmas: "In a second, the air became black, peals of thunder echoed among the hills, lightning danced about the buildings, and the inhabitants in the darkened rooms heard the clatter of hoofs and the weird shrieks of the hosts of the gods."

From Fur to Rags

It is not possible to separate the various beliefs that combined and recombined over the years to make the end of the year a time of both magic and dread. We do know that the Wild Man and his entourage of life and death underwent drastic changes in some areas, while remaining fairly well intact in others. It is apparent that folk custom adapted the basic Wild Man themes to fit local preferences, giving different names and explanations to the basic rituals. The same transformation to suit local tastes also occurred with the physical appearance of the Wild Man figure.

It is noteworthy that when the Wild Man does discard his old features, he always retains at least one distinctive trademark. On the European continent, where Harlequin rose to become a central figure on the professional stage, the "cleaning up" of the Wild Man went through stages that make sense in light of an acting troupe's need to appeal to local sensitivities and tastes. One of the most flagrant symbols of the Wild Man, and one that was sure to offend polite audiences, was an enlarged phallus. This often was moved backward to become a tail, or it was modified into a stick, wand, or "fool's bauble." The horns also posed a problem; they, as much as any part of the Wild Man, symbolized the devil for Christian clerics. The asses' ears on fools' caps are but one adaptation of these withering horns.

The Wild Man's hairy costume changed as well. Although drawings of early mumming plays are rare, the earliest costumes depicted are beast costumes. The normal evolution is from hairy costume to leafy or grass costumes or hair substitutes, usually tatters as in Trinidad's Pierrot Grenade, or irregular patches as in Harlequin's early outfits. Changes in the Wild Man's costume have been studied by Bernheimer, Margaret Dean-Smith, and Samuel Sumberg, and all agree the rags, fringes, and patterns of later fools are modifications or simulations of real fur. Sumberg says: "In the case of folk festivals we observe a transition from the hairy skin to a pure design." This full possible range of costume transformation did not take place everywhere, but we can see the whole array of change from fur to diamond lozenges in the figure of Harlequin.

Harlequin's place at the head of the wild hunt apparently had been forgotten by the mid–1800s, when it was replaced by a children's tale, at least in France. Larousse's 1865 *Dictionnaire Universal de XIX Siecle* relates how Harlequin got his costume of patches that evolved into the exotic diamonds of today. The story was inspired by a seventeenth-century picture showing Harlequin's suit splattered with irregular patches, and a 1973 children's story, *Harlequin and the Gift of Many Colors,* uses Larousse's story as its basis.

The story relates that Harlequin was a poor but popular village boy who would have to miss the annual carnival because he did not have the necessary "splendid new costume'" every villager wore. His friends, knowing his financial pinch, decided each child would contribute a piece of their own outfit. When the children saw the pieces in Harlequin's hands, however, they looked like just what they were — a pile of rags.

In despair, Harlequin threw the rags into the air, but one piece landed on his white shirt and gave him an idea. He carefully placed each piece on the shirt, and his mother worked far into the night to sew them on. Harlequin donned the unique outfit, and — club in hand and black mask on his face — dashed into the town square. There he danced with joy in the midst of an enchanted crowd. The children were delighted to see their friend, but "Harlequin was the happiest of them all on this happy night, for he was clothed in the love of his friends."

Thus the conversion was complete: The Wild Man, once the ruler of all nature's forces, becomes an athletic comic servant and a likeable boy grateful for the cast-offs of his betters.

Chapter 7
On Board
the Ship of Fools

As the Wild Man evolved, Santa, Satan, Robin Goodfellow, Robin Hood, and Harlequin were exceptions; they provided legitimate new personas for this forest creature after he divorced himself from his clamorous wild horde. Each essentially became independent and self-supporting, establishing a life outside the confines of some sort of mass gathering or celebration. Santa Claus has this independence: He lives at the North Pole, has a workshop, employs industrious elves, and has settled down with Mrs. Claus. His alter ego Satan also has established his own realm of influence. Robin Goodfellow stands ready to inherit the throne of the fairy world; Robin Hood presides over his Sherwood Forest crew as the symbol of romantic outlawry and independence; and Harlequin enjoyed an active life on stage until the twentieth century.

Most descendants of the Wild Man ended up in roles that were more symbol than substance. A few became mere spear-carriers in the drama of life, like Black Pete, who traveled around as St. Nicholas's servant. Another offshoot, however, assumed an important symbolic role in society by becoming the fool. The fool was not foolish; rather, he was a caustic commentator, someone worth listening to and laughing with. Among the more durable fool figures still recognized in the modern world is the court jester, and this court jester helped coach the Wild Man for his new fool role.

Enid Welsford in *The Fool: His Social and Literary History*, comments:

> For centuries, the honest countryman on certain days of the year blackened his face, dressed up and talked nonsense, for no other reason except that his fathers had done it before him, and that in some undefined way it would bring good luck. ... [B]y the 15th century, hardly anything remained of the old religious awe, except a feeling that the figure of the fool was in some way significant. The village clown is obviously a survival, and his words and deeds became ever more meaningless with the passing years.

When a lively young clerk took the part of the traditional fool, he was not likely to rest content with an unintelligent repetition of the actions of his predecessors; on the contrary, the role would afford him an admirable opportunity for dramatic experiment and satirical comment. He was a fool, the elected "King of Fools"; very well, then, he would exercise the fool's right of free speech, and he would model himself on the ways of the court rather than of the country village. He would adopt the dress, assume the role and claim the privileges of the court-jester.

This mutation of Wild Man into fool and social critic sprang up in many communities as Europe was moving out of the plague-stained Middle Ages and into the Renaissance. The fool was a reaction to events in the 1400s: Europe was in a state of turmoil, marred by the Black Death and social upheaval. With perhaps half of Europe's population destroyed by the plague and sometimes whole villages wiped out, human aspirations and hope seemed pretentious and doomed. In this era of fools, it became fashionable to view the world as a stage of fools, and all of humanity's aspirations and vices could be reduced to one symbol — the fool.

Welsford says the idea of the fool that appeared in the fourteenth and fifteenth centuries "caused the dramatic activities of the fool societies, he appeared frequently in art, he inspired a whole section of literature which was little else but an exceedingly simple and direct criticism of life." As society became self-conscious enough to treat itself as subject matter, humanists and Christians looked round them, and what they saw was not a pretty sight. In fool literature and plays, these enlightened intelligentsia held humanity's puny pretensions up to a mirror and ridiculed them.

After the church exorcised the Feast of Fools, fool societies took to the streets in French and German cities, perpetuating the old festivals. Throughout Europe, fool societies flourished from the fifteenth through the seventeenth centuries. These societies organized into "kingdoms" for the purpose of keeping up the old customs, especially activities like the charivari, which gave them license to comment on their neighbors' affairs and satirize society. These groups organized enormous parades built around the theme of humanity's foolishness, personified by the fool. From these societies rose the *sottie,* a comedy play in which the fool provided both the actors and theme. The unrelenting theme was the universal sway of the fool, and the Fasnet and carnival activities provided the ideal medium in which to chide humanity for its hubris.

Fool societies, and the fool as social commentator, began in the sophisticated cities and courts of Europe, were emulated by European towns, and were exported to the New World, reshaping festivals while spreading them around the planet. The French brought these pageants with them to their colonial empire, and their influence is still reflected in such New World events as the New Orleans Mardi Gras and the Trinidad carnival.

Fifteenth-century literature picked up the theme of humanity's foolish-ness as well, and the fool became a common literary motif. One very popular book of this type is Sebastian Brant's *Narrenschiff*, or *Ship of Fools*, written in 1494. Brant, a German, wrote his moralistic account after viewing the Nurem-berg carnival's central float, a ship of fools. The book was quickly translated and imitated in other languages, and its appeal still persists. In the twentieth century, Katherine Anne Porter resurrected the old motif in her *Ship of Fools*, which also was made into a movie, featuring vignettes of ocean voyagers doomed to frustration.

The perfect symbol and spokesperson for this worldview was the Wild Man turned fool: as a creature outside the pale of human norms and conven-tions, the Wild Man's gibberish turned into scathing commentary on the world's, and community's, inhabitants and weaknesses. The Wild Man was ready for this new opportunity. As leader of the festival parade, he was the log-ical spokesperson; as a figure never limited by the strictures of civilization, he was a keen observer of human weakness. Under these circumstances, his orig-inal gibberish and animal-like behavior gave way to a speaking role that dis-played his earthy humor and pithy wisdom, signs of foolhood.

The Wild Man turned fool, then, was a personification of human foibles as well as a reaction of turmoil and chaos. As a symbol for humanity's vices, the Wild Man gained a new life and glory, however dubious that glory might be. As a personification of human weakness, the Wild Man turned fool remained above or outside normal social laws; from this unique vantage point, he could point with impunity at humanity's excesses and ridicule them — with an effect much more devastating than religious moralizing.

Nonsense Night

Even before the fool societies and the Wild Man's new role, the Wild Man and his troupe had invaded German communities in spring, personifying free-dom from drudgery and the promise of new life. In Germany this pre–Easter celebration is sometimes called *Fastnacht* or *Fasnet*, from *fassen*, meaning "to talk nonsense," and *Nacht*, meaning "night." Nonsense night is an apt name for a celebration of beast-men whose trademark was gibberish and maniacal possession and the nonsense that marked these celebrations of reversal and abandonment. In Nuremberg, the Wild Man's peregrination was called *Schem-bartlauf*, literally meaning a run (*Laufen*) of bearded, hairy men (*Schembart*).

By the time we have woodcuts of this festival in the fifteenth century, the Schembartlauf had undergone significant changes, including the death and res-urrection of the festival itself. The Schembartlauf was abolished by authorities in 1339, then revived in 1349 under the sponsorship of the butcher's guild. Later, sons of rich merchants took over the celebration, until, under fire from

Christianity, it was abolished again in 1539. Samuel Sumberg in *The Nuremberg Schembart Carnival* gives an account of the Schembartlauf of the early 1500s:

> The main body of dancers was ushered in by fools, whose shouts, as they beat the boys pursuing them, roused the crowd to view the festivals. Now came the heralds of the Schembartlauf, on horse and on foot, throwing nuts to the boys and eggs filled with rose water to the ladies in the windows. A howling mob of devil guisers followed them, amazing and frightening the crowd by their rough, theriomorphic [animal] costumes and the fire and ashes they threw. A way was thus cleared for the troop of handsomely masked dancers who came leaping through the streets to the rhythmic jingle of strings of bells on their person and the music of fife and tabor.

As the Schembartlauf runners paraded, they, like their Greek counterparts, would stop at inns or public areas to perform rough, ribald, sexually explicit horseplay that revolved around the mating, mock death, and resurrection of either the Wild Man himself or one of his offspring.

Walter French in *Mediaeval Civilization as Illustrated by the Fastnachtspiele* [Fools' Night Plays] *of Hans Sachs* examines these plays' dialogues and divides them into several types, the most common being the "review," which originally served simply to introduce a round or sword dance. French reports that a Wild Man/presenter, sometimes simply called the fool, led the troupe of local folks conducting the annual ritual. He greeted the landlord, told people not to be afraid, warned the audience the play might be a little offensive, and demanded silence.

As Nuremberg strove to restrain the wilder aspects of its revels, sponsoring guilds began supplying "scripts" for the actors to follow. Under the sponsorship of the butchers, there were important commercial interests at stake in the festivals, somewhat like our modern corporate sponsorship of college football bowl games.

As the Nuremberg festival became more regulated, these Fools' Night plays became more structured and followed a format that would keep the players within acceptable bounds rather than risk the wrath of authorities through the excessive words and actions of some improvising amateur.

Writers were brought on board to produce scripts, and these authors garnered some name recognition. Two of these authors, says French, were Hans Rosenpluet and Hans Folz, who continued the old racy dialogue. The nature of the plays changed drastically, however, when a shoemaker named Hans Sachs began writing scripts for the Schembartlauf plays. Sachs had fallen victim to the educated classes' romance with humanism, one of the strong philosophical movements that grew out of the Italian Renaissance. Nuremberg was a free, imperial city and a major business center in Bavaria. The bustling German city was a key point on the trade route with Italy, and it resonated with the influences of Italy's vibrant Renaissance culture, a culture that was to take its toll on the Wild Man's behavior and shape the play's dialogue.

Appalled at the rough-and-tumble, erotic world of the carnival, Sachs and the Nurembergers sought to emulate the great centers and courts of Europe with their lifestyle, their philosophy, and their carnivals, incorporating classical and religious themes into their plays. The characters of these plays were drawn from Italian literature, or they were gods and goddesses from Greek and Roman mythology, rechristened with German names.

Scriptwriters like Sachs felt it was their humanistic duty to instruct the great unwashed lower classes on a more appropriate world view. French says,

> With the beginning of the Sixteenth Century and the growth of Humanism in Germany, the old immoral [plays] began to lose influence. It was felt that lofty ideas should deal with lofty people and not with those of baser stamp. Since the people as a whole could not become familiar with the new trend of thought, it was fortunate that the masses produced a man who was capable of grasping the essence and of presenting to the people in terms well known to all. ... Sachs chose the [carnival plays] as a chief means of doing this teaching as the form was familiar to the people, who could enjoy their favorite form of amusement and at the same time, unconsciously, be morally uplifted. With Sachs the material, to a large extent, was worked over to free it from anything that might be offensive.

Comparable changes took place throughout the larger metropolitan areas of Europe. According to Mikhail Bakhtin in *Rabelais and His World*, Greek, Roman, and Italian classics dominated the festivals in larger cities, turning the original carnival celebrations into "small and trivial" events, irrelevant, crude, anachronistic peasant entertainments. Elaborate formal balls and parades became *de rigeur* for the "citified" privileged classes distancing themselves from their peasant roots.

Humanism and its ideals were the property of the educated upper classes, and Sachs's plays reflected a contempt for the peasant. They also reflected the upper classes' fear of peasant unrest. The peasants were increasingly resentful of rising taxes, interminable barons' wars for which they paid with their toil, and regulation of all phases of life by the ruling classes. At the same time, says French, peasants were becoming aware that they held power in their hands. The combination of lower status and potential power made the peasant, considered subhuman and morally stunted, the object of vicious ridicule in the carnival plays. The celebration, originally a primitive attempt to renew agricultural, animal, and human life, consciously distanced itself from both its peasant roots and the primitive peasant god, the Wild Man, who, with his uncouth animal ways, was obviously unfit for the more urbane citizenry.

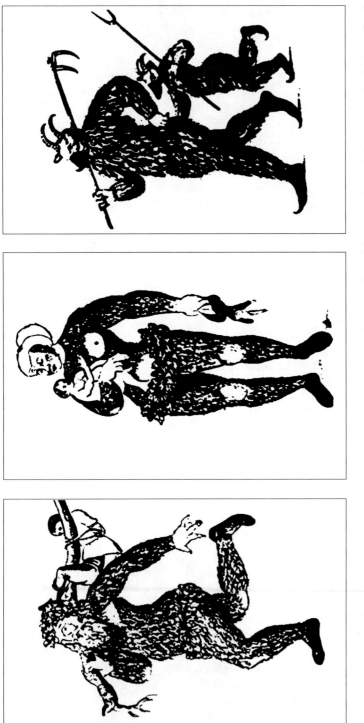

Left: The Wild Man adds substance to parental warnings as he carries a lad on his tree. The Wild Woman (*center*), in contrast, her hair confined in a neat chignon, cradles a hairless human child while she dangles a woman from her other hand in these woodcuts from a Nuremberg carnival about 500 years ago. *Right:* Sixteenth-century father and son goat-men parade down the Nuremberg streets with their pitchforks, standard agricultural implements for these gods of fertility.

Nevertheless, despite his transformation to fool, the Wild Man also still paraded in his archaic roles, and carnival woodcuts record these roles for posterity. The woodcuts of the Nuremberg carnival show us a time of transition, when old and new elements were combined in the festival. Even the wild thrashings and runnings of the Wild Men–devils remained. These woodcuts show the Wild Man clearing the way for more comely dancers, the old fertility god doing his magical copulation, the bogeyman snatching children, the old man, the noble savage, and the sophisticated fool of humanity's vices. Dozens of Wild Men types paraded, and woodcuts preserve the variety of forms he assumed. Samuel Sumberg in *The Nuremberg Schembart Carnival* says the club and the "rough coat" made of skin, leaves, moss, or flax, were essential to all representations of the Wild Man–fool.

A fifteenth-century woodcut of a Nuremberg carnival shows the Wild Man with a "naughty" boy firmly tied to the uprooted tree he carries, reinforcing parental threats. There is a Wild Woman, too, who carries a human child, though her mask is more loving than malicious, and the child's attitude seems to be one of trust. The child's hand is raised in a caress of the Wild Woman's comely face, but in her left hand she carelessly dangles a red-clad woman by the legs.

The Wild Man on his way to being a devil is seen in "Father and Son," where the goatish Wild Man and his son parade. The horns, hairy hide and pitchfork-rake are common symbols for the devil. The pitchfork would evolve into the mystical trident of the old sea god Poseidon, symbolizing power over land, sea, and air, but in this father and son tableau we see the devil's trident in its original form — a simple pitchfork, a farm implement, a fitting tool for a god of fertility.

Another evolution the woodcuts reveal is Wild Man turned noble savage. This was the era of exploration, and bold seafarers were venturing on uncharted oceans to claim new worlds for their monarchs. These adventurers returned with exotic tales of aboriginal tribes living at one with nature in peace and harmony. City life, with its crowding, disease, unsanitary conditions and stress, had begun to pall for many, and tales of people living in harmony with an unpolluted environment had a strong appeal. As a result, the Wild Man sometimes became idealized and softened, transformed from a wild demon into a tame Rousseauian noble savage.

This Wild Man as noble, unspoiled patriarch of a woods-dwelling family entered art and literature, and in plays the Wild Man often carried his children proudly on his back. One example of this evolution is found in a 1540s Bavarian festival, where the Wild Man, his mate, and their child are found in the woods. Unfettered by chains, they politely accompany the townspeople. As they calmly walk in the place of honor at the parade's head, the Yule Log is pulled behind them. The parade moves through the village, stopping at inns, where the paraders courteously introduce the woods family to the local inhabitants.

By the end of the sixteenth century, the Wild Family took on a tamer, more human aspect as noble savages, living at peace in nature. This woodcut by Hans Schäuffelein illustrates a poem by Hans Sachs, scriptwriter for the Nuremberg carnival skits.

This taming of the wild family, although stripping it of its terror, retained the essential nuclear family of regeneration.

The role of Wild Man as devoted father changed the meaning of the children he carried around. Early Christmas cards often show Santa Claus carrying a box instead of a bag on his back, with mannikins or little dolls peeking out. Johnny Jack's stock lines in a representative British mumming play, "Here comes I Humping Jack/My wife and family at my back," refer to the Wild Man's habit of carrying these mannikins. Harlequin also appeared in fourteenth-century German processions carrying "children" on his back.

These little people often were puppets that performed scenes. In the demon puppeteer we see an example of the Wild Man as puppeteer, as an old woman and a goatish devil battle each other, much as their cousins Punch and Judy fight even today in some parts of England. It's impossible to tell whether the

A less robust Wild Couple and their children relax in their Edenic environment in this fifteenth-century German engraving.

This eighteenth-century depiction of a Swiss carnival scene by Daniel Burckhardt-Wildt is called "Signs of Honor" and includes the Wild Man. With him travels a boar man as well as a fantastic bird figure.

puppets came first, then were explained as naughty children, or the other way around, but these little people became dolls intended as gifts for the children themselves when the Wild Man became a gift-giver, a transformation that could only benefit the shuddering youth of Europe.

The mannikin in the basket sometimes served as a gift-giver as well. The old woman was a prominent part of carnival processions in some Teutonic areas. She was known as *die Burgl* in one Tyrolese Fasnacht procession and was driven along by a fool with a bladder whip. As the *Butzenbrechtl,* she used to be a Yuletide visitor in Munich, where she went from house to house with a basket on her back containing a child and apples. The child threw apples to people in the house. In Munich's annual cooper-sponsored celebration, a fool sometimes occupied the old woman's basket. Sumberg comments: "Here the fertility motif was evidently present, for the clown offered his admirers a bit of a long sausage he held in his hand, and a rime was sung, asking the 'Gretel' [woman] for her eggs."

In keeping with the new moralistic worldview and the Nuremberg carnival's revised mission to illuminate evil and foolish ways, the Wild Man as fool also personified the human vices and folly that could undermine the unenlightened, inattentive human spirit. Card and dice costumes illustrated the fool turned moral symbol.

Although the runners were essential to the carnival and performed skits at inns, the main focus of the Nuremberg festival parade became an elaborate float pulled on a sleigh. The float featured a tableau with costumed persons, or

The puppeteer was a common sight in fourteenth- and fifteenth-century German carnivals. Here the demon puppeteer strides through the streets, while on his back a demonic Wild Man fights with a woman, just like their descendants, Punch and Judy.

it might have mechanical creatures doing the same action over and over (as we see in modern pageants such as the Rose Bowl Parade or Macy's Christmas Parade). The high point of the Schembartlauf, says Sumberg, was pulling the pageant-sleigh into the square. There the runners put ladders against the float, stormed it, set fire to it, "and thus buried their carnival."

These pageant sleighs often featured the Wild Man as center of the carnival in his most devilish role, the child eater or *Kinderfresser,* who rolled along the Nuremberg streets, blithely munching on naughty boys and girls. As parents reminded their wayward offspring, the Wild Man not only snatched children, he ate them. If the presence of a child-snatching Wild Man stalking the streets in the old-style Schembartlauf were not enough to keep children in line, the pageant's main float with the giant Kinderfresser was sure to bring the point home. In the 1516 Nuremberg Schembart float, the child eater is a devilish Wild Man. In the 1522 float, he has become a standard Fool, but his actions are the same; like his predecessor, he is voraciously gulping down children.

The child in the child eater's mouth and the reserve supply of children in

This eighteenth-century depiction of a float from an earlier Nuremberg carnival includes a devil, a Wild Man and Woman with their clubs, a transitional Wild Man–Fool following the float with his fireworks, and the Fool–Wild Man atop the "castle," while a Fool is dragged along by the devil figure.

his bag were conventional carnival figures by the sixteenth century. This devilish child eater was commemorated on a fountain built in the mid–1500s in
Berne, Switzerland, about 250 miles from Nuremberg. This ogre, called the
Kindlifresser in the local tongue, is shown gobbling up children. A sixteenth-
century Swiss almanac explains the Kindlifresser's intention to swallow up all
bad children "even though he might choke on one." The almanac shows a picture of a bearded, humanoid Kindlifresser being attacked by children with
bows and ropes, but he already has stuffed several in his pocket and one is in
the process of going to his huge stomach.

A cousin of the child eater was the Narrenfresser, "fool eater," who fed on
human foibles by literally consuming fools as the Schembartlauf progressed.
A 1508 woodcut from the carnival shows a giant Narrenfresser, part Wild Man
and part fool, picking fools out of a castle for a snack.

In other Teutonic areas the Wild Man retained his original appearance as
well as his ancient position as the symbol of fertility, freedom from inhibition,
and new life. Sheep or goat skins were the most common covering of the German Wild Man, and Perchta runners of Bavaria included Ugly Perchten who
wore what Sumberg calls "the guise of devils"—black sheepskins and horned
masks. These Perchta runs continue today in Austria, and William Sansom in
A Book of Christmas tells us: "The double-edged demons or Perchten who come
screaming and running on one of the Advent Thursdays through Austrian villages ... are half inimical, yet half helpful if persuaded to dance on your fields
to ensure a fruitful harvest." The pictures in Sansom's book show a bearded
figure resuscitating one of the troupe's fallen members while a deer and other
characters look on.

Villages and towns in the Tyrol region of Western Austria take turns
putting on the famous Tyrol carnival *Laufen* or runs. About every fourth year,
Imst organizes the *Schemenlaufen,* a run of ghosts or masks. On other years,
Telfs has the *Schleicherlaufen,* or sneakers' run; Thaur presents the *Muller-
laufen,* or beating run, and used to also have a *Huttlerlaufen,* or run of ragged
men, *Huttler* meaning rag costumes. The fourth village, Axams, holds a
Wampelerreiten, or wampeler ride, wampeler being plump clowns.

Maskers in Austria are of two basic types. One is the beautiful Perchtas
or *Schönperchten,* which includes the *Schellers,* figures with big bells (*Schellen*),
and *Rollers,* figures with small bells (*Rollen*). These runners are characterized by elaborate headdresses. The other basic type is the ugly masks or *Schi-
ache,* which include witches, jesters, chimney sweeps, bears, horses, and Wild
Men.

When carnival ends at midnight on Shrove Tuesday, a puppet or representative of carnival is buried or burned. In a Schemenlaufen picture we see
this form as the Wild Man in a wheelbarrow, a monster made of straw, who
will be summarily dispatched at the end of the festival.

The Kinderfresser or Child Eater stuffs his pockets with children and seems intent
on further treats, even while devouring a hapless victim. The other intended morsels
run to their unperturbed mother for protection.

The carnival's connection with fertility and marriage is seen in the
Blochziehen, or log pulling. The Austrian federal chancellery notes this pulling
traditionally took place only in villages where no one had been married during the past year and is interpreted as "compensating marriage." Although this
log pulling has become the central feature of regular carnival activities in some
areas, in other parts of southern Austria it is still dragged around only when
no marriages have taken place. The log, a relative of the Yule Log, was part of

The Wild Man accompanies a *Schönperchten* or Beautiful Perchta in this modern Tyrolean carnival called the *Schleicherlaufen*. The world *schleichen* means "to sneak," and a *Lauf* is a run. Courtesy of the Austrian Cultural Institute.

the basic Wild Man festival, as he dragged this symbol of fertility and super-human strength through villages.

The chancellery publication *Austria Folk Customs* notes the "traditional masks" also make their appearance in Lower Austrian regions on May Day for the cutting of the May Pole, which is erected secretly during the night. There the jester, doctor, and bear or Wild Man perform comic skits.

In this extraordinarily tradition-rich country, the wild hunt even roams the streets of Salzburg on the second Thursday in Advent, with masks representing figures from Untersberg folklore. On December 5 or 21, several interesting Saint Nicholas processions take place. In one of them, the *Nikospiel* or Nicholas play at Mitterndorf, a goat-man leads a procession of straw men. In

Two witches or *Hexen* with large bells are part of the Schellerlaufen (bell run) in this Austrian scene. Courtesy of the Austrian Cultural Institute.

other areas the *Klaubaufgehen* or "going" of the Klaubauf Wild Man character takes place. In Oberdrauburg this is called the *Bartel-Lauf*, Bartel being one of the Austrian names for the Wild Man–devil. The Wild Man also lives on as the *Thomasniklo* or Thomas Nicholas and other names as well. In other areas, the processions have incorporated the sanctioned Catholic bishop into their festivals.

In Munich, paraders used to don sheepskins as well, but, as happened in Nuremberg, Munich's celebrations changed, heavily influenced by the carnival

The Schemenlaufen is a run of masks or ghosts that takes place about every fourth year in Imst. In this festival, the Wild Man–Monster is being rolled through the village in a wheelbarrow, while the other maskers celebrate. Courtesy of the Austrian Cultural Institute.

and splendor of Venice, according to Jennifer Russ in *German Festivals and Customs*. In 1893, a "fashing society" was formed in that city to plan elaborate balls and parades; in the parade of that year a handsome *fashing* (foolish) prince wore a crown and ermine robes, carrying a vestige of the original parade — a scepter decorated with the head of a jester. Today, says Russ, the "costumes are typical of the baroque splendor of the Viennese Balls."

Black Forest Survivals

The older rough-and-tumble primal carnival events continued in outlying communities in the southwestern part of Germany. Peter Tokofsky, an

American folklorist who studied and participated in the Fasnet activities in 1988 and 1989, describes this area of Germany in *The Rules of Fools: Carnival in Southwest Germany:*

> This portion of the state contains no metropolises and consists primarily of smaller towns and villages dotting the valleys of the Black Forest, the banks of Lake Constance, and hilly Swabian landscapes. Pre-19th century mapmakers would have required a stock of at least 600 colors to depict the administrative diversity of this region filled with tiny principalities, foreign holdings, and independent cities....

In this pocket of independent villages, which reflect the population patterns of centuries past, the Wild Man continued to roam, although he and his fellow masqueraders were roundly condemned by the better-off burghers. The masqueraders, called *Schuttig* in Elzach, were covered with hair or red rags and went house to house wearing heavy bells. Their behavior, more restrained now, used to be stereotypically Wild Man: they ran around, leaped into the air, and beat people and the ground. Although more sophisticated elements ridiculed the Schuttig and railed against the festivals, two events made the Schuttig not only acceptable, but a source of pride for the best known of the modern Fasnet villages, Elzach.

One of these events was a nineteenth-century movement that romanticized and idealized the past. Germans such as Jacob Grimm began collecting folklore, stories, songs, and activities that reflected their Aryan heritage. The old festivals gained further prestige when German historical revisionists decided they were indigenous to the Aryan race and were modern survivals of worship of the Germanic all-father, Odin. Tokofsky says offshoots of idealization of an ethnic past were *Heimatschutz* in Switzerland and Nazism in Germany, as ethnic pride became a call for ethnic purity. Tokofsky said the Nazis' rise to power in 1933 "cast a false sense of renewal and tradition over the nation," resulting in the resurrection and strengthening of fool societies and festival activities.

The other main stimulus came from French occupational forces in the Napoleonic era in the 1800s, when Germany was still a jumble of independent states, bound more by customs than politics. Germany's defeat in World War I again put the local people under French control, and the French banned the Fasnet activities. Facing the imminent loss of an integral part of their cultural past, Germans rallied together to regain their roots and formed fools guilds to perpetuate, and tame, the Fasnet celebrations. This spread, and by 1924, fools guilds were organizing across villages; that year, Fasnet organizations from 13 different areas assembled in the Black Forest to form a coalition to gain greater governmental support.

Tokofsky says this initiative, taken in part to cast off the yoke of foreign domination, cast Fasnet and other carnival activities in a new role as preservers of a unique cultural past, putting them into the third of German historian Norbert Schindler's three stages of urban carnival activities:

1. A folk carnival in the fifteenth and sixteenth centuries, a parody of folly;

2. A "domestication" of carnival in which it became a public show, composed of audience and spectators, with a resultant purging of the wilder erotic and physical elements.

3. Romantic reintroduction in which the old symbols are displayed for their own sake.

Following the interruptions of world wars and occupation, the southwestern German communities dusted off Fasnet activities in the 1940s and 1950s. Today these draw large crowds of tourists, especially in Elzach. Fasnet became an integral part of southwestern Germany's reinventing itself as tourist delight; nestled in the Black Forest area, the villages became shrines to a romanticized early Germany. The effort to attract tourists had a stronger civilizing effect than all previous outcries of church and state, as, in Tokofsky's words, carnival became a "commodity." By the 1950s, with the spread of prosperity and the financial rewards of tourism, villages that had not possessed or preserved Fasnet events quickly established them.

The same evolution of community festival to tourist attraction that occurred in southwest Germany took place in the conservative southwestern Ausserrhoden area of Switzerland, which had stubbornly pursued its traditional ways throughout the centuries, even refusing to adopt the Julian calendar until the occupying French forced it upon them. There, in Urnäsch, we find the Chläus who, with their white beards and mustaches, appear to be Santa Claus's very close cousins. A glimpse of these paraders is provided by Regina Bendix in *Progress and Nostalgia: Silvesterklausen in Urnäsch, Switzerland*. Bendix shows us three kinds of Chläus: the pretty Chläus, the ugly Chläus, and the pretty-ugly Chläus, a combination of the other two. The ugly Chläus are completely covered in hair or vegetation as they go from house to house on New Year's Eve. Shaking their heavy bells rhythmically and yodeling, they announce their arrival and are greeted with food and drink.

These seeming anachronisms, like most mumming troupes, travel in all-male groups, with some of the participants dressed as women. The young men are considered the only people capable of physically enduring the hours of leaping and running while wearing costumes that weigh as much as 50 pounds; and, as Bendix points out, the Urnäsch women would consider it unseemly to participate. Bendix says *Chlause* (the name of the activity) used to be an opportunity for the better off to share with the poor, "but as the poor disappeared and Chläus started investing more in their outfits in both time and money, the custom bearers became those who could afford it and wanted to see the custom continue."

Bendix finds the earliest mentions of the Chläus in denouncements. In

In Urnäsch, Switzerland, three kinds of Chläus parade: Ugly, Pretty, and Pretty-Ugly. This picture is from a postcard probably from the 1930s or 1940s and shows a Chläus mumming group. The hostess (right) offers the masqueraders food and drink. From *Progress and Nostalgia: Silvesterklausen in Urnäsch, Switzerland*; courtesy of the University of California Press.

A Pretty-Ugly Chläus group forms a circle to yodel in the center of town. The large protrusions on their stomachs are huge bells. From *Progress and Nostalgia: Silvesterklausen in Urnäsch, Switzerland*; courtesy of the University of California Press.

An Ugly Chläus drinks through a straw, with some help from a village woman, in this scene from Urnäsch, Switzerland. From *Progress and Nostalgia: Silvesterklausen in Urnäsch, Switzerland*. Reprinted by permission of the University of California Press.

1663, clergy criticized the "walking around at night with bells and making noise in the manner of St. Nicholas," and in 1744 the state council decreed that the "obscene and aggravating disguisement on the occasion of the so-called Klausen at Christmas and New Year be forbidden and punished." Taking part in Chlause remained a punishable offense from 1776 to 1808. The *Appenzeller Zeitung (APZ)* newspaper of Ausserrhoden in 1836 said the "Klausen custom deserves to be condemned as a remnant of a barbaric age, but, fortunately, the custom is not as popular as one might think."

Bendix chronicled the effect of ethnic pride on the celebrations by tracking the changes in the *APZ*'s attitudes toward the Chläus, and in 1920, *APZ* was delighted to see the Klausen revived after World War I, finding it "as worthy of Heimatschutz as anything else." After World War II, the Chläus returned from a wartime absence to find themselves a tourist attraction, as busloads of city people swarmed to see original Swiss-German customs preserved in the hinterlands. As Bendix says, "Today one of Urnäsch's hopes lies in tourism. The town has ski lifts and hiking paths, but, most importantly, it has living customs. Urnäsch has preserved customs that are no longer seen elsewhere." Although tourists are tolerated, the Chläus see them as a hindrance to their ancient "magic effects."

Not only does the magic disappear, so does the seemingly infinite adaptability of the Wild Man and his festival, which Tokofsky fears will dissolve as tourist-seeking villages "freeze" the custom into a dramatic display with rigid

Federle, or the Feathered Man, is one of the original Fasnet masks in Waldsee, Germany. Old accounts describe him as a "neat and gallant figure," usually dressed as a hunter, with feathers in his hat, although he also is known as the "evil one" from Waldsee. Federle uses his stick to jump and prod people. Photograph by K. Furtner; courtesy of Städt. Kurverwaltung, Bad Waldsee.

The Schuttig costumes in Elzach, Germany, include overlapping rows of red felt rec-tangles and a hand-carved dark mask of wood. The special Schuttig hat is made of woven straw covered with snail shells. Courtesy of Peter Tokofsky.

rules, scripts, and costumes, rather than the flexible folk festival of old. The problem with Fasnet being a commodity, according to Tokofsky, is that the celebrations, which absorbed millennia of influences and adapted themselves to the religious, political, and economic realities of each era, become static public displays.

Bendix sees the Chlause as an amalgam of old and new, a constantly evolv-ing work in progress: "While outsiders may come and regard the whole thing as a tourist attraction, insiders do not. ... While a folklorist may pessimisti-cally consider this a spoiling of development of the event, they never stand still, these spectacles, and they have the capacity to add further layers to their per-formance without necessarily losing the ones they already had."

Whether tourism is desirable or not, the Elzach, Waldsee, and Rottweil Fasnet celebrations that Tokofsky writes about retain much of the original ele-ments and characters. Chief among these are the Elzach Schuttig, the fools who caper about, skipping, taunting, and growling, with broomsticks and ugly wooden masks, sometimes led by a black devil. The Schuttigs' behavior has been toned down; they don't attack people viciously as they used to, but Elzach fool societies pride themselves on preserving the original characters as closely as possible. The Schuttig are covered with bright red flannel strips and beat the

The *Narrensprung* or Leaping Fools of Rottweil, Germany, used to run through the village in a "chaotic storm." In 1888 Rottweil began the Narrhalla carnival society and ordered the fools to be more restrained. The impressive carved masks show tusk-like horns projecting from the jaw and a curled beard on a large-nosed brown face. Feathers adorn the cape, and the Narrensprung used the pole to vault down the street. Photographed by Karl-Heinz Raach; courtesy of Städt. Kurverwaltung, Bad Waldsee.

ground with inflated pig bladders as they and witches parade through the streets. The Schuttig at one time were "rag fools," dressing in dark, uneven rags; today they wear clean, uniform rows of felt.

Tokofsky relates that during Fasnet in nearby Waldsee, some of the all-male groups dress as women in ugly masks and red flannel hoods They carry broomsticks, which they use as leverage for vaults and leaps during the parade. Also at Waldsee, there is a death and resurrection of the carnival figure. At the beginning of Fasnet, a group of fools carries a young girl, dressed in a clown outfit, on a stretcher onto a stage. A doctor tells the audience the girl is in a deep, year-long sleep and needs the Fasnet spirit to rouse her. As the audience provides the energy and excitement, the girl slowly revives. Rejoicing in their success, the fools dance around a bit, then leave. In the final drama of Fasnet, all participants dress in black, and the community mourns Fasnet's death, which is symbolized by throwing a doll dressed like the girl into the river, thus "burying their carnival."

Just as we saw Robin Hood emerging from Robin Goodfellow in the British plays, his counterpart in Waldsee is Hans Federle, or Feathered Hans. Tokofsky says Hans Federle is the evildoer who once lived in the forests of Upper Swabia: "From the history of witch trials, we know that he was a young man who emerged from the forest wearing an unusual costume." Hans Federle wears a brown velour cap with a Robin Hood–style feather stuck in it; curly locks of graying black hair and a grimacing wooden face complete the look. His green cape is dotted with red and yellow feathers, and he carries a forked branch. In neighboring Rottweil, Hans Federle's cousin has curved fangs and a cape covered with white feathers. The Städt. Kurverwaltung from Waldsee reports *der Federle* is one of the original masks from Waldsee's Fasnet.

In still another German area, Hamelin, we see this same figure embodied in the Pied Piper of Hamelin, whose story is reenacted for tourists every summer Sunday in the public square. The piper's story, known to us through a Robert Browning poem, was one of those collected by the brothers Jacob and Wilhelm Grimm in their folklore-gathering efforts. The legend relates that in 1284 a man came to Hamelin wearing a multi-colored or "pied" coat. The pied man offered to help the village get rid of its plague of rats in return for a goodly sum of money. The citizens were delighted and agreed, so the pied man started piping away. Mice and rats swarmed to him and docilely followed him to the local river, where they plunged in and drowned. The citizens, however, reneged on their bargain and refused to pay the piper. Insulted and furious, the piper left, only to return June 26 dressed as a huntsman. While the adults were at church, the piper started his irresistible tune, and the village's 130 children followed him into a hill and disappeared.

Russ relates that "serious researchers have dedicated a good deal of time to trying to establish whether there is any truth in the legend and have come up with weird and wonderful theories in an attempt to demythologise it." At the heart of the story, these theories suggest, is everything from a ritual murder of Jews to the capture of the young people by some fanatical group.

The Wild Man, whether called Perchten, Chläus, Ruprecht, Schuttig, or Hans Federle, *was* carnival for Germans and neighboring ethnic groups in the forested mountains. No matter what religious, bourgeois, courtly, or monetary influences would modify him over the centuries, the Wild Man remained central to carnival celebrations.

The Fool and Bessy also continued to frolic in Scotland, and Mrs. M. MacLeod Banks gives some information on Scottish activities in her 1941 *British Calendar Customs*. In Scotland, as in Germany and France, the Wild Man was an important fertility symbol. He was a standard member of wedding celebrations, but he made his other year-end rounds as well. At the close of the sixteenth century, says Banks, it was common for young people to go "guising," or roaming in disguises. In Rosburgshire beribboned dancers, accompanied by a broom-carrying Bessy and a fool "in grotesque costume" visited houses. The fool was often equated with the devil in Scotland, and the fool's outfit was often called the "devil's coat."

By the time we have written accounts of this Scottish mumming, it is under fire by the church. In 1598 the deacon of Perth blasted mumming as "blasphemous and heathenism" and threatened that those participating would be punished and banished. If this seems a bit stiff for a night of communal fun, we should remember that witchcraft hysteria was in high swing in the 1500s, and these recreations were synonymous with heresy against God and church.

Remnants of worship of the old horned god also persisted in the Hebrides, a region of about 500 islands off the Scottish coast. Here sacred cakes were baked on Michaelmas Day (an old year's end); the first harvest grains were made into a loaf, and the first piece of this loaf was cast into the fire as an offering to Old Hornie or Donas.

In Scottish Michaelmas activities, the death-resurrection theme from Wild Man festivals evolved into a romantic, ballet-like pantomime performance called "Carlin of the Mill-dust." In the play the Wild Man's wooden rod had become the magic wand that held the power of regeneration and life. A man and woman danced, "gesticulating and posing before one another, crossing and recrossing, and exchanging places," says Banks. The man waved the wand above their heads, but as he touched the woman, she fell dead at his feet. He danced, lamenting, then breathed on her left palm and touched it with the wand. The left hand revived, and the man rejoiced. After capering a bit, he finished the resurrection by touching her right hand, then both feet. He then knelt, breathed into her mouth and touched her heart with the wand. She revived, and they danced joyously. This more aesthetic version recalls the beginning of ballet, which some have traced to the Wild Man festivals. We saw this same evolution of prancing to choreographed dancing in the evolution of Harlequin.

In Ireland, the old mumming activities existed into the 1800s. In *Hibernian Country Pastimes and Festivals* we learn that a dozen couples, with ribbons piled on their shoulders to make them look humpbacked, paraded in celebration. The fool, with a "frightful mask" and goat's beard, paraded with Bessy, who wore a tanned, ugly mask. The writer, though he knew who the fool "really" was, "could hardly refrain from taking flight, most country children not being able to look on an ugly mask without extreme terror." The fool gave an "Indian yell," charged around, and thrashed the crowd with an inflated bladder hung from a stick as Bessy used her broom to discourage spectators who ventured too near. A vestige of the battle over a woman occurred as brave youths sidled up to Bessy to flirt with her. The enraged fool chased the intruders through the crowd, then lovingly reconciled with his grotesque mate.

In Killorglin, Ireland, King Puck, a goat, is hoisted on a platform 50 feet over the town as the sign that the three-day Puck Fair has begun. Sharon Bohn Gmelch visited the fair and wrote about the event in a 1988 *Kansas City Star* newspaper travel section. The first days of the fair are devoted to horse trading and cattle buying and selling, and a carnival atmosphere reigns as "sideshow performers lift weights and wriggle out of chains. The music is loud and the pubs are crowded."

The central event, says Gmelch, is the crowning of the Puck, who is captured in nearby mountains, decorated with bells and flowers, placed on a wagon, paraded through town in the early evening, then hoisted in the air, to remain there throughout the fair. Throughout Ireland in the twelfth and thirteenth centuries, says Gmelch, these fairs were times of relief; people were exempt from trading tariffs and arrest for debt as long as Puck remained on high.

"Despite the pagan connotations of paying homage to a male goat, symbol of fertility and licentiousness, several accounts of the custom's origins are decidedly tamer," writes Gmelch. The dominant local myth is that a puck, or goat, saved the people of Killorglin from the English, for as Oliver Cromwell's forces plundered the countryside, they startled some goats who were grazing outside Killorglin. One of the male goats fled into town, alerting the townspeople and giving them time to save themselves.

Like the festivals in Switzerland and Germany, the Puck Fair today is a major tourist event. Gmelch says in 1987 fair organizers were planning two weeks of activities around the event and built a large entertainment dome to accommodate live bands.

Beastly mummers carrying out a death and resurrection theme were common in Poland as well. Barbara Bazielichowna in "Further Notes on the Polish Guisers" tells us the mummers' function was to bid the old year farewell and greet the new year. These mummers were divided into two groups of maskers, the dead faces and the bears, in this ancestors' procession. At homes, a "priest" announced the New Year was coming and sprinkled everyone with "consecrated water." Then horses, grooms, and gypsies entered. The horses kicked, stamped, neighed, and pranced, shaking their bells. One of them fell to the floor; the groom struck the floor and tugged on the horse's reins to revive the beast. Failing, he called for a gypsy woman, who revived the horse, after which the dead faces ran around beating people with sticks. Then the bears entered and rolled around on the floor; if they caught a girl they carried her out and threw her in the snow. This ancestors' procession still takes place in some parts of Poland.

In Russia, the same fertility festivals with parallel themes took place. Lisa Warner in "The Russian Folk Play Tsar Maximillian" says the play *Tsar Maximillian* is a descendant of the same rites that spawned European mumming plays. Warner states this play is one of the last remnants of an indigenous people's theater, which came to an end under persecution in 1648. Like other modern survivals, the original fertility ritual was overlaid with local celebrities and Christianity, characters, and motifs, and the Wild Man survived only in comic interludes, as Markusha the gravedigger, just as Dionysus was relegated to comic relief in the tragedies that had originated to honor him.

The King of the Puck Fair is hoisted 50 feet above the town in Killorglin, Ireland, signaling the beginning of the three-day celebration. Courtesy of the Irish Tourist Board.

The plot of *Tsar Maximillian* concerns the religious conflict between the pagan tsar and his recalcitrant Christian son Adolf. The father three times ordered Adolf to worship a pagan god; each time the son refused. After the third refusal the tsar banished Adolf to the wilderness to reconsider, but later he apparently lost patience and decided to end Adolf's dilemma by having an executioner slay him. The second part of the play consisted of dueling, including the stock character of the black Arab fighting Anika the knight. Anika is the consistent victor, until Death's scythe defeats even him.

Warner's interest lies in the comic interludes, where Markusha is the key buffoon figure. Markusha's part in the play consists of his removing the figures of Adolf and the executioner, who committed suicide after he killed Adolf. Markusha appeared with a troupe that included his old wife, a Devil, and a doctor, who cures Markusha of his aches and pains. Markusha was distinguished by his humpback, his sheepskin coat worn wooly side out, the phallus he carried, and his generally tattered appearance. Warner says the comic scenes are "overtly erotic" and sees Markusha as the Russian variation of Beelzebub and the fool.

Warner says Markusha is a derivative of the "Russian ritual bear whose dance was originally intended to promote fertility and whose costume, like that of the other Russian ritual animal the goat, was also made from inverted sheep-skin garments. The erotic play of the Gravedigger, who is sometimes adorned with a phallic symbol, and his connection with death is a direct parallel to the often exaggerated sexual nature of the spring vegetation figures and the enact-ment of their death and subsequent resurrection during the ritual."

In Georgia, which abuts northern Turkey and Iran in the Caucasus Moun-tains, the *Berikaoba* preserved the festival tradition. Juliet Rukhadze and Georgi Chitaya show us the Berikaoba-Keyenoba festival in "Festivals and Tradition in the Georgian Soviet Socialist Republic." The chief *berika* or bridegroom wears a black felt mask, a beard and mustache of goat's hair, and a pair of goat horns. As the groom and his retinue go from house to house, the homeowner greets the mummers, invites them to his table, tells them his troubles, and asks for help. After hearing the homeowner's litany of woes, the troupe dances to protect the house. Carrier boys, also wearing masks and sheepskin coats, then collect gifts of meat, flour, bread, or cheese. "No matter how generous the gifts," say Rukhadze and Chitaya, "the Berika and his retinue feel honor bound to loot something from the house, while the host tries to pluck a tuft of wool from the Berika's beard or moustache, to be put into the cattle trough or hen's nest to increase fertility." At the home of a miserly or unreceptive host, one of Berika's retinue rolls on the ground, an action calculated to bring on bad har-vests, illness, and other evils to the family.

As they parade, the group enacts a courtship ritual in which the berika courts the bride, and they marry. Amid singing and dancing, the happy cou-ple "enact the scene of the wedding night." But the blissful state ends as the male wedding guests try to win the bride's considerable favors. Two of the ungrate-ful guests, the Arab and the Tatar, slay the bridegroom, after which the bride and wedding guests mourn inconsolably. While the rest of the guests are wail-ing, the dastardly Arab and Tatar attempt to carry off the bride; this act revives berika, who leaps up, pursues the villains, battles with them, and regains the bride.

The Keyenoba part of the festival occurs on the eighth day, and "none but the tallest, strongest, cleverest and handsomest man in the village can play the part of the keyen; and he must be eloquent and successful as well, since only a man 'with a lucky touch' can bring luck to the village, ward off drought and ensure a good crop." The keyen, of course, wears a sheepskin coat and is smeared with soot.

Rukhadze and Chitaya say the festival is "an echo of the Greek myth of the Argonaut's voyage to Colchis, in Western Georgia, to capture the Golden fleece, a sacred Georgian relic." The authors say the berika is connected with Bosseli or Bosla, a Georgian deity replaced by a Christian saint, Basel, who was considered the patron saint of fertility for both humans and fauna.

Serafim Severniak takes us north of Greece to Bulgaria in "Bulgarian Fes-tivals, Old and New" in which the *koukeri,* strapping young men dressed in animal skins and colored cloth, perform athletic dances on the Sunday before Lent, Christmas or New Year's Eve, the spring equinox, and the night before the harvests. Severniak traces the dance back nine millennia to a scene in the cave of Magura in which a young hunter, "endowed with well-defined viral attributes is jumping just like a kouker, while a group of women dances around him." The leader of the koukeri often wears a gigantic phallus hidden under an apron, which he pulls out to touch the legs of young women without children.

On the island of Ceylon (now Sri Lanka), a traditional fertility drama also bears a striking resemblance to the basic Wild Man rituals. M. H. Goonatilleka in "Mime, Mask and Satire in Kolam of Ceylon" says the *Kolam* or playlet supposedly was begun to help the queen conceive a child, and that the original masks were commissioned by the Indian god Indra.

Leader of the acting troupe is Tom Tom Beater, a potbellied "decrepit," a satirical figure. The play describes him with

> Staff in hand and talipot leaf,
> Turkey red waist band
> And drum slung over the shoulders,
> Bowling all round in a drunken fit

Tom Tom Beater has a flowing white beard, sagging cheeks, and wrinkles, and he is accompanied by his old wife, with white matted hair and hanging breasts. In the play, the woman enters the assembly with her son, hunting for her husband, Tom Tom Beater. The play includes drunk and boisterous policemen who quarrel. One of the policemen is struck down; a doctor enters and diagnoses the illness as malaria, and the patient is removed. It is notable that the irrational behavior of Tom Tom Beater and his troupe is explained as a result of drunkenness, any idea of divine possession having been forgotten long ago.

From this sampling we can see the near universality of the festival and of its main character, the Wild Man. In these rituals a Wild Man and earth goddess — representatives of life — paraded; the god was killed and resurrected or replaced by his "son." These characters paraded throughout ancient and modern Europe, from Scotland to Russia from Greece to India. As their significance was degraded or forgotten in more metropolitan areas, the Wild Man shed his furs and horns to become master of ceremonies, a fool, and the personification of holiday.

Many original festivals and their offshoots died off from causes other than humanism and Christianity; often the motive was more practical than moralistic or philosophical. As mummers' disguises were a perfect opportunity for enemies of the crown in England, mumming was outlawed there during the Scottish wars of Edward II and in the reigns of Richard II, Henry IV, and Henry V.

A severe blow to the ancient masquerade came when supporters of Richard II reportedly tried to assassinate Henry IV while disguised as Christmas mummers. Henry V was the target of a similar plot, and in 1418 Henry declared false beards, painted faces, mumming plays, and parades illegal. Later, they were resurrected, but the continuity had been broken, and the significance was gone.

Mumming plays had had a hard time co-existing with the Catholic Church, but the Puritan regime of England banned all Christmas festivities in the mid–1600s, as we saw in Father Christmas's imprisonment during this time. Christmas reemerged during Queen Victoria's reign, but the virile Christmas had become a decrepit; the fool altered from sensual young man into aged buffoon. On the Continent, the Teutonic sword dancing succumbed to religious opposition in the seventeenth century. In France it died earlier, but enjoyed a diluted revival in the 1700s with the 1717 play "Harlequin Executed."

The festivals changed throughout Europe. Sometimes they were banned as obscene, obnoxious events; sometimes they died from obsolescence or lack of interest as the young lost the understanding of the parents' old customs. In the 1800s, however, revisionists and folklorists showed a renewed interest in the old festivals. In England, the May Pole was resurrected to become a dance of gentlemen and gentlewomen; in many communities the old ritual became children's paradings, such as Halloween activities today; in others, it became a modern tourist attraction. The world wars interrupted many of those pageants that survived into the twentieth century, sometimes eradicating them, as it eradicated the strong young men who performed them.

Despite the many obstacles and influences, however, the Wild Man still cavorts through mountainous and forested areas of the earth, as he does in America's skies, visiting from house to house, just as he did when he was a fertility god distributing the boons of the earth. A thousand years of political, social, economic, and religious pressures have somehow failed to eradicate this hardy heathen.

Chapter 8
European Gift-Givers

In its most primitive forms, a major part of the Wild Man's presence among humans included sharing the fruits of the earth with them. It was this role of gift-giver that proved most resilient to change, and we find the Wild Man's descendants playing this part at Christmas throughout Europe. This gift-giving behavior persisted even when all that remained of the original ritual and its festive parades were a saint and a sinner, Saint Nick and Old Nick, the same odd couple who visited Dutch households as Saint Nicholas and Black Pete.

In Germany, the Christmas men sometimes are called the Knecht Ruprechte or Servant Roberts. The first written record we have of Knecht Ruprecht is as Christ's servant in a 1600s Nuremberg Christmas procession, where he had been cast in a subservient role to the nobler powers. We also find Ruprecht accompanying Saint Nicholas and Saint Martin in their nineteenth- and early twentieth-century German house calls. A typical house call from Ruprecht and a saint was identical to the Dutch Nicholas-Black Pete visit: After the children had welcomed the saint with praises, the saint had the children repeat a prayer and show their lesson books. Ruprecht didn't do much — just stood by growling, his lolling tongue obviously ready to taste the flesh of young wrongdoers. The children shakingly knelt before the saint and kissed his ring, after which the Nicholas told them to put their shoes outside; later they would find them filled with either fruit or sticks.

Ruprecht here plays the part of the bogeyman, a black, hairy, horned, cannibalistic, stick-carrying nightmare. His role and character are of unmitigated evil, the ultimate horror that could befall children who had been remiss in learning their prayers and doing their lessons. He was hell on earth. When a holy figure was present, this was the old Wild Man's role, servant and satanic foil. Their fellow paraders gone, these two continued their ancient rounds.

We find the Klaubauf of Austria filling this role in the Tyrol, where as Clement Miles notes, Saint Nicholas "in all the splendor of a church image; a revered grey-haired figure with flowing beard, gold-broidered cape and

155

Germany's Knecht Ruprecht, shown in this 1784 German engraving, grabs one child while the others scamper away. Instead of helping Saint Nicholas deliver gifts, this Ruprecht has the good saint tucked away in his bag, along with the Christmas tree.

pastoral staff" comes to visit the children with the terrifying Klaubauf in tow. This monster is covered with a shaggy hide and wears horns: he has a black face, fiery eyes, and a long red tongue; and he clanks in chains.

Actually, this Saint-Satan duo was fairly well confined to Teutonic countries. As Clement Miles comments, the Saint-Satan combination was uniquely Germanic:

> The difference between the orderliness of the German mind and the happy-go-lucky tolerance of the English is well shown in the German insistence upon the punishers of the bad children being as important characters in the Nicholas Myth as the rewarders of the good. ... In England, of course, there is only the Rewarder in the Christmas fable; the bad, if they are punished, are punished in a negative, typically English way, by the mere absence of reward. ... Father Christmas never has a Hans Trapp or a Klaubauf with him; German St. Nicholas is never without something of the sort.

Although Saint Nicholas might never go out without his hairy companion, Ruprecht and Pelznichol managed to exclude the dour saint from their house visits in other areas, or else the church-initiated saints reverted to type and melded back into the more primitive Wild Man costume and manner. In these places the Wild Man continued his fertility visits alone, with his troupe, or with Bessy, or the woman herself visited homes without a Wild Man escort. A look at European Christmas figures that lingered on after the ball shows how widespread the Wild Man's visits remained and gives us a close look at Santa's immediate kin.

Writers and folklorists have marveled over the variety and numbers of these Christmas creatures, but what seems more marvelous is that all variations of the Christmas Man followed a basic pattern. All were dressed in fur or in tatters to simulate hair; all had blackened faces or grotesque masks; and all carried bells and whips, sticks and sacks.

In most German communities, Knecht Ruprecht appeared as a slightly frightening but not totally hellish figure. In goatskins, this bag-carrying bearded figure went about examining Teutonic children. If they could not say their prayers perfectly, he punished them with his whip or bundle of sticks; if they performed well, he gave them apples, nuts, and gingerbreads. He was both the rewarder and punisher and contained within himself both the blessedness of forgiveness and the terror of the unknown. He was sometimes comical, rough and crude, but not entirely satanic. He was generally a strange, bearded figure who carried forgiveness and condemnation in his little sack of goodies and sticks.

In northern Germany this man was known under names such as Ru Claus (Claus in "rough" clothes), Joseph Claus, Claws, Bullerklaas. The bag of ashes he carried gave him the name of Aschenklas (Claus with ashes) in parts of Austria.

In southern Germany he often wandered as Pelzmärte (Martin in furs), Pelzni-chol or Bellsnichol, a name he carried to the United States. No matter which name he bore, he was the same personage — bearded, humpbacked, dressed in goatskins, and carrying a stick, whip, or ash-filled bundle, and bells.

In addition to creating Saints Nicholas and Martin to replace their hea-then forebears, Christianity made other other attempts in Germany to replace the Wild Man with holy figures. Beginning in the sixteenth century, the Lutheran Church promoted Christ as the children's gift-giver, hoping to draw attention to the child for whom Christmas was named. Christkind (Christ Child) was not, however, a babe in swaddling; it was a teen-aged girl who drifted gracefully about in a flowing white gown, with a gold crown and can-dle, creating an effect Clement Miles describes as "hovering between the char-acter of the Divine Infant and that of an Angel."

Christkind sometimes traveled with other holy figures, as in parts of Aus-tria, where the archangel Gabriel and Saint Peter joined the visitational pro-cessions. Before handing out presents, the three performed a skit in which Christkind announced she had presents for the good and sticks for the bad. Saint Peter complained of the children's naughtiness, but when the children's mother pleaded their basic goodness, he relented and gave gifts.

Christkind's usual companion, however, was no saint, but the Wild Man, lurking beside her like an unbanishable memory. In what is now French Alsace, a region that borders Germany and displays strong Germanic influence, he was known as Hans Trapp. Dressed in bearskins, a blackened face, and long beard, and carrying a rod, Hans Trapp accompanied the angelic Christkind to local houses, frightening and threatening naughty tots.

The most common consequence of the effort to replace the Wild Man Ruprecht with Christkind was that Ruprecht confiscated Christkind's name and left her in the dust. Under the name of Christkind, Christmann and Christ-puppe (Christ Elf), the Wild Man wandered through German communities. In the Ruppin district, Christmann visited local homes in beribboned white clothes, accompanied by creatures called *Fein,* men in tattered women's clothes and blackened faces. Christmann made the children repeat some scripture or recite a hymn. If they knew the proper response, they received gingerbread; if not, he beat them with an ash-filled bundle. After he left, the Fein entered, jumped around, and frightened the children.

In Scandinavia, clerics battled him under the names of *Julbok* (Yule buck), *Julsvenn,* or *Julgubben* (Yule goblin). As in Germany, an angelic figure was cho-sen to take the Wild Man's place. This character took the name Santa Lucia or Saint Lussi, from the Latin word *lux* for "light." Lussi reportedly achieved sainthood after passing the ultimate test. According to legend Lussi was a Chris-tian maiden in ancient Rome. She was courted by a pagan, but rejected him because of his heathenism. Her spurned lover reported Lussi to the proper officials, who tortured and blinded her. Lussi held to her faith through the torture, was killed, and later was declared a saint. Legend relates that Christian teachers carried Lussi's story to Sweden, whereupon the Swedes took the martyred Lussi into their hearts and created a day in her memory. Because this day happened to fall on the shortest day of the year in this land of wintry darkness, and because of her blindness, Lussi became the symbol of victory over darkness — the queen of light.

A second Swedish legend relates that Lussi singlehandedly saved Sweden from starvation. The country was suffering from a severe famine when Lussi, in white robes and candled crown, stepped across the frozen lakes, bringing food to the starving nation.

Today Lussi is a young woman in white robes who wears candles in a wire crown. In each house the girl selected to play Lussi awakens her family at dawn and offers coffee and *lussekatter,* a special wheat cake. This custom, which spread from western Sweden, has been adopted by businesses, and each commercial establishment has its in-house Lussi at Christmas time.

Lussi, like other holy figures, began her Christmas reign by taking part in traditional heathen festivals, and at one time even led the raucous wild horde. Later, townspeople annually selected a Saint Lussi, who roamed the countryside with a horseback rider and men with blackened faces and hairy costumes. These Wild Men were called star boys and were said to be the demons and trolls conquered by the reviving sun, represented by Lussi.

These star boys were a constant butt of official civic antagonism. In 1721 the magistrate of Stockholm warned against the "irresponsible boys and other loose persons who gather together and run about the streets and alleys and prowl about the houses with the so-called Christmas goats, stars, and other vanities." Parading around with demons and trolls gave Lussi a bad name in Norway, where she is considered an unmitigated witch. Folklore puts Lussi at the head of the wild horde in Norway, where she ruled the evil spirits that prowled the Norwegian countryside on the longest nights of the year.

Just as was Christkind's fate, the name "Saint Lussi" was adopted by some very unsaintlike figures, including the Julbok (Yule buck) himself. In the Boehmerwald, St. Lussi was a man dressed in goatskins, a devil's mask and horns, who gave fruit to children who had behaved; he threatened to rip open the stomachs of those who had not. A cow with a lighted candle on its head was Saint Lussi in other areas.

The Yule buck kept his name and identity in many places, however, until the last of the nineteenth century. Dressed in goatskins and wearing a frightening mask and horns, the Yule buck visited children's houses, giving gifts and threatening the nonconformists. Sometimes this character, wearing a buck's head, "went after" children. In some areas the Julbok survived as a straw puppet tossed from hand to hand in games; in still others he lived on only as a buck-shaped cake.

According to Ruth Cole Kainen in *America's Christmas Heritage,* the Yule buck is one European Christmas creature who made the crossing to America, where he lived on on Hatteras Island, North Carolina, into the 1700s. Christmas there began with a parade of fifes and drums, and shortly before dark the townfolk dressed in "grotesque" costumes. Then Old Buck emerged from the woods, where he had lived all year. With a steer's head and horns on a pole body covered with quilts and adorned with a bell, Old Buck rushed at the crowd awaiting him.

Today the wild wanderings of the Scandinavian Julbok and his companions have been taken over by small children who, dressed like American Halloweeners, go from house to house in witch and goat costumes, begging treats. The star boys are now fresh-faced carolers, with little apparent heathenism as they sing lilting hymns. The observant spectator, however, will notice a toy goat in the hand of at least one singer — the Julbok making a last stand.

The Julbok also survived in another capacity, pulling a sled for the gift-giver known as Jultomten, a Yule elf. Jultomten had been on the Swedish scene a long time as a house sprite and achieved widespread popularity in the 1870s through a book, *Little Vigg's Christmas Eve*, written by a scholar and mythologist, Viktor Rydberg. Helge Åkerhielm sees today's Jultomten, whom she calls Sweden's Father Christmas, as a blending of the old land sprite with the now popular Father Christmas and Santa Claus figures.

Despite Jultomten's popularization as a fun-loving gift-giver, however, an undercurrent of fear lives on at Swedish Christmas. Adults in the mid-twentieth century considered Jultomten a destructive spirit and set out porridge and milk on Christmas Eve in the hopes of warding off his malevolence. And, although Yule goblin brings gifts, there is a dark side to the visit as well, and the whole family sleeps together on the floor on Christmas Eve as a protection against the goblins who roam the earth during Yuletide.

In Norway, the Wild Man Julsvenn made the transition from ogre to gift-giver rather well. There Julsvenn was considered a bringer of luck and plenty who came to houses on Christmas Eve to hide a lucky tuft of barley, which the residents found in the morning. Today, Julsvenn looks just like Santa Claus or Father Christmas, bringing gifts in a horse-drawn sleigh. Because he sometimes sleeps in the barn at night, a wooden bowl of porridge is placed in the hayloft as a midnight snack. Similarly, leaving a snack of cookies and milk for the Christmas Man survives today in many American homes. On Christmas Eve, however, like the Swedes, Norwegian families also slept together on the floor, on a layer of straw, because it was dangerous to sleep by oneself on this goblin-filled night.

In Sweden, Julsvenn remained a monster, and Åkerhielm says an important Christmas task in Sweden was the chopping of Christmas wood. If too little wood were chopped, Julsvenn, a monster with one eye in the middle of his forehead, would appear. Fires were kindled to keep the goblins away while the wood was being chopped.

In Finland, the Christmas goat, dressed in a long fur coat, a hoodlike cap, a white beard, and a goat's mask, also evolved into a grandfatherly Santa Claus figure named *Joulupukki* (Yule pixie). Joulupukki inquires at each house: "Are there any good children here?" Of course, the children all shout, "Yes!" and Joulupukki opens his sack of presents. Younger children dress like Christmas elves and help distribute gifts.

The Christmas goat's cousin, *Klapperbock* (rattly buck), used to visit children on the German island of Usedom in the Baltic Sea. Klapperbock was a large man in goatskins and a buck's head with a moveable, clattering jaw — hence the name Klapperbock. Like the Julbok, Klapperbock took the role of Christmas judge and attacked children who could not recite their prayers on demand.

A common explanation for Santa's having reindeer is that the beasts were adopted from the Lapland gift-giver, for Lapp life has centered around these animals and their migrations for four thousand years. A look at traditional Lapp Yuletide, however, shows no trace of reindeer, gift-giving, or festivity. Lapland is an area rather than a nation, within the Arctic circle, covering the tips of Norway, Sweden, Finland and the Kola Peninsula of Russia. In this harsh, isolated area, with little pressure from such modern amenities as gift-giving and humanism, the Wild Man survived as the terrible Stallo, untainted by beneficence. The Lapp Christmas Man was an unmitigated monster, a creature who had no use for presents and festivity as he terrified Laplanders into the twentieth century.

Like the Swedes, the Lapps carefully tended their woodpile on Christmas Eve. If one piece of wood stuck out, the one-eyed Stallo might catch his sleigh on it. A branch was carefully placed by an abundant water supply so Stallo could tie his sledge and drink as he made his Christmas rounds. This was more than a hospitable gesture, for if Stallo found no water he would suck out brains or drink a child's blood to sate his thirst. Stallo's sleigh was not pulled by reindeer, either, but by Lapland's destructive lemmings.

Christmas Eve was considered the most dangerous of all Lapp nights, for this was the night Stallo and other evil beings were on the loose, looking for naughty children to stuff into their sacks. In *Turi's Book of Lapland,* author Johan Turi relates the kind of tale that kept him and other Lapp children quiet and well-behaved on Christmas Eve: Three children decided to play games while their parents attended church. They would kill and gut a reindeer, as they had seen their father do scores of times. Since there were no reindeer handy, one of the children volunteered to take the beast's place. "Then the one that was bound at the slaughtering place began to freeze, and so he shouted: 'Come quick and kill me, I'm fwesing!' ... [H]e was so little he could not say his words properly." After his siblings had killed and gutted their brother, they began to cook his flesh. That was Stallo's cue, and he appeared, horrid and hairy. The children tried to escape, but all were killed; one child who tried to hide in a chest was roasted when Stallo blew embers through the keyhole.

Of course, Stallo's watchful eye also picked up smaller moral infractions, and Turi says when he was young "most folks were talking about this happening and not a single one doubted it; ... [a]nd the children were always told ... 'If you make a noise and a disturbance at Yuletide you will see the evil spirits.' And Lapps live a quiet and beautiful life at Yuletide."

Stallo was a lone bogeyman and child-threatener in the twentieth century, but he was the remnant of a less gruesome parade. A survival of this parade existed in Finland in the early 1800s, when young men visited area houses. The strongest and biggest dressed in black rags or skins and called himself Stallo. Stallo prodded girls with a wooden phallus commanding them to pay a "tax." In southern Norway a similar Christmas procession was led by the "Christmas Stoale."

The Feminine Touch

We have witnessed two types of beings roaming the earth during the Twelve Days of Christmas — fur- or hair-clad men and saintly men and women. But not all women who roamed during these most sacred and most dangerous nights were saints. The old earth mother-Wild Woman once traveled where the soft-treading Lussi now steps. Hunchbacked, with dirty, tangled hair, a hooked nose, and a blackened face, and clothed in black rags or hair, she was as horrifying as any of her male counterparts.

This woman went by various names as she made her rounds, often with a pot of starch or a sack of ashes for smearing children's faces. In central Germany and parts of Austria she was Frau Holda or Holle, whom we met as leader of the wild horde and whose name Grimm tells us means "gracious." In southern Germany and the Tyrol she was Frau Perchta, meaning "bright" or "luminous," ironic appellations for a witch. Perchta, of course, survives today in the Perchtenlaufen of Austria. In northern Germany she was Frau Free or Frick, Gode, or Harke; Budelfau in Lower Austria. Whatever her name, she was the same in appearance and mannerisms.

During their Christmas rounds, Holda and her counterparts carried out the traditional giving and judging functions, rewarding "good" children with nuts and apples and punishing the "bad" ones. In Germany Holda or Berchta judged adults as well, especially the women's conduct of their households. Women hastened to finish their spinning before the Twelves, for if it had not been completed, Holda would spoil it. A table was set for Holda and her traveling companions, and the house was cleaned so she would be pleased.

Holda and Berchta were very particular about what food was eaten on their festival day. Berchta demanded that mortals eat fish and oat-grits. Those who ate other food courted disaster, for the indignant Berchta would cut open their stomachs, fill them with chopped straw, and sew up the gash with a plow. Borne's *Folktales of the Orlagu* relates that Berchta's sister Perchta had the same rather intense reaction: If everyone did not eat *zemmede,* a dish of flour and milk, Perchta would slash open the malefactor's stomach, take out everything, and fill the space with hay, straw or bricks, using the plowshare to sew him up again. Misbehaving children were threatened with these women; Bavarian children were warned that if they were naughty on the eve of Epiphany (January 6, Twelfth Night), Berchta would cut their stomachs open. In the Franchonian and Swabian districts of Germany, children believed Berchta walked around the house at night looking for bad boys to tear to pieces.

These frauen, like their male companions the Julgubben, Christpuppe, Jultomten, and Joulupukki, are identified as elves or associated with elves. Holda was queen of the *Huldrefolk* or mountain sprites in Norway and Denmark; in Germany, Holda was considered the princess of a subterranean people called the *Holden,* who Grimm says were considered friendly to humans. Grimm says Holda ruled over the elves in an underground cave where "some men still find their way in, and live with her in bliss."

In spite of a massive effort to "witchify" this goddess, her beneficial aspects keep surfacing. Grimm sees Holda's name as an epithet for Frigg, the German fertility goddess. As we saw with Pan, in writing or speaking about the gods, people felt it wise to avoid calling them by name because it might summon them. In the case of the fertility god and goddess, these deities were given the utmost respect, for they were god and goddess of death as well as life. In Frigg's case, *Holda* or Gracious One was used in place of her name, and later this epithet was considered the name of a separate being.

To support his contention that Holda and her counterpart Berchta are transformed versions of the gracious Frigg, Grimm enumerates the similarities between the Holda and the Germanic goddess (italics are Grimm's):

> They drive about in *waggons,* like Mother Earth, and promote agriculture and navigation among men; a *plough,* from which fall chips of gold, is their sacred implement ... [T]hey appear *suddenly,* and Berhta especially hands her gifts in at the window. Both Holda and Berhta/ Berchtal have spinning and weaving at heart, they insist on diligence and the keeping of festivals holy, on the transgressor grim penalties are executed. ... [T]hey rule over *elves* and *dwarfs,* but *night-hags* and *enchantresses* also follow in their train.

In Upper Franconia, a young man dressed as Berta at Christmas gave nuts to good children and a rod to bad ones. In the mountains of Salzburg, Perchta-running was held in honor of this goddess, and the Perchta runs persist today. In the Pinzgau region of Germany, several hundred men called *Berchten* roamed about in what Grimm calls the "oddest disguises," carrying cow bells and cracking whips. Knecht Ruprecht, under his own name or a half-dozen other names, traveled with Holda in central Germany, the Wild Man as companion of the earth mother.

This same gift-giving hag is found in Italy as *La Befana* and in Russia as *Babushka* (grandmother). Legend tells us that these aged wanderers are destined to spend eternity trudging from house to house during the twelve days of Christmas. La Befana reputedly refused to go to Bethlehem with the Wise Men when they passed her door, and the hapless Babushka misdirected them. For penance, they are condemned to find the Christ Child. As they wander from house to house, peering into the face of each child, they also give gifts. In Grimm's time La Befana was a terror, a misshapen black "fairy" dressed in rags, but more recently she has become a kindly grandmother.

In our glance at recent European gift-givers we see all the non-saint male figures are variations of a theme: They are blackened, hairy, part beast (usually goat), and associated with elves or goblins; they carry bells, whips, sticks, apples, ashes, nuts. They carry bags or are humpbacked, and they bring both terror and gifts to humanity. The women, hags and witches, are seen upon closer look to be beneficent, but dangerous, fertility goddesses. Fortunately for misbehaving children, who were threatened with some pretty gruesome punishments throughout Europe, both the Wild Man and the earth goddess softened to become charitable gift-givers.

Chapter 9
A Right Jolly Old Elf

A look at the Wild Man and his descendants answers many questions regarding Santa's identity and characteristics — his furry clothes, bells, bag of dolls and gifts, whip, reindeer names, sleigh, home visits, and "Ho! Ho! Ho!" But many questions remain. For example, why does Santa go up and down chimneys instead of in and out by more conventional passages? And why does he live at the North Pole?

We know Santa Claus as a "jolly old elf" who rules a band of industrious elves in the Arctic Circle. He comes at the "fairy hour" of midnight and carries a "fairy whip." His Northern European descendants have elves' names — Christpuppe, Jultomten, Joulupukki (Yule pixie). There is a constant association of the Wild Man and his descendants with elves and fairies. To answer the remaining riddles, therefore, we need to visit fairyland.

Although the terms *elves, fairies,* and *good people* were used in the Middle Ages to refer to people who continued their pre–Christian festivals (much as the word *heathen* is used today), the terms also referred to specific peoples so different from the later Europeans they were considered non-human in many ways. Some scholars contend these elves and fairies were very early — perhaps aboriginal — Europeans, and that the fertility rites that gave birth to Santa and other folk characters were more ancient than we once suspected, either pre-dating the Greek goat-god Dionysus or not related to him at all.

When we think of fairies, pixies, and dwarfs we are apt to think of Peter Pan's Tinkerbell or Grumpy, Sleepy, Happy and crew from Disney's *Snow White and the Seven Dwarfs.* Originally, however, fairies were neither minuscule nor sparkling, and dwarfs were not as amenable to human interference as Snow White found them to be.

This idea that elves, witches, and fairies were an indigenous European people was first advanced in the 1800s. In the early 1900s, some anthropologists and folklorists concluded that "witchcraft" was based on fertility observances practiced by early Europeans later referred to as elves and fairies. This idea became so accepted that Dr. Margaret Murray could state: "It is now a commonplace of anthropology that the tales of fairies and elves preserve the tradition of a dwarf race which once inhabited Northern and Western Europe."

Actually, it's not that clear-cut. As John MacCulloch points out in *Eddic Mythology*, "The origin of the elves and fairies of popular belief, including the older Alfar, has been sought in different directions. They were souls of the dead, nature spirits, lesser divinities, reminiscences of older races, products of dreams or imagination. Probably all these mingle together in the elfin belief wherever found." These elements all intertwine, and at different times each has been the most popular or most academically acceptable explanation. One of the many threads that interweave to form these tales, however, apparently had its origin in an actual people or peoples who inhabited Europe thousands of years ago.

Murray and some others believe these people were a short, dark-skinned people who came from northern Africa and took up residence in Egypt, where their culture and religion formed the basis of the great Egyptian religions. In this scenario, they migrated from Egypt to Europe and arrived in Britain around 2000 B.C., when they constructed Stonehenge and the other monoliths that dot the British Isles and Europe. Harold Bayley in *Archaic England* believes that these early settlers were Trojans, for London's old name was New Troy. Others believe they were a unique culture that survives today only in the Basque area.

This idea that Trojans or other Mediterranean or African people traveled up the coast of Europe, bringing civilization in their train, was the only explanation that made sense in the intellectual and scientific climate of the early 1900s. Until the late 1940s, there was no reliable way to date remains, so prehistorians started with the premise that civilization began in northern Africa, southern Europe, and Asia. By comparing monuments, graves, and other cultural markings, scientists inferred a spread of civilized people and their culture from the Mediterranean outward and northward; this dissemination of people and culture was called the diffusionist theory.

Prehistorians had no way to date what they saw in northwestern Europe as they struggled to make sense of Stonehenge and other monoliths and artifacts. They therefore used a chronological reference point — in this case, classical literature — which was the only source that could be dated. The Romans Caesar and Tacitus had referred to the "barbarian peoples" of Europe and their Druid sacrifices; when prehistorians looked at the huge tombs and monoliths dotting the land, they tried to relate these artifacts to this sparse literature and concluded the monoliths were sites of bloody Druid sacrifices.

After Champollion deciphered the Egyptian hieroglyphs in 1822, prehistorians began building a more comprehensive picture of early Europe, but this history was based on the assumption that cultural similarities in separate areas resulted from a link between these cultures. Any cultural developments in northwestern Europe were considered to have come from the more advanced

Mediterranean world, the "cradle of civilization." "Child summed up this view when he stated that 'The sole unifying theme of European prehistory is the irradiation of European Barbarism by Oriental Civilisation,'" writes Mark Patton in *Statements in Stone: Monuments and Society in Neolithic Brittany*.

But whereas students of the past once thought that metallurgy, monument building, religion, and other aspects of advanced civilization were brought into Europe by more advanced Mediterranean peoples, recent data summarily dismiss this conclusion. Megaliths in western Europe and Britain apparently predate the Egyptian pyramids; a metal industry was fully developed in Europe before it even began in the Aegean. The earliest gold treasures found to date come not from Egyptian tombs but from Bulgarian graves.

Professor Colin Renfrew, who is in the forefront of the new archeology, says, "We now know, too, that three thousand years before the Greeks, the Romans, or the Celts, European farmers had discovered the principle of copper metallurgy and were using gold to make precious objects."

This new look at Europe is a result of the "radiocarbon revolution." Willard F. Libby developed radiocarbon dating in the 1940s as an outgrowth of atomic bomb research. Radiocarbon dating is based on the fact that all living things, whether plant or animal, contain the element carbon. A small proportion of that carbon is radioactive carbon 14. Radiocarbon dating is based on the idea that once the organism dies, the proportion of carbon 14 in its cells drops lower and lower, at a fixed rate, as time passes. Therefore, if persons could determine the percentage of carbon 14 in a cell, they could calculate when the organism died. Inorganic objects such as metals are dated by association; a metal knife found in a wooden box, for example, would be dated by determining the carbon 14 found in the wood of the box, and this date would be applied to the knife. Radiocarbon dating finally enabled archeologists to date artifacts objectively, and the diffusionist theory began to look a little shaky.

The diffusionist theory crumbled completely, however, with the discovery that carbon 14 dating assumptions were erroneous. This discovery came about when Dr. Hans Seuss of the University of California compared radiocarbon datings with tree ring analysis of the world's oldest trees, the California bristlecone pine. Seuss discovered that beyond 1000 B.C. the radiocarbon dates fell increasingly short of the real dates.

Renfrew says, "While original radiocarbon dates had already cast doubts on theories of Europe's chronology, the new dates make them untenable." Renfrew calls this the "eclipse of the diffusionist view." The impact of this redating of prehistoric remains can't be overestimated: It means *every assumption* about European prehistory had to be reevaluated. Renfrew says the oldest portions of Stonehenge would be dated at 2100 B.C. instead of 1650 B.C.; the oldest stone structure anywhere in the world dates from 4000 B.C. and is in Brittany, a peninsula that juts off the western coast of France, due south of the

British Isles. What this means is that in western Europe — before Egypt, before Greece and Rome — a civilization had developed that wasn't the result of more advanced southern peoples bringing their cultural niceties with them.

Renfrew says western Europe's civilization was a stratified society, probably a chiefdom. It was a society of classes and tradespeople, where the exotic artistry of goldsmithing reached a peak. These people's identity is a mystery, and today their huge monuments stand as mute testimony to a now-vanished civilization.

To archeologist Mark Patton, however, these monuments are not as mute as laypeople might think. Patton in *Statements in Stone* finds the monuments and huge stones, or megaliths, of Brittany remarkably eloquent; from their size, placement, and other archeological and anthropological data, Patton has reconstructed four phases of Europe's prehistoric societies.

The first or oldest phase was the Early Neolithic, from 4850 to 4250 B.C., marked by the beginning of farming, animal husbandry, and tribal societies. In these societies, elders held the reins of power, a power based on the control of religion and socially valued objects — in this case, stone axes — which were important symbols of status.

In the next 1,000 years, from 4250 to 3250 B.C., power became more centralized as tribes or societies vied for influence, a competition that saw such conspicuous displays of might as the large stone monoliths that Renfrew believes were territorial markers. Leaders became more jealous of their power, and religious rituals became secretive, the property of an elite group.

Then things changed. Under the old anthropological paradigm of social evolution, in which groups of people inexorably move from a less to a more developed organization, societies should have stepped up to a "higher," more civilized plane — but that didn't happen. In the next era, the Late Neolithic, from 3250 to 2850 B.C., the powerful elite societies of Brittany collapsed.

Patton says that after this collapse, the next era, from 2850 to 2250 B.C., was marked by a rapidly expanding exchange network that involved copper axes and daggers, gold jewelry, and other symbolic or adornment items, which probably served as symbols of prestige. Society became more stratified, and power became more centralized in the hands of a few. In this same third millennium, says Renfrew, Britain's large henge monuments, like Stonehenge, were built — the result of powerful tribal chiefdoms.

There is some evidence that writing existed as well in some early European societies. Harold Bayley in *Archaic England* says that Saxon monks examined old caves at St. Albans, near London, "bringing to light many curious and extraordinary things," including artifacts the monks pawned off as saintly relics. They also found manuscripts, which could only be read by one monk. That monk informed the abbot the manuscripts were pagan, idolatrous documents, so the abbot burned the offensive literature and had all passageways to the caves filled in. Beyley notes the word *Albans* means *Elfland*.

It is in this prehistoric Europe that we look to the elves and fairies for clues about Santa. These little people are not entirely lost to us; in addition to the megalithic messages that tell us the size and structure of the society, we can glimpse these people through shrouds of mythology and oral tradition. Unfortunately, oral tradition makes little distinction between 5000 years ago and 2000 years ago, after later Europeans had overrun their country.

The Icelandic *Eddas*, a collection of Scandinavian poems and prose written from about 800 to 1200 A.D., says the alfar or elves were a separate race, with a language of their own. In Devon and Cornwall, pixies are believed to be the old inhabitants of England. David MacRitchie says Scottish tales of fairies and brownies preserve memories of the Picts, a race that dwelt in hills and earthen houses. Herbert Robinson and Knox Wilson say the Scots know these people as the Siths. Grimm says dwarfs in Germany are considered to be the race that preceded the Germans and Celts and that Scandinavians equate the dwarfs with the Lapps. Snorri Sturluson, Icelandic poet and historian who compiled the prose *Elder Edda*, identified two tribes of peoples — the dwarfs and the dark elves — in his early thirteenth century work.

Jan Machal in *Slavic Mythology* says the Lusatian Serbs believe the *Ludki* (little people) were the first inhabitants of Lausitz, where they lived in ages past and had their own king. The Ludki are described as small, with disproportionately large heads. They grew corn and baked bread, spoke their own language, and lived partly in "human" dwellings and partly in the woods. Later they left the country and were rarely seen again. The Poles call similar beings *Krasnoludi* or *Krasnoludki*; the Hungarian Slovaks knew them as the *Lucky*.

Machal said the Russians called these people *Lesiy*. A Lesiy was depicted as an old man with long hair and beard whose body was covered by a thick coat of hair and who carried a whip. These people lived in the woods and were ruled by a tsar. Although the deer and birds enjoyed their protection, their favorite animal was the bear, "with whom they feast and revel."

The people who spread into Europe and encountered these fairies and elves probably were a far cry from the sophisticated seafarers postulated by Murray and others. In fact, they found themselves in the same situation as Europeans who came to America to settle: woefully ill-equipped to subsist in a New World. Jack Weatherford, in *Native Roots: How the Indians Enriched America*, shows the essential role of Native American guidance in helping European immigrants, who usually emigrated from cities and were equipped with little or no knowledge of the rudiments of subsistence. Earlier immigrants to northern Europe found themselves in the same dire straits, but the fairies and elves shared their knowledge with these less advanced humans. As shown in tales of the Wild Men, humans depended on the Wild Folk for agricultural knowledge, when to sow and reap, how to plant. Fairies taught humans weaving and husbandry. According to Machal, the Serbian Ludki taught humans the art of building houses. Robinson and Wilson say the fairies could cure most diseases and knew herbs, plants, minerals, birds, and beasts, and Grimm says dwarfs taught humans how to weave and bake.

Murray says these fairy people raised cattle and plowed the land. They were esteemed and respected by the newcomers, who stood in awe of their civilization, accomplishments, and seemingly magical efficacy. From tales about dwarfs and leprechauns we see that a major enterprise was goldmining and goldsmithing, and intricate goldworks are found in abundance in Europe. They apparently were superb metalsmiths and supplied the high gods of Germany themselves with their most prized assets. Odin went to the dwarfs for his magical spear. The dwarf Brokk made Thor's hammer, the magical ring Draupnir that was given to Odin, and Freyr's magical ship *Skidbladnir,* which was so large it could hold all the gods, along with their household and battle equipment, but could be folded small enough to fit into a pocket. Four dwarfs created Freyja's prized necklace, rings of gem-studded gold, and golden ornaments for the kings. MacCulloch comments on the dwarfs' metalworking skills: "None could forge such swords, weapons, and armour as they. ... The dwarfs, as skilful artificers, were thus necessary to the gods for some of their most cherished possessions." Powerful fairy swords permeate mythology and folklore, for the making of metal objects was probably a well-kept secret handed on from generation to generation through master smiths, although dwarfs taught smithery to "humans" as well.

There appear to be several types of little people, some not so little. Grimm makes a distinction between light, dark, and hairy elves and dwarfs. Folklore of other countries also makes distinctions, but the different types of little people have become confused with time. In other words, in prehistoric Europe we have the same wide range of physical types we have today. Some were quite tall, dark and hairy (the brownies); others are light and hairy; dark, short and hairy; and "Iberian" or Spanish types. Most of the Little People are described as short, stocky, hairy, and darker skinned. Kathryn Briggs relates a tale from the British Isles in which a farmer's wife peeked at the pixies as they helped thrash corn. She was not afraid of their "skinny eyes and hairy bodies" but thought it a shame they should go naked. German dwarfs and elves are hairy, as are the Slovak house goblins. The house sprite Puck is compared to a satyr, that is, a goatman.

They are sometimes described as having oversized heads and being humpbacked. Grimm says the dwarf was shorter than "people" and sometimes "misshapen"; he "adds to his repulsive [greyish] hue an ill-shaped body, a humped back, and coarse clothing." Machal says the Serbs' Ludki had disproportionately large heads and wore red caps. We see vestiges of this large cranium in Big Head, one of the "supernumeraries" found in British mumming plays. Big Head's standard lines are

In this old woodcut, a knight comes to an esteemed group of fairies with his hat in hand. The fairy queen and her group apparently live in the side of a mountain or hill.

In comes I, as ain't been yet
With my big head and my little wit —
My head so big, my wit so small,
I will dance a jig to please you all.

Grimm says later dwarf tales show "a downtrodden, afflicted, conquered race, which is on the point of abandoning its ancestral home to new and more powerful invaders. There is stamped on their character something shy and heathenish which estranges them from intercourse with Christians." Through folklore, then, we can glimpse two eras: when the fairies lived in societies, helping the unskilled immigrant, and thousands of years later, when immigrants were pressing the last fairies out of their ancestral homeland.

German mythology indicates these elves at first were regarded as superior to immigrating people; in fact, there is a lot of confusion between the elves, called the *Alfar* in German, and the gods themselves. The German *Vanir,* one of two major families of gods, are equated with elves in some earlier sagas. The other god clan was the *Aesir,* dominated by Odin or Wotan, all-father of the gods, after whom the day Wednesday is named. Turville-Petre in *Myth and Religion of the North: The Religion of Ancient Scandinavia* believes Odin was introduced to the Northland somewhere between 200 and 800 A.D., perhaps from the Far East. After arriving, Odin and his Aesir gods quickly assimilated the duties and power of the Vanir; for example, although De Vries says the first cup of Yuletide had been drunk to the Vanir, later Odin held that honor.

As a newcomer to the North, Odin did not come equipped with omniscience or omnipotence; elves and dwarves mentored him. Just as the Aryan immigrants had to learn to subsist in a new world, Odin worked hard to earn a god's power, one time piercing his side with a sword and hanging himself to learn the secret of the runes; another time trading one of his eyes for wisdom from a dwarf. The Vanir also tutored the new god in less painful ways. Turville-Petre says Freyja, Vanir goddess of fertility, taught Odin magic by which he could see into the future and cause death, misfortune. The dwarf Mimir forged Odin's powerful spear.

MacCulloch says this tenth-century image of Freyr from Sweden was carried in its owner's purse and buried with him.

The Vanir were equated with the elves in several early poems, such as one in which the gods are drinking together and a toast is made to the "Aesir and elves who are here within." John MacCulloch in *Eddic Mythology* says the elves were "akin to divine beings. They dwell in Heaven, in Alfheim, which is ruled by Freyr, and they act with gods and share their feasts." Robinson and Wilcox tell us Frey, god of fruitfulness, sunshine, and rain and brother of Freyja, lived in Alfheim (Elf Home), where he was king of the elves. (Freyja lives on in the name Friday.) In other old sagas, the elves are separate from both the Vanir and the Aesir, as in one saga which says the runes were given to Aesir, Vanir, Alfar, and humans.

Although the Vanir and Alfar or elves blend and become confused, there is no doubt the Vanir and Aesir were separate categories of deities. In fact, they only began to coexist somewhat peaceably after a cult war, after which each group of gods gave one of its main deities to the other. MacCulloch says this legendary battle probably reflected conquering peoples and their accompanying gods vying for power with an indigenous people in northwest Germany, then reaching a fairly peaceable accord. The earliest Swedish kings, leaders of a people called the *Ynglings,* regarded themselves as descendants of Freyr, who also was known as *Yngvi.*

Apparently "swarthy" victims were sacrificed to Freyr at Upsala, Sweden, and Adam of Bremen says "unseemly songs" were sung at nine-year festivals to the god. Each year, at the end of winter, a priestess took an image of Freyr

This Paleolithic beast-man from a cave in France holds what some believe is a small bow, much like the elf bow of later years.

throughout the land in a wagon, and MacCulloch reports, "the procession traversed the land, and was everywhere received with joy and with sacrifices, in expectation of a fruitful year." Elves also were worshiped, and *alfablot,* sacrifices to the elves, persisted in some Germanic countries into the twelfth century. Turville-Petre says the alfablot took place at the same time as the disablot, which was a sacrifice to the fertility god Freyr. Hilda Roderick Ellis in *The Road to Hel: A Study of the Dead in Old Norse Literature* relates a story by Sigvat the Skald, who visited a farm where elf sacrifice was in progress about 1019. The Christian poet was driven away from the household because the woman there said she was holding a sacrifice to the elves.

Machal says the Greek historian Procopius wrote that the ancient Slavs and Czechs worshiped fairies called *Vila;* these Vila lived on as the archer god in Valhalla and the wild hunter who chased the Wild Woman through the woods. Eventually the foreigner Odin and other gods assumed the Vanirs' duties in Germany and elsewhere, and the elves abandoned Alfheim. Hilda Ellis says the elves then "forsook their high calling and became little creatures of the earth."

Thus, if one believes the evidence of ancient stone structures and folklore handed down through generations, western Europe was home to a thriving civilization in pre–Christian, pre–Roman, pre–Celtic times. These little people lived in peace and splendor until later immigrants came into western Europe. Apparently the first immigrants eventually blended with the impressive aborigines. After the more bellicose invaders entered Europe, however, fairyland was soon to fall, though not without a fight.

The eighth-century Anglo-Saxon epic *Beowulf* tells us that the elves and Anglo-Saxons fought and that the elves were a formidable foe. Beowulf comes to Denmark to rid the country of the beast Grendel, who has been killing the Danish warriors. Upon meeting King Hrothgar, Beowulf immediately breaks into a panegyric praising himself and reciting his most impressive victories. One of his first boasts, and therefore his most proud, is "I am the one who crushed the wicked Elves." The sheer majesty of his boast shows that these "wicked elves" were a major power and their "crushing" required heroic dimensions. Hrothgar is terrified of the hairy Grendel, and his warriors have lost their nerve, so mercenaries are imported to defeat the hairy one and his mother.

So we can thank Beowulf — or the action on which the poem is based — for helping break the backbone of this European civilization. *Beowulf* shows that in Europe the new kings found not stone-wielding barbarians, but organized societies with formidable military forces.

Other tales indicate that after the little people's civilization had been crushed, they fought a guerrilla war from the hills into which they had been pushed. The invaders feared the elves and fairies and their magic, and the little people did everything within their power to give that fear substance. One of the little people's most feared weapons was a tiny arrow tipped with poison. These arrowheads have been found in the old mounds and are so small they could only be shot with a tiny bow. A flesh wound would be the worst harm they could inflict, yet Murray says, "To be shot with an elf bolt meant death or at least severe illness, usually paralysis." An example of a more modern people that uses small, poisoned arrows and bows for bringing down quite large animals is the South African Kalahari bushmen, whose poison enters the animal's bloodstream and kills it — yet the meat can be safely eaten, because the poison affects only the bloodstream.

From Selkirkshire folklore we learn a tale that "one day very many years ago a farmer of the Ettrick Forest while ploughing in one of his fields heard a buzzing sound in the air, and looking up he saw a small stone falling in the direction of one of his horses. He drove quickly forward, and it fell harmlessly by the animal's side. He stopped and picked up the stone which was slightly translucent and yellow. It was shaped like a small spearhead, and its angles were so sharp it cut into his hand as it lay there, 'even though its weight was only an ounce.'" The farmer had good reason to hurry his team at the approach of such a seemingly harmless mite, for his common sense told him this might be a deadly elf arrow.

We find the infamous elf arrow appearing in witchcraft trials as late as the seventeenth century, where Isobel Gowdie of Auldearne, Scotland, reported the devil had personally shaped these arrows with his own hands and delivered them to "elf-boys." Gowdie claimed to have killed a plowman with one of these arrows. A witch in 1662 reported that the devil had given her an "elf arrow stone" to shoot a seven-year-old child, and that the child had died immediately.

From the few clues that remain, we know the aborigines resisted the later invaders, but the races eventually did interact and even blend. One interaction came about through marriage. H. N. Gibbon in "The Human-Fairy Marriage" in the journal *Folklore* says tales about human-fairy marriages were based on the reality of marriage by force or capture, with the invading Aryans taking the aboriginal females. Gibbon says these human-fairy marriage stories have recurring common elements: The overwhelming majority of them make the fairy female and the human male. The fairy is always reluctant to marry the man, and there is often the suggestion of force on his part. He lures her near, grabs her, and refuses to let her go until she consents to marriage. The marriage always has a condition attached to it: He must not strike her, reproach her for her origin, etc. If he breaks the condition, his wife will disappear to fairyland.

Gibbon says most invaders were single young men, usually from the more populous areas that were suffering poor economic conditions. In this situation, Gibbon says, "two peoples, at entirely different cultural levels, existed side by side with at first no interrelationship of any kind." The fairy's reluctance and the trickery and force used by the male, says Gibbon, "are romantic symbols of a marriage by capture, which, since the two peoples had no social relationship of any kind, is precisely what any marriage between them must necessarily have been." In this way aboriginal and invading blood fused, and the children inherited characteristics of both races, resulting in the eventual absorption of much of the aboriginal race. "Fairy blood" was no stigma, either; in the Middle Ages those who could trace their lineage to fairies did so with pride, and many of the noblest families, including the Plantagenet kings, prided themselves on their fairy blood.

The Aryans and aborigines eventually interacted in another way as well, for the little people ultimately became servants for the intruders. The astounding amount of work done by the little people in historical Europe can hardly be attributed to imaginary sprites. The fairies became menial laborers, working for a small portion of food or harvest and a roof over their heads.

Grimm says that in certain parts of the world every person had his own fairy, goblin, elf, or brownie to do menial work — carry water, cut wood, and fetch beer. The *Kobold* (goblin) did this in parts of Germany. He (for it was usually a male) cleaned the kitchen, fought vermin, and asked only for a little food in return. Grimm says:

> The goblin is an obliging hardworking sprite, who takes a pleasure in waiting on the men and maids at their housework and secretly dispatching some of it himself. He curries the horses, combs out their manes, lays fodder before the cattle, draws water from the well and brings it, and cleans out the stable. For the maids he makes up the fire, rinses out the dishes, cleaves and carries wood, sweeps and scrubs. His presence brings prosperity to the home, his departure removes it.

The English had the brownies and pixies to help them. Briggs says earlier brownies were often of "human" size or larger, but later were seen as small and shaggy, dressed in rags or naked. "They are ready to do any work around a house or farm: sweeping, churning, spinning, weaving, mowing, thrashing and herding." That these "goodfellows" became a race of household helpers is reflected in Burton's *Anatomy of Melancholy*, which says, "a bigger kinde there is of them, called with us hobgoblins and Robin Goodfellows, that would, in superstitious times grinde corn for a mess of milk, cut wood, or do any manner of drudgery work." In the fairy's address to Robin Goodfellow in "A Midsummer Night's Dream," we saw his reduced, servant status:

Those that Hobgoblin call you, and sweet Puck,
You do their work, and they shall have good luck.
Are not you he?

Robinson and Wilson say Robin Goodfellow, although originally a forest creature, visited families and helped them do their chores, "doing in one night ten
men's work. For these labors his standing fee was a bowl of cream and white
bread." If mortals noticed his nakedness and put clothes out besides his bread
and cream, Robin would become mortally offended. On such an occasion he
would declare, "Hemton hamten/here will I never more tread nor stampen,"
and depart.

The Slavs also had these menials. The Russians called them *Deduska
Domovoy* (Grandfather House-Lord). The Domovoy is represented as an old
man with a grizzled, bushy head of hair and flashing eyes; his whole body is
covered with a thick, soft coat of hair, and his garments consist of a long cloak
girded with a red belt. Jan Machal in "Slavic Mythology" says the Domovoy lives
behind the oven or in the closet, courtyard, stable, or bathroom. The Domovoy
takes care of the herds and works in the house, sweeping the floors and weaving. The Domovoy's ego was easily bruised, however, and if he wasn't treated
with the respect and honor he felt he deserved, he would destroy the cattle or
storm out of the house, damning the inhabitants to sickness and ultimately
death. Robinson and Wilson relate that the Domovoy also was a protector of
the family and god of the house and hearth.

The Ukrainians called this figure the *Didko* or *Domovyk;* the Czechs knew
him as well; to the Silesians he was the *Djadek.* Another Slavish menial elf was
Shrítek (hobgoblin), whose name is related to the German *Schrat,* or hairy elf,
and "Old Scratch," a name for the devil. We saw this Schrat as a major mask,
the Schrättele, in the Black Forest Fasnet festivals. The Styrian Slovenians had
this same character, the *Skrat,* as did the Bohemians with their *Setek.* These
sprites often live in some out-of-the-way corner of the house or in the barn,
the customary quarters for a laborer.

Sometimes the elves or fairies lived off the farm and came to harvest or
help plant. Dwarfs on the German Ramsflue reportedly lived in caves, cooked
nothing, and ate only roots and berries. Grimm says:

> Often when honest folk cut hay or tied corn, dwarfs helped them to
> finish and get it under shelter; or in the night, if rain came on, they
> brought in what was lying about. ... One severe winter they came
> every night to a house at Arlisbach, slept on the oven, departed before
> dawn; wore scarlet cloaks reaching to the ground, so that their feet
> were never seen.

Grimm also says the kobolds, "like the wild folk," "have in them, something
of the nature of apes which also are trained to perform household tasks."

The Setek from Bohemia protects the flocks from disease and brings good harvests and money. Styrian Slovenians left part of their meal for this sprite. The Setek was also known as the Skrat, who brought money and corn to people. The Skrat dwells in mountains and dense forests and is covered with hair. At night he forges things at the local human smithery.

Murray says the fairies and elves were reduced to household drudgery as much from economic as from militaristic reasons. After the Black Death of the 1400s, the feudal system broke down because not enough people remained to support it. Gillian Tindall writes:

> It is not known with any exactness how many actually perished from this scourge. Some authorities put the figure at over 25 per cent of Europe's total population. In France, according to one contemporary writer, two-thirds of the people died, others put the figure at one-half, but it is known that towns and villages were totally depopulated. In the English countryside it was not quite so bad, but in London and Bristol hardly one in ten remained alive.

This clay statue is modeled after Czech Djadek statuettes. These often crudely made forms were placed in the home to protect the inhabitants, much the way saint statues are used in some Catholic homes.

Landowners, unable to continue their old way of life, let their lands to tenant farmers, who began raising sheep because sheep require less supervision than cattle. Murray says that since sheep eat the grass almost to the roots, the fairies' cattle found little grazing, because cattle must be able to wrap their tongues around a bunch of grass and break it off. This new sheep-raising industry eliminated many "human" jobs, and the increase in the number of unemployed workers brought forth the peasant revolt and guild revolts of Europe. Sir Thomas Moore, seeing the connection between sheep-raising and unemployment, commented, "The sheep have eaten up the men." Murray adds, "The sheep have eaten up the fairies."

The fairies' way of life had been destroyed — by invaders, the Black Death, and sheepherding. These people then took whatever means of survival was open to them — generally the most menial labor for room, board, and a token "wage."

The little people became household helpers, but there is never any suggestion of humility, obsequiousness, or slavishness about them. They appear very independent, and their goodwill is courted by the mortals they serve. They were regarded not only as workers, but as protectors of the home and its occupants. If an elf was offended, he was likely to pack up and leave, or he might storm about, damaging the flocks, harming people and crops. And, of course, people had to consider the elf arrows as a possible retribution.

In the 1400s and 1500s, then, the remaining elves and fairies were doing the most menial chores, but the immense pains taken to keep these little people happy around the house cannot be explained by a mere labor shortage or the fact they were willing to work so much for so little. These little people's names show their state of sacredness; they sometimes were called by the same name as their god.

An example of this transference of a god's name to its people is found in the word *Puck*. Murray relates the English Puck to the Welsh *Boucca* meaning little people, derived from an old Welsh word for god, *Bog*. *Bog*, in turn, "becomes our own Bogey and the Scotch Bogle," names for the Wild Man–devil. The bogeyman and a "mind-boggling" experience come from this same *Bog*. The old fertility god's name remains in the Lincolnshire Plough Monday play, where the men who pull the fertility plow are called *boggons*.

T. F. Dyer says Puck, as in Robin Goodfellow, becomes *pixie* in Britain and *pooka* in Ireland — words meaning the little people. In Teutonic lands little people were also known as *pooka* or *pookie*. In Swabia, the little people were called *poppele, popel,* or *pucci,* and our word *puppet* for "little person" comes from this root. Another humpbacked holdover from this elfish clan is the Italian stage character Pulcinella, who evolved into Punch, an actor in Punch and Judy shows and the symbol for a British publication.

Homage was paid to the little people and statues of them placed in niches in the home. Statues of these kobolds, domovoys, and other little people protected the home, and there is as much of the household god as the servant in people's attitude toward them. In fact, there is a great deal of confusion between these aborigines and the fertility gods they worshiped.

Humans courted these elves' favor by setting aside a portion of their meals for them, especially on Thursdays and at Christmas, a practice that continued after the elves stopped being real helpers. If the Schratt didn't receive his Christmas or Thursday meal, he would storm about, damage the flocks, and harm the house's master. Writing of his time, long after the elves had ceased their menial chores, Grimm stated that "many Christians still believe in such home sprites and present them an offering each year, 'pay them their wage,' as they call it," a vestige of the small extra portion they actually gave on holidays a long time ago. This custom lives on in Teutonic and American homes, when children leave a snack of milk and cookies for Santa Claus as he makes his rounds.

Many Germanic Christmas figures retain their elf identity in their names: Christpuppe delivers gifts in parts of Germany; in Finland Old Man Christmas is called Joulupukki, the Yule Puck. Åkerhielm says the Swedish helper, the *nisse,* now the Christmas gift-bringer *Julenisse,* liked porridge and milk, but tobacco and liquor as well. The Swedish sprite Jultomten has ceased his labors, but lives on today as a Swedish gift-giver. The Swedes leave porridge, milk, drink, and tobacco on Christmas, in exchange for Jultomten's gifts. The same fate awaited the Norwegian elf Julsvenn. Grimm traces the name Nicholas for these sprites from the German elf or *Niclas.* This is the same elfish Nicholas who inspired the creation of Saint Nicholas in the Catholic pantheon.

England's Puck also was associated with gift-giving, as we see in *The Mad Pranks and Merry Jests of Robin Goodfellow,* which tells us that "a great while ago, once upon a time, fairies used to dance in the hills. These fairies spent their time doing basically harmless pranks, like pinching lazy girls and making messy homes messier. They gave silver and toys to women who kept their houses clean, however." Spencer and Wilson relate that fairies in the British Isles were bountiful and rewarded virtue "and left unexpected gifts in the bottom of pails and bowls."

Humans left token gifts for fairies and elves, but they expected, and received, goods in return, as implied in their continued existence as Christmas gifters. Briggs in *The Fairies in Tradition and Literature* says fairies and goblins in the British Isles gave "prosperity" if their ways were respected — and this usually came in the form of tangible gifts. Machal in 1916 commented that the "Slovenians in Styria likewise believe that the Skrat brings money and corn.... [He] will bring whatever a man may wish, placing these things on the window-sill, although when he carries money, he comes in the shape of a fiery broom, flying down the chimney." The Bohemian house sprite brought food and money for his human household as well. The leprechauns of Ireland have been known to bless people with gold and good luck, and in Robin Goodfellow's *The Mad Pranks,* we find that fairies left silver and gifts for "mortals."

The tenth century *Corrector,* the archbishop of Worms' checklist for backsliding Christians, refers to the little people who traded goods and prosperity for more practical food and clothing. The Corrector inquires: "Hast thou made little boys' size bows and boys' shoes and cast them into thy storeroom or thy barn so that satyrs or goblins might sport with them in order that they might bring to thee the goods of others so that thou shouldst become richer?"

We see here that the "satyrs," or hairy people, and "goblins" did more than bestow an amorphous prosperity; they brought presents and money. These gifts did not come from fairyland, either; they usually came from other homes. Just as the dead of Sicily in the twentieth century were believed to rob shopkeepers to bring Christmas presents to their descendants, these tenth-century goblins robbed from the better-offs and gave to those that helped them, behaviors that explain Robin Hood's activities. The Russian Domovoy was considered so eager to please his human family he would do anything, "even to the extent of stealing from other people in order to increase his master's wealth."

The fairies that rode with the god and goddess of fertility were sometimes called Hellequins, and these Hellequins invaded cellars, where they ate and drank the food set out for them and gave "prosperity" in return. Unlike the humble household elf, who reportedly was content with table scraps and cast-off clothing, these bold night visitors demanded gifts. In the thirteenth century we hear of male masqueraders dressing as women, entering the homes of rich farmers, dancing and singing: "We take one and give back a hundred." They took what they pleased, leaving "prosperity" in exchange. In 1370 the Inquisition indicted a Milan woman for saying that as a member of the society of Diana — the Romanized name for the mother goddess — she and others went out at night to eat, drink, and steal from homes of the wealthy. In 1395 in another Italian village, we learn that revelers gathered every three years, elected a king, and went about doing this same kind of mischief.

An essential ingredient of surviving mumming plays and Wild Man festivals was expecting money or gifts from homes and citizens. Georgian mummers felt compelled to steal something from a house, no matter how generously they were treated. In some areas of Europe, however, any reciprocal "prosperity" motive disappeared, and all that remained was the masqueraders' habit of invading homes, taking things, and vandalizing the property of those who refused to acknowledge their right to do so.

A penitential of the bishop of Exeter in the twelfth century condemns throwing gifts into the granary for "fauns" in the hope they would bring the giver more grain. Again, this was often more than a wish for a good harvest, for this extra grain often came from other fields. Like the German *Bilwiss* or shaggy elf, these little people stole others' grain. Grimm states categorically: "All dwarfs and elves are thievish," and the word *good-fellows,* according to the *Dictionary of Obsolete and Provincial English*, is "an old cant word for thieves." We see here the basis for Pelznichol's habit of collecting items from richer homes and redistributing those boons to others.

In these visits we find the beginning of Santa's peculiar practice of coming down the chimney. As the elves became more and more prolific at their Yuletide stealing, they became more devious. Their burglarizing was so professional, their coming and going so subtle, that mortals began to imagine the fairies came through doors and walls. This added to the mystical aura surrounding these beings.

Mamoris, a fifteenth-century cleric, helped the church confront this belief by explaining that fairies, elves, and witches flew down the chimney. This was somewhat based on reality, because "fairies" often lived in houses which were partially underground. The entrance to these homes was often through the roofs, so fairies like the Skrat were said to enter through the roof or chimney (for the smoke hole and entrance were usually the same). After Mamoris's explanation, chimney-sliding became the standard explanation for how fairies got into houses, and remains so today for Santa Claus. It also provides an explanation or excuse for Santa to soil his red garments with black, and to blacken his face, like the village celebrants of old.

This ceremonial wagon from the early Iron Age was found in Denmark. MacCulloch says the wagon may have been used to carry around an image of Freyr. It also may have been a wagon which would be buried with the deceased for use on the Hel-way or road in the afterlife.

Banshees and Boons

Lamentations against women riding in groups echo throughout the centuries. In the ninth century, clerics decried the wicked women "perverted by the devil" who rode with Diana, "the goddess of the pagans, and innumerable multitudes of women." This lament continued, and in the fourteenth century another cleric complained:

> But, I ask, what is to be said of those wretched and superstitious persons who say that by night they see most fair queens and other maidens tripping with the lady Diana and leading the dances with the goddess of the pagans, who in our vulgar tongue are called Elves, and believe that the latter transform men and women into other shapes and conduct them to Elvelond.

Diana as the mother goddess was equated with Aphrodite, Isis, Demeter, the Irish Keridwen and the Germanic Freyja. In the words of Isis in initiation ceremonies of her cult: "I am she that is the natural mother of all things, mistress and governess of all the elements, the initial progeny of worlds, queen of the powers divine, queen of all that are in hell, and principal of them that dwell in heaven."

Before Odin's takeover, German Yuletide was the night of the Vanir, headed by the mother goddess Freyja and the fertility god Freyr, who presided over rain, sunshine, and the fruits of the earth, and ruled the elves in Alfheim. Eighth-century Anglo-Saxons worshiped the mother goddess on Christmas Eve, which was known as *Modranichts*, Night of the Mothers, and honored the divine mothers. These mothers traveled about, teaching humanity house-keeping, husbandry, spinning, weaving, hearth tending, reaping, and sowing. Edward Anwyl says these goddesses were called simply *Y Mamau*, the moth-ers, in Wales, and that this name reveals a religious worship so ancient that the fertility powers had not been personified with specific names. *Y Mamau*, says Anwyl in *Celtic Religion and Pre-Christian Times*, is also a Welsh name for fairies.

The ancient goddess worship is found in the Scandinavian goddesses, the *disir*, whom Turville-Petre dates to prehistoric times and who are also associ-ated with the god Freyr. Chambers says these disir are called *Matrona* by the Celts and Holda, Perchta, and Berchta by the Germans. These are the same women we met leading the wild horde in Germany and in the Austrian Per-chtenlaufen. The disir are described as superior beings, detached from human-ity but intimately concerned with human life. Humanity must revere them or incur their terrible wrath, an idea that persisted in later tales about Berchta and Holda.

Murray associates the mother goddesses with the aboriginal Europeans and sees Saint Lussi and other white-draped women that visited homes during Yuletide as holdovers from the original fairy queens. The extreme whiteness of their garments persists in legends about mysterious white ladies who appear all over Europe at strategic times, usually at year's end. Jane Beck in "The White Lady of Great Britain and Ireland" says these white ladies were fertility god-desses; in Yorkshire a white lady appears at Halloween with her arm around a deer. Beck says Somerset boasts three white ladies. In Dorsetshire, the white lady drives around in a wagon, like her German counterparts Holda and Freyja.

In Scotland, Ireland, and Wales the woman is sometimes called the ban-shee, and it is said that one can hear her scream before a death in the family. This legend has led to a common simile in the English language: "Screaming like a banshee." The name *banshee* is from "bean sidhe" (*sidhe* is pronounced *shee*), meaning a woman who dwelt in mounds or *sidhe*. In Shropshire, these white fairies were still expected at Yuletide at the time of Beck's 1970 article. In Finland these wise women, or *trullit*, went abroad on the eves of Shrove Tuesday and Easter. Elsa Enäjärvi-Haavio in "Finnish Shrovetide" says there are about 250 stories of these women in Finland.

The English white ladies are always associated with fairies, as their Ger-man counterparts are associated with elves. Grimm equates Berchta and Holda with the wood wife, Wild Woman or elf woman "who acts along with the wild man and to whom the people still offer up gifts." In Germany, the Wild Man–god that accompanied Holda was Ruprecht; in England it was Robin

Goodfellow and his fellow fairies. These earth goddesses and the Wild Man, along with their worshipers, roamed the countryside at year's end, blessing households with fertility and dispensing the fruits of the earth — acorns, apples, and other vegetation — as well as manmade goods.

Lady Godiva's Ride

Sometimes a historical person's name replaced that of the mother goddess, and the riding persisted into Christian times. According to Lewis Spence in *The Mysteries of Britain*, this is how Lady Godiva received immortality. Most of us have heard of Lady Godiva, if from no other source than the 1970s song by Peter and Gordon. According to legend, Godiva's husband, Leofric, imposed heavy taxes on Coventry, where they lived. Godiva appealed to him to lessen the taxes; Leofric promised to comply if she would ride naked through the town. On horseback, her long golden hair covering everything but her lovely legs, Godiva made the journey. Some accounts state that although everyone was ordered to remain indoors with windows closed, Godiva was seen by a Peeping Tom.

Godiva, or *Godgifu,* meaning "gift of God," was an actual person but did not make this undignified ride. The first story of the ride is found in an account by Roger of Wendover in the early thirteenth century, 150 years after Godiva's death.

At the time Godiva lived, Coventry was a village of some 300 serfs living in wood huts with no marketplace to ride through and no burdensome taxes, says Spence. The town began to blossom when Godiva and her husband, the earl of Mercia, restored the monastery of St. Osburg there, marking the beginning of Coventry's prosperity. Godiva was considered a benefactress whose actions brought real prosperity, and over the years, says Spence, her story became confused with the myth of the ancient British goddess Brigit, "who in the Keltic period ... rode through the village of Coventry at the end of May. After the Keltic divinity had been subdued by Saxon invaders, her feast and attributes were confounded and laterally absorbed by the legend of the Saxon countess."

The Celtic priestess representing the goddess Brigit appeared naked in her annual ride, but her body was sacred and not to be spied upon by "mortal" eyes. Spence says the legend of the Peeping Tom originated with Brigit's shrine in nearby Ireland. The shrine was enclosed by a fence "which no man might pass or peep through"; if any "peeping Tom" dared to look, the outraged goddess would instantly blind him.

In a celebration near Coventry, in Southam, two Godivas used to ride through the streets in a parade led by the Wild Man, Old Brazen Face, a priest wearing a bull's-head mask with horns. One Godiva was light-skinned with long golden hair, representing the Saxon countess. The other Godiva was completely blackened, a blackness as essential to the sacredness of the earth goddess as it was to the essense of the Wild Man. (The Roman scholar Pliny related that the women of ancient Britain decorated themselves by painting their bodies black on religious festivals, smearing their bodies with woad [a plant] "so that they resembled the swarthy Ethiopians.") Because Godiva was available to take the goddess's place in the old perambulation, Coventry's parade lived on into the twentieth century. In most places, however, no local heroine existed, and the ride of the gods disappeared or degenerated into a ride of heathen demons.

Little is known about this goddess worship, but we do know that in Scandinavia the goddess was considered an elf and a three-day disablot and alfablot (sacrifice to the elves and disir) was held at the beginning of winter. Sacrifice formed part of Scandinavians' worship not only at the household level, as related by Sigvat the Skald, but on a higher level as well, and no less a personage than the Scandinavian king apparently was sacrificed to the glory of the supreme dis, the earth goddess.

Turville-Petre relates a story about the disablot from the *Ynglinga Saga,* in which the king of Sweden was riding his horse around the goddess's hall when the horse stumbled and the king fell, striking his head on the stone. "His skull was broken, and the king's brains were left on the stone." This is a very matter-of-fact rendering of what would appear to be a tragic accident, but the saga says the death was caused by a "witch," whom Turville-Petre identifies with the mother goddess. Another version of the death places the event in the Hall of Diana, "Diana" being the generic Roman name writers applied to the local goddess.

There is evidence that Swedish kings were killed at nine-year intervals, and this kingship may have evolved from a priesthood in service to the earth goddess. Thus the king was priest-king and consort to the earth mother, the supreme creator. He was expendable; she was eternal. It was the king, the ancient priest, who lived a life of sacrifice, not the eternal goddess. This method of dying from horseback is preserved in a Goatland mumming play, where the victim's "death" results from his fall from a horse.

Pacts and Pucks

Some scholars, as we saw, view the death and resurrection plays that formed the basis of most of the mumming plays as holdovers from king-killing, when the beast-king or vegetation deity was killed periodically. Others believe this is an unwarranted generalization resulting from the phenomenal influence of Frazer's *Golden Bough.* Still others see the white women or goddess rituals as unconnected to the Wild Man activities, although they may have blended in some areas, perhaps a result of Celtic and "aboriginal" merger. At any rate, there is evidence that human sacrifice did take place in some areas and that the sacrificial victim was often the king or priest.

As human sacrifice became less palatable, often the animal that defined part of the Wild Man's nature died in his place. If the Wild Man was a goat-man, a goat was sacrificed; if a bear-man, a bear; if a stag-man, a deer. In western Europe, the Wild Man's most frequent costume was goatskins or a "satyr" outfit. The goat was his favorite French and German costume, and the English Robin Goodfellow was a goat-man, as were the old Balkan gods. Although this fertility god was sometimes originally sacrificed, by the time we have written records of the custom — in the sixteenth and seventeenth centuries — a goat had been substituted for the divine victim in France, Belgium, and parts of Germany. Gillian Tindall cites one report in which the "devil" himself was sacrificed by fire, the traditional method of sacrifice, and Grimm says in Germany the Great Goat burned himself to ashes at the climax of a great meeting, and the ashes were distributed "to work mischief with." Most of the time, however, the leader had substituted an animal or person in his stead.

The idea of a pact with the devil originated from this practice of giving temporary power to a "mock king" who died in the priest-king's place, says Murray. In such pacts, mortals traditionally can sign their soul to the prince of evil, in return for riches, prosperity, and earthly power. At the end of a certain period — usually seven years — the mortal is "taken" by the devil. Well-known stories with this theme are "The Devil and Daniel Webster" and *Faust,* and more recently the stage play *Damn Yankees.* In reality, says Murray, the pact-signer died in place of the devil or fertility deity after living like a king for a seven- or nine-year span. Murray says British Isles witch trials show the devil promising a witch wealth and power for a certain number of years, after which he would claim him or her; that is, the chosen one would die in place of the old god. When the number of years is given in the British Isles, it is seven or multiples of seven, coinciding with the seven-year cycle of death for royal kings in the British Isles. This seven-year sacrificial cycle lives on in a Cumberland tale that says every seven years "the elves and fairies pay Kane [tax], or make an offering of one of their children, to the grand enemy of salvation, and they are permitted to purloin one of the children of men to present to the fiend."

Before learning to pass off this rather odious aspect of kingship to a substitute, some British kings may have died as representatives of the godhead every seven years, according to Murray, who says King Edmund's death at Pucklechurch (Puck's Church) in May 946 and Edmund Ironside's death in 1016 show they were victims of the ancient pact of the king and his people. Edmund Ironside was killed at Pucklechurch by an arrow after a vote of the Witan (senate).

In August 1100 another British king, Rufus, son of William the Conqueror, fell in the New Forest, the victim of the "chance flight" of an arrow. Accounts of his death vary, but they agree Rufus was killed by an arrow shot by one of his own people, Tyrel. While hunting in the forest, Tyrel shot at a stag and hit the king instead. According to William of Malmesbury's account of the incident, "on receiving the wound the king uttered not a word; but breaking off the shaft of the weapon where it projected from his body, fell upon the wound by which he accelerated his death." Murray says his death was expected as the obligation of a divine king whose death sealed the ancient pact of a king with his people and his god, Lucci, one of the white women.

Irish kings apparently also died every seven years, on Samhain or Halloween, the last night of the year. C. F. Dalton investigates Irish king-killing in "The Ritual Killing of the Irish Kings" and "Kings Dying on Tuesday: Irish King Killing" in the journal *Folklore*. Dalton says the Irish kings were murdered at the seven-year festival of Tara on Samhain. At this four-day festival, the main events were killing the old king, inaugurating his successor, and celebrating the successor's sacred marriage to the earth mother. Two kings abdicated after a seven-year reign, thereby avoiding death, but Dalton says a mock king probably died in their stead. Regarding mock kings, Dalton points to the "high proportion of very short reigns of one year or less" which ended at the festival. We have one record of the prescient decision to use a mock king when Cormac, "foreseeing his death," dressed his court fool in his royal robes to die in his place.

The Irish kings' mode of death is significant says Dalton, for they were killed in one of two ways: by a priest's sacred spear, which was anointed with a "witches brew," or by the "fairy folk," who assembled in animal and woman disguises to dispatch the monarch. An example of the second was the "self-willed and overbearing" Eochaid Airem, who was killed by the "fairy folk" of Sid Neanta. Another king, Conn Cetcathach, was killed on the eve of Samhain by 50 disguised warriors.

Muiercetach, the first Irish king to embrace Christianity, forsook his Christian wife and children at the end of his life and took in a "witch woman" named Sin. Sin allegedly gave him drugged food and drink to sap his strength, and he seemed to see battalions of grotesque masked enemies attacking his house. Included were headless men, beast-men, black men, and some with the heads of ghosts. Although later writers explained these as hallucinations caused by Sin's drugs, Dalton notes that "they seem to have been real enough; for the king and his troops received wounds while fighting against them." As shown by his resistance, Muiercetach apparently was not eager to die for his people, but finally masqueraders set the house on fire and the king perished, all on Samhain, 530 A.D.

Although not all kings were killed by fairies, a significant number met their doom in this "masquerade of the plebes." Dalton says, "Lower class people might gather at night, put themselves under the protection of some proletarian goddess, and attack the king's house."

Dalton says there probably was a mock attack each year or each festival year, and if the people were dissatisfied with their ruler, the attack became real. The last Festival of Tara was held in 635 A.D., but kings abdicated at seven-year intervals into the eighth century, symbolically continuing the end of the ruler's life as representative of the godhead. The old king-killing custom was revived for a special occasion in 845, when the Danish king Turgeis was killed by Irish "fairy folk." Turgeis had ordered the king of Meath to send him his daughter for the night. When the daughter arrived, she was accompanied by a retinue of men dressed as women; they seized the palace and drowned the king. As in Scandinavia, the king was probably sacrificed originally in the name of the earth goddess, and Dalton comments that more than a chance number of kings died in the flames of their own homes.

Although the national festival ended in the seventh century, fairy disguising continued locally. From Lecky's *History of Ireland* we learn that in 1762 more than 500 men assembled as "fairies" and roamed around doing as they pleased. With blackened faces and stout hazel sticks, they attacked houses and drove unpopular neighbors out of the country. Today, says Dalton,

> on the last night of October in any year, in any street after dark, one can meet the characters from the old tales in miniature — the "headless men" with blackened faces, the "cat-heads" and "dog-heads" and the "warriors dressed as women" all played by young boys and girls. They go round from house to house, banging on the doors and are presented with fruit and nuts or a little money. This looks like a reminiscence of the mock attacks on houses, which became very real.

Murray finds a modern survival of the goat-god's worship in Ireland at the Puck Fair of Killorglin in Kerry County. Murray says, "It seems clear that this ceremony of the Puck king of Ireland is a survival of the worship of the Divine King and Incarnate God, with an animal as a substitute for the man."

Murray says that in Normandy, Scandinavia, and France, kings died every nine years, and Swedish kings seem to have been sacrificed at that interval, originally to the earth mother. Chambers says the great event of Teutonic heathenism, just before Christianity's influence in northern Europe, was the overshadowing of earlier cults by Odin's. Because of this takeover, historical Swedish kings were sacrificed to Odin. For example, Odin himself supposedly told King Aun his life could continue as long as he sacrificed one of his sons every nine years in his place. Aun therefore dispatched them at the required intervals, sacrificing nine in succession.

After the seventh son's death, Aun was so feeble he could not walk and had to be carried in a chair. He sacrificed his eighth, then his ninth, but by then was so debilitated that he had to drink from a horn like a child. As Aun prepared to sacrifice number ten, the people balked — Odin or no Odin — and refused to let him do it. So the old king died and was buried at Upsala, the Swedish sacrificial center.

After the ritual sacrifice of Swedish kings ceased, they were still held responsible for fertility. When a famine covered the land, the chiefs decided King Domalde must be responsible, so they killed Domalde and smeared the gods' altar with the king's blood.

The house visits by people disguised as women and satyrs (Wild Men) give us an insight into the early mumming activities. It is unknown whether the Wild Man festival was part of the original mothers' visits and sacrifice of their earthly consorts, or a later addition; what is clear is that both shaped Santa's habits and appearance.

The fairy influence not only lived on in European gift-givers, it also shaped Santa's means of conveyance and residence. Santa Claus resides in the Arctic, at the North Pole, where Mrs. Claus keeps him well supplied with cookies. This seems a rather inhospitable place for a fertility god to live; however, in view of what we know about the fairies and their advanced, seemingly magical, northern European civilization, it shouldn't be too surprising to find that the North has always been associated with gods. After the Wild Man became a devil, Satan's dwelling place moved north as well.

In Hindu mythology, the gods live in the North; in the biblical book of Isaiah, the North is the dwelling place of the devil; in Job we learn that hell is somewhere in the far North. Rudwin tells us that the oldest English morality play stage directions place the devil's scaffold in the North. England itself was considered the chief abode of evil spirits, and Scandinavia was counted among the devil's homes, while others believed the devil preferred Germany. Wherever the god, Wild Man, or devil lived, the location was sure to be in the North. After progressive waves of immigrants moved into Germany, Scandinavia, and England, "North" moved farther toward the pole, to Lapland.

Lapland has long been considered the special place of witches, and is as close to the North Pole as humans usually get. Lapland not only influenced Santa's address, but is responsible for his means of transportation as well. The last known "wizards" lived in Lapland, where people have depended on their reindeer for thousands of years. Teutonic people considered the Lapps powerful shamans. Sailors from northern Europe would consult Lapp shamans for advice and information about the future; these sailors also would purchase handkerchief-wrapped winds for voyages from them. Because of this and the fact the Scandinavians considered the Lapps to be fairies, it makes sense that Teutons would give the Santa reindeer for his magical flights.

The reindeer is a stag, which is the traditional steed of the Wild Man. There is a long association of fairies, Wild Folk, and elves with deer. The first protest against disguising as a stag comes from 370 A.D. and continues through the millennia. The stag was a favorite costume in some Wild Man festivals and persists in some Austrian Perchta festivals. British fairies were associated with deer, so much that a hero pursuing a deer in stories became a commonplace literary convention to show he was nearing fairyland. The mother goddess often appeared with her animal, the deer. The Scottish highland fairies, also associated with deer, were visited by hunters and fishermen to get the fairies' blessing for their expeditions.

European civilization predated Mediterranean influence; a developed people lived and prospered in Europe before the Celts or Anglo-Saxons arrived. Thus we have an advanced people whom immigrants considered superior, dangerous, or both. When the Celts and other immigrants descended upon the land, these fairies helped the neophytes learn the basics of survival, although they generally kept apart from the rougher greenhorns.

Then later immigrants, "civilization," the plague, mercenaries, and economic catastrophes changed everything. The old gods became devils, and the people that carried the old gods' names became menial helpers. Robin Goodfellow became a buffoon and household helper, and Oberon's fairyland fell. Still, however, the elves and fairies retained an aura of magic, power, and fertility; though their influence was diminished, it was still wise to propitiate them as household gods. From these fairy and elf activities came Santa's reindeer, chimney-sliding, gift-giving, and secretive comings and goings. Although elves and fairies no longer rule in Europe, they live on at Christmas in their ancient role as bringers of bounty.

Chapter 10

The Fairy
and the Wild Man

Early Europeans, groups of people who live on in folklore as fairies and elves, apparently created a civilization that carried out rituals of death and rebirth, dances, and perambulations to spread fertility to the land. Central to many of these was a Wild Man, often part bear or goat, who was slain and reborn or replaced so life on earth could continue.

Many scholars, seeing the similarity between the European Wild Man and Dionysian festivals, point to Greece and Rome as the origin of these festivals. This line of thinking implies that the rituals accompanied the Roman Empire's tenuous spread throughout Europe and somehow were assimilated by thousands of isolated communities. Other prehistorians and folklorists believe the European rituals are home-grown religious rites and that any similarity arises from similar circumstances and aims. Still others see the Celts' handiwork in these festivals.

It is implausible to believe that all the European festivals we have just examined came from one single source, yet there are similarities too striking to ignore or chalk up to coincidence. Speculation about the origin of rituals that involve sacrificing a beast-man is just that — speculation. We are asking questions for which no firm answers exist. Yet the overwhelming similarities of these rituals, and the astonishing pervasiveness of their spread throughout Europe, imply an origin so ancient and so deeply rooted it may have predated any European civilization, indigenous or imported.

Joseph Campbell, certainly the best known and most eloquent of modern mythologists, looked for origins of similar rituals. Although Campbell was not seeking Wild Man sources, his *The Masks of God: Primitive Mythology* points us in a promising direction.

The Masks of God, which covers the many forms of humanity's religion, goes back to Neanderthal rites and traces their survivals into the twentieth century. It is impossible to follow Campbell's trail and not see a link between his festivals and rituals and those of the Wild Man. This scenario looks back more than 50,000 years at rituals that took place in Europe and survived in some form into the twentieth century in many parts of the world. These rituals involve the death and resurrection of cave bears, ancient goats, and Neanderthal humans, and evidence indicates a rite that involved sacrifice of a Wild Man in the form of a bear or goat has existed in Europe for 75,000 years. Further, this ritual survived into the twentieth century in polar regions and Japan, and it is to this ancient bear or goat sacrifice that we turn for the beginnings of the Wild Man.

Campbell cites the evidence of bear worship in Europe from about 75,000 B.C. Between 1903 and 1927, archeologist Emil Bächler excavated three caves in the virtually inaccessible High Alps. There Bächler found the earliest altars known anywhere in the world, altars to the bear. Two of the caves, *Wildkirchi* (Savage or Wild Church) and *Wildermanlisloch* (Wild Man Cave), are 7,000 feet above sea level; the third, *Drachenloch* (Dragon's Cave), looms 8,000 feet in the Austrian Alps. The finds were dated at 75,000 B.C. at the latest because the caves presumably could not have been entered during the Würm glaciation period and so have been assigned to the Riss-Würm interglacial period.

Campbell says the caves contained flagstone flooring, benches, work tables, and altars for a bear ritual. In Dragon's Cave and Wild Man's Cave, walls of stone enclosed bins with carefully arranged cave bear skulls. Campbell relates, "Some of these skulls had little stones arranged around them; other were set on slabs; one, very carefully placed, had the long bones of a cave bear (no doubt its own) placed beneath its snout; another had the long bones pushed through the orbits of its eyes." Both skulls still had two vertebrae attached.

Konrad Hörmann discovered similar cave bear skulls in a cave near Velden, Germany, which he excavated between 1916 and 1922. This cave had five skulls in wall niches; again the leg bones were placed beneath the snout, says Campbell. The most elaborate bear cult remains come from Regourou in Southern France, where excavators found a complete bear skeleton, minus the skull, along with the remains of more than 20 cave bears in a rectangular pit covered by a stone slab that weighed a ton.

Campbell cites archeologist Herbert Kühn's conclusions, written in 1926: "The location of the sites in remote caves, where they would be most readily concealed, indicated their reference to a cult; and so it immediately occurred to their excavators that they were uncovering the evidence of a sacrificial offering, storage places of the cave-bear skulls used in primitive service honoring a divinity of the hunt, to whom the offerings were rendered."

Besides their antiquity, an intriguing aspect about these discoveries is that the worshipers appear to have been Neanderthals. In other Neanderthal areas, we see worship of the goat instead of the bear; a cave in the mountains of Uzbek in Central Asia has the shallow grave of a young Neanderthal boy with half a dozen pairs of ibex horns placed around the head of the grave. This indicates a goat cult more than 50,000 years ago, and the historical Wild Man in that area was a goat man.

Neanderthals have presented a problem for anthropologists. Until recently, the Neanderthal was considered an evolutionary dead-end, a now-dissolved link in the ascending chain that led to Magnons — modern humans. The Neanderthal was supposed to have existed from about 200,000 to about 35,000 B.C. at the latest, at which time Cro-Magnons entered southern Europe, and Neanderthals obligingly became extinct. John Pfeiffer phrases this viewpoint: "The Neanderthals of Western Europe had no chance against these people and these institutions. In any competition for the best living places and hunting grounds, and competitions must have occurred on many occasions, they came out second best." Pfeiffer does find it "doubtful" that the Neanderthals were wiped out quickly, for "it is unlikely that capacity for systematic mass extermination evolved so early."

Some anthropologists, sticking to one-track evolution, now believe the Neanderthals probably didn't simply disappear; instead, they evolved into modern humans along with their Cro-Magnon cousins. But this, too, presents a problem, for 30,000 or even 50,000 years is just not enough time for evolution to work such miracles. Some anthropologists have attempted to slip between the horns of the Neanderthal extinction dilemma by stating that the human species, whether Neanderthal or Cro-Magnon, is a continuum, with all characteristics blending smoothly into each other.

First we need to rid ourselves of any false ideas about Neanderthals — that they were stupid, apelike creatures. They have been called "archaic humans," and it is implied that they are lower on the evolutionary scale and therefore inferior. Their heads were shorter and wider than ours, but there is no reason to assume they were less intelligent. Neanderthals' brain capacity was generally larger than ours, and archeological remains point to an intelligent human with burial practices and religious rites 75,000 years ago.

As Joseph Campbell phrases it: "The picture is no longer that of a lot of scattered families of moronic ape-men, but of an extraordinarily sturdy race of human beings, perhaps of a slightly higher mental order than ourselves, fighting it out, at the dawn of what may be considered to be our properly human history, in a landscape calling for every bit of wit and spunk at their disposal."

The evolutionary picture painted by early archeologists and anthropologists reflected the philosophical and scientific milieu in which they lived. This world view was heavily influenced by Darwinism and philosophies that believed the European was the pinnacle of evolution — physically, intellectually, and morally. This evolutionary philosophy served as the underpinning for European economic expansionism and colonialism; since the aborigines in "uncivilized" areas were subhuman, the superior Europeans were justified in subjugating them. In addition, the anthropological ladder that leads from primates to humanity was built on very slim rungs and braced by a Eurocentric philosophy. Excavation sites usually were "chosen" because they were discovered during quarrying or construction operations. Often one site would result in extensive excavations of surrounding areas, such as the Dordogne area of southwestern France. Today, just as archeologists are struggling to reconstruct a more objective past, biological anthropologists are contending with old prejudices as they try to construct a path from hominid to human.

Ritual Continuity

This Neanderthal goat and bear ritual didn't end with the Neanderthal; it also is found associated with Cro-Magnon about 30,000 B.C. The earliest cave paintings or engravings are placed next to cave bear marks, says Campbell, for bears' marks were the marks of god. Two explorers, Count Bégouën and N. Casteret, explored a French cave and found the clay form of a crouching bear at the end of a long passage. This clay form lacked a head, but it had a hole in the neck area for inserting a stick. Between the bear's forepaws lay a bear's skull. Campbell cites Leo Frobenius's evaluation of the clay form: "The coarse, mushy form of the whole thing pointed to one specific conclusion, namely that the piece had served as supporting form for a freshly flayed bear pelt with the head still attached." This bearskin probably was donned in a rite that reenacted the bear's death for the good of his people.

Not only was this bear cult found in the Upper Paleolithic, it persisted substantially unchanged in parts of the world into recent decades, a fact that has caused considerable scholarly amazement. Kühn and Campbell notice the old bear rituals have twentieth-century counterparts that include, among other things, taking off and putting on bearskins — in other words a shaman "changing into" a bear. Modern hunting societies within the Arctic Circle prepared the bear remains exactly the same as the Neanderthals, and their bear worship can give us a clue as to what went on in Neanderthal ceremonies.

Campbell cites Kühn's conclusion:

> [T]he usages and customs of the Interglacial Period have been retained up to the very present in these peripheral regions of the earth. ... The same offering is still made today. The bear skulls still are flayed and preserved in sacred places, offering places. They are covered and set round with slabs of stone, even today. Special ceremonies still are celebrated at the offering places. Even today two vertebrae of the neck are allowed to remain attached to the skull, just as then. And even today we find that the large molar of the bear has been ground down, precisely as Zotz found the case to be in the course of an excavation of a series of caves in the glacial mountain heights of Silesia.

Such details among the contemporary Asiatic hunters as the grinding down of the teeth of the bear and leaving of two vertebrae attached to the skull, just as in the European Interglacial period, proves that the continuity has actually remained unbroken for tens of thousands of years.

The Finno-Ugric peoples who live in the Arctic Circle regarded the bear as the holiest of all animals. Ostyaks and Voguls swore oaths by the bear.

Until historic times a vigorous bear cult and ritual existed in Lapland, where the beast was killed in the spring. Actually the Lapps didn't really kill the beast; they released its spirit from its body. The Lapps, like many Native American and Eurasian people, call the bear Grandfather. In his book *The Lapps*, Björn Collinder reports on the Lapp ritual, which is no longer carried out. Lapp hunters roused a hibernating bear in March or April. The bear, bewildered and drowsy, stumbled out of the den's opening. Instead of spring, however, he found a spear aimed at his breast. After the Lapps had killed the bear, they thanked him for his cooperation and beat him with birch twigs to restore and renew life. "The purpose of this obviously was to confer vital force upon the bear, to give him a kind of substitute or compensation for the life which he had been deprived of," says Collinder.

The hunters then brought the bear back for a three-day festival. First they cooked the blood, which the hunters smeared on themselves, their family and the tent poles. The Lapps were careful neither to break any of the bones nor sever arteries and large tendons, and after the banquet the men carefully buried the bones, muzzle, head, genitals, and tailskin. Saving vital parts of a sacrificial animal is thought necessary for its continued life; if everything were destroyed, the death and rebirth cycle of the god would end.

Then the Lapps put the bear hide against a tree or snowdrift and decorated it. Blindfolded women shot arrows at the skin. The first woman to hit the hide, if unmarried, would marry a distinguished bear hunter. If she was married, her husband would be the next one honored with the task of dispatching the bear. The Lapps also performed a ceremony in which a person played the part of the bear and dressed in its head and skins, and the ritual killing was reenacted. This ceremony also persisted among the Voguls and Ostyaks in northwestern Siberia. After the ceremony, the bear blesses the people and "withdraws with joy over mountains and hillsides."

We see here the possible beginnings of Wild Man festival plays, as the hunter, the one empowered with the mystical job of dispatching the god, dresses in bearskins, and the hunters reenact the death of their divinity. But the god is not dead; in joy he returns to his mountain home, to return again to his people.

This same bear ritual existed into the twentieth century among the Ainu of Japan, who inhabited all of that land until the Japanese arrived. The Ainu believe the human world is so much nicer than that of the gods that the deities come to visit them in disguise. Of all the gods that come to visit, the most important is the bear, a visiting mountain god. John Batchelor, a missionary who lived with the Ainu in the late 1800s and early 1900s, developed close relationships with these people and wrote about their lives and ceremonies in several books. He gives the following description of the bear ritual.

When a young cub was caught in the mountains, the hunters brought it back in triumph. It lived with a family, where a woman suckled it, and it played with the children and was treated with affection. As it grew larger and more dangerous, the bear was caged and fed on fish and millet porridge for two years. In September the people decided it was time to release the bear's spirit from its body and send it back to its mountain home. This was the occasion for a festival called "to send away," a joyous send-off in which the the bear, as guest of honor, participated. Guests from surrounding villages were invited to this grand celebration, and men wore special head ornaments made from sacred willow shavings with a small bear's head symbol in front.

The people whittled *inao,* religious symbols. No prayer or sacrifice was acceptable to the gods without these sticks, which look suspiciously like the "brooms" carried in some mumming pageants. These were placed in the ground and two large "strangling poles" put near them. The men approached the bear cage, with the women and children dancing and singing behind them. They sat in a circle around the bear, while one person told the bear the joyous event that was about to happen:

> O Divine One, you were sent into this world for us to hunt. Precious little divinity, we adore thee; pray, hear our prayer. We have nourished and brought you up with a deal of pains and trouble, because we love you so. And now that you have grown big, we are about to send you back to your father and mother. When you come to them, please speak well of us and tell them how kind we have been. Please come to us again and we shall again do you the honor of a sacrifice.

The men tied the bear with ropes and took it from the cage. As he was led around, people shot blunt arrows at the bear until he became enraged. Then the bear was led to a decorated stake, where two men seized him and a third thrust a stick between his jaws. They grabbed his front and back legs, and the strangling poles were readied. A perfect marksman shot an arrow into the bear's heart so no blood fell on the ground; then the poles were squeezed together, and the bear died.

The hunters then removed the bear's head with the whole hide attached — a custom observed throughout the bear cult areas. The dead bear was not excluded from the feast; he was still the honored guest. The head and hide were taken into the house through the "god's window" — a window in some areas, the smoke hole in others. Then, as Campbell phrases it, "a succulent morsel of its own flesh is placed beneath its snout, along with a hearty helping of dried fish, some millet dumplings, a cup of sake or beer, and a bowl of its own stew. And then it was honored with another speech." This speech admonished the god to go straight home and tell his mother and father how good the Ainu had been to their son. After this, there was dancing, and the woman who raised the bear alternately wept and laughed. After the bear "finished" another hearty meal, its head was separated from its skin and placed on a pole with other bear skulls.

Anthropologist M. Inez Hilger, in her 1971 book *Together with the Ainu, a Vanishing People*, relates the prayer with which they dispatch the bear after this three-day *Iomande* ceremony: "Oh, bear! You are of benefit to us. You give us your fur for clothing and bedding; you give us meat for food. In order to show our gratitude we shall now send you back to your own country with many, many gifts for your bear relatives there. We are going to perform for you a variety of interesting dances with this in mind."

Hilger says that hunters showed this same reverence when they killed a bear under "normal" or nonritual circumstances. First they sat down and admired it, worshiped it, and offered presents of inao. After they skinned it, and decorated the head with inao, they thanked the bear. When an Ainu hunter saw a bear, he bowed to him as to a deity, and fixed his attention on the bear's eyes, for it was there he aimed his arrow, and the bear "had to be felled by the first arrow." This death was hastened by the monkshood or wolfsbane, a poison put on the tips of their arrows. To prevent blood from entering the flesh, any blood on the head was removed as soon as the bear was dead.

The Ainu no longer ritually execute a bear, but summer tourists to the Japanese island of Hokkaido and its first-class hotels and spas can see the play enacted for them in the Bear Festival. Hilger says some Ainu find this pantomime an offensive sacrilege and quotes an Ainu named Sasaki:

> The *Iomande,* like our other rituals, was sacred to our ancestors. Why should they now be put on as shows for commercial purposes? Especially the *Iomande*! I think of this as a desecration. ... All authentic Ainu festivals were inaugurated by our ancestors. If we perform them as tourist attractions, that is, for commercial purposes, we shall have no words with which to apologize to our ancestors!

Sasaki told Hilger the bear-killing ritual originated in ancient times when the Ainu were starving. The top god, *Kamui Ekashi,* saw the Ainu's plight and told his lesser gods to appear to the Ainus as bears to supply them food. The Ainu gratefully sent the spirits of the bears back with millet dumplings and millet sake, and after that the god-bear appeared regularly.

The *Iomande* ritual shows many similarities to historical mumming plays. The bear is captured, led among the people with ropes, and shot with an arrow. The woman who raised the bear (a mother substitute instead of a bride) laments his death; but his death is not permanent, for his spirit returns to the mountains and will come back to the people in the future.

The character of the woman leads a bear character in this Vogul turn-of-the-century bear dance in the Arctic Circle. The bear mask was made of birch bark and had a large nose and often a beard.

We gain even more of an insight when we look at the nearby Gilyak, who worship the "master of the mountain" who sends the bear to them. This master is a man on one hand, and on the other a real bear of unusually large size. Here we see the bear as an emissary that can appear as a man or a bear. In a similar bear ceremony in western Siberia, people sang songs about the animals' life in former mythological times and of how things were different then. These songs talk about how the bear walked in the forest, found a mate, and made a den.

The Gilyaks not only sang about these events, they showed them in a play form that included a dance representing the episodes of the hunt, with one of the men taking the part of the bear and mimicking its motions. The Voguls held a drama in which men wore birch-bark masks, with large noses and beards, painted with charcoal. A Bishop Rothovius was concerned about the Finns' customs, and in 1640 mentioned during his inauguration at the University of Abo that "when they capture a bear, they must hold a feast in the dark, drinking the health of the bear from its skull, acting and growling like the bear, procuring in this way further success." The Finns called the bear feast a "wedding," and a human bride or groom (depending on the sex of the bear) sat with the dead beast at the place of honor.

From these different twentieth-century bear ceremonies we can piece together what the original Wild Man–bear ritual might have been like. The bear was captured and sacrificed. Then men donned bear costumes and performed a play telling of the bear's life — how it mated, had a child, and eventually was found by people. The ceremony then depicted how it was killed by a master archer, but in body only, for the bear remained eternal — the spirit returned to its master to reappear in the future.

There is even an intriguing suggestion that the Wild Man himself could have been a Neanderthal, and Campbell shows us archeological evidence that Neanderthals were sometimes sacrificed in exactly the same way as the bear. Campbell tells us that 80 miles from Rome, on the coast of Italy, excavators found a Neanderthal skeleton that had been treated in exactly the same way as sacrificed bears. "The head had been removed, a hole had been tapped in it for the removal of the brain; the remains of sacrificed animals were preserved in receptacles round about the grotto, and the skeleton itself was surrounded by a circle of stones," says Campbell.

Through this ritual the Wild Man would become identified with the bear or goat and regarded as the master of faunal life. In the Pyrenees, Russia, Poland, and parts of Europe the Wild Man is identified with the bear above all animals; in other parts he is a goat-god. No matter what animal the Wild Man became identified with, it is this Wild Man as master of the animals that people worshiped and propitiated. Thus, we have fascinating implications that a bear and goat cult of at least 75,000 years ago evolved into the Wild Man rituals that covered Europe in historical times. And we have tantalizing hints that the Wild Man was originally a Neanderthal.

Last of the Fairies?

A big hindrance in learning about the fairies is that they are assumed to be extinct. But there is a group of people so different from other living peoples that they have been declared unique, and to them, through possible parallels, we will look for clues about what happened to the fairies. These people are the bear-worshiping Ainu of Japan.

The Ainu live in northern Japan and were there before the Japanese arrived. The oldest Japanese writings tell us that when the Japanese arrived they had to fight the aborigines, the Ainu. The Ainu were not easy to conquer and rebelled against Japanese domination until 1789. Takakura Shinichiro relates that the first clash between the colonizing Japanese and the Ainu happened in 1456, when a Japanese blacksmith on the island Hakodate argued with and killed an Ainu chieftain; in retaliation, the natives massacred the immigrants, and the next year a chieftain assaulted nearby Fukuyama. "The natives were so powerful that settlement after settlement fell into their hands. The immigrants were driven out of all their bases and those who escaped from the slaughter

Batchelor was intrigued by the Ainu's famed hairiness and tried somewhat unsuccessfully to capture it on film. Ainu men took great pride in their prolific beards.

assembled. ... This is the turning point when the relations between immigrants and natives became serious," says Shinichiro. The Japanese then began a strategy of assimilation that rewarded Ainu for adopting Japanese ways and appearance. Those who did so, however, were considered a disgrace to their people.

The Ainu are not Japanese. Kyosuke Kindaiti writes, "The Ainu are a specific race that lives only in some parts of the Japanese territory and is not found in any other part of the world." He continues, "The Ainu race which exists today is an interesting and rare specimen of the human race that lived from the stone age until recent years." In 1926 Dr. Tanemoto Huruhata, an authority on serology, said blood analysis shows the Ainu were vastly different from any other race in the world and formed a "racial solitary island." This is not universally accepted today, but there is dispute as to which people or "racial category" they should be assigned.

One thing is certain, however: They are disappearing as a distinct people. In her 1971 book, Hilger related that only about 300 full-blooded Ainu remained at that time. Hilger wrote that Ainu, accepting the inevitable, approved of marriages between themselves and Japanese. One of her Ainu sources stated: "Ainu and Japanese should marry. The Ainu should be absorbed by the Japanese. Japanese and Ainu should be one people."

John Batchelor lived with the Ainu as a missionary in the 1880s and 1890s and wrote about their lives, beliefs, and customs in *The Ainu and Their Folk-Lore*, published in 1901. Batchelor calls this portrait of an Ainu with a ceremonial headdress simply "An Old Ainu Friend."

Early descriptions of the Ainu echo those of the fairies. Both are described as short, stocky, and full-chested. The fairies were known for their hairiness and bushy grey beards, and their deep-set, flashing dark eyes. The single most distinctive feature of the Ainu is their hairiness, and they have been called "the hairiest people on earth." Batchelor says of the Ainu's famed hairiness that the hair of the really hairy specimens is "not so thick the skin can't be seen." Campbell, commenting on their hirsute appearance, says, "Indeed their proud and sturdy old chieftains, copiously bearded, with their broad noses, bushy brows, and spirited eyes, look very much like a child's version of Santa Claus."

Batchelor says: "The Ainu people are not a handsome nation, though, as individuals. The race is strong, thickset, squarely-built and full-chested. The chief thing that strikes one on meeting an Ainu for the first time is his fine beard, moppy hair, and sparkling eyes." The men have bushy beards, prominent cheekbones, and bushy heads of hair. Their hair and beards turn grey early, giving young men an older appearance.

Ainu once honored their ancestors by putting beards on their carved bear heads. This, Batchelor says, was an appropriate gesture: "Now when we

This drawing by Batchelor is captioned "A Village Father."

consider that the Ainu regard the bear as 'king of the forest,' that he is worshiped by the people, we can see at once the appropriateness of carving bears'
heads with human beards and placing them as ornaments upon their festive and
sacerdotal crowns; for the bear would appear as an emblem or symbol of
power."

When the Japanese first ordered the Ainu to cut their hair, the Ainu chiefs
held a great meeting and sent an emissary to beg that this not be done, "for we

The Ainu women used to consider tattooing their face around the mouth a sign of beauty. This woman is rearing a bear cub. Ainu in the 1970s still raised cubs until they were about two years old, for luck.

could not go contrary to the customs of our ancestors without bringing down upon the wrath of the gods." The Japanese governor relented, and the men kept their treasured beards.

Although they no longer ritually kill a bear, except in pantomime, the bear is a revered part of Ainu life. Hilger notes many homes have fenced-in bears on the property and show affection for these young animals. Hilger's companion stated, "It is well to have a bear nearby. It brings blessings on the home."

Batchelor says the Ainu usually were considered to be light brown but are actually rather light-skinned; their skin browned in response to the sea and wind. Writing about dwarfs, Grimm commented that they were greyish, wore coarse clothing, and were hairy and thick. Batchelor says the Ainu were often grey, too, from layers of dirt. Their garments were traditionally made from bark and were very rough. Before they learned textile-making from the

Japanese, they also wore clothing made of animal skin, feathers, and fish skins sewn together, or straw coats.

Murray says fairy women are regarded by Aryans as quite lovely when they are young, but "are always commented on with horror when they are older." We find this same comment about Ainu women. Batchelor says "It would be a calumny to assert that all the hard-working Ainu women are ugly. Some of them, especially the younger ones, are quite good-looking. The repulsiveness of the older ones is enhanced by tattooing." This tattooing looks like black lipstick smeared widely around the mouth, somewhat like a clown's mouth. Some writers have suggested that the fairy women tattooed their face as well.

The Ainu women's facial tattooing made acculturation difficult, and Shinichiro cites Yamazaki Hanzo's statement that Ainu mistresses of Japanese guards attempted to emulate the Japanese in their hairstyle and clothing, and "were attired in beautiful costumes and in no way appeared like country women from the back. However, their tattooed faces made a shocking contrast to the way in which they were dressed." Today young Ainu women don't tattoo their faces, and in modern haircuts, the Ainu are as comely a people as any other.

The Japanese considered the Ainu the most savage and barbarous of peoples, yet the Ainu's oral knowledge reveals some remarkable things. Whereas the ancient Chinese and Japanese believed the world was flat, the Ainu have always known it is round. Their legends say the world is a vast round ocean with islands, worlds, and countries on it. The Ainu told Batchelor they once knew how to read and write, but that this knowledge had been lost.

Although they lived in communities of seven to ten families in historical times, their legends remember a life in thriving villages, and Shinichiro says there are remnants of scores of semi-underground houses scattered around the remains of a chief's large, palisaded house, which had formed the center of a large community. The chieftainship was hereditary and legitimized by the chief's close relationship to the community's common ancestor. "Therefore," says Shinichiro, "the family line of descent was highly important and those chiefs who possessed power called themselves descendants of God."

The Ainu also said their ancestors could travel through the air and carry on warfare far above the earth. This same tradition exists among America's Hopi Indians, who say their ancestors at one time flew on "shields" and attacked faraway cities, during the age they call the Third World. Batchelor's account was written in 1892.

In writing about the similarity between the Neanderthal and Ainu rituals, Campbell writes that "no one has yet suggested that the Ainus are their descendants; nor the Gilyaks, Goldi, peoples of Kamchatka, Ostyaks, Vogul, Orotchi of the Amur river, Lapps, or Finns. All who have written on the subject express amazement; and yet the facts remain."

The Ainu and the fairies bear strong physical resemblances to each other;

both perpetuated bear–Wild Man rituals that blessed their land and people; both had an exalted past and knowledge far beyond their conquerors'. This doesn't "prove" the Ainu are the last of the fairies; at the least, however, it does show the fate of a similar people, a race who lived in a seeming paradise, then lost that world.

Today fairyland and Elfheim have vanished. At Christmas, however, a jolly old elf still comes to visit, bringing the last vestiges of a magic more ancient than any civilization.

Bibliography

Abrahams, Roger, and Bauman, Richard. "Ranges of Festival Behavior." In Barbara Babcock, ed., *The Reversible World: Symbolic Inversion in Art and Society*. Ithaca: Cornell University Press, 1978.

Åkerhielm, Helge *Swedish Christmas*. New York: Holt.

Alford, Violet. "Carnival at Binche." *Folklore* 66 (1955).

____. "The Hobby Horse and Other Animal Masks." *Folklore* 79 (Summer 1968).

____. "Some Other Hobby Horses." *Folklore* 78 (Autumn 1967).

____. "Springtime Bear in the Pyrenees." *Folklore* 66 (1955).

Anwyl, Edward. *Celtic Religion in Pre-Christian Times*. London: Constable, 1906.

Arent, A. Margaret. "The Heroic Pattern: Old Germanic Helmets, Beowulf and Grettis Saga." In *Old Norse Literature and Mythology, a Symposium*. Austin: University of Texas Press.

Armstrong, Lucille. "The Carnival at Basel, Switzerland, Spring 1981." *Folklore* 95 (1984).

Ashton, John. *Chap-Books of the Eighteenth Century*. 1882. Reprint, New York: Kelley, 1970.

____. *A Righte Merrie Christmasse!! The Story of Christ-tide*. N.d. Reprint, New York: Blom, 1968.

Austrian Federal Press Service. *Folk Customs*. Vienna: Federal Press Service, 1993.

Balter, Michael S. "New Look at Neolithic Sites Reveals Complex Societies." *Science* 272 (8 October 1993).

Banks, Mrs. M. MacLeod. *British Calendar Customs: Scotland*. Glasgow University Press, 1941.

Barnett, James H. *The American Christmas*. New York: Macmillan, 1954.

Barnouw, Adriaan J. *The Dutch*. New York: Columbia University, 1940.

Barth, Edna. *Holly, Reindeer and Colored Lights*. New York: Seabury, 1971.

Batchelor, Rev. John. *The Ainu and Their Folklore*. London: Religious Tract Society, 1901.

____. *The Ainu of Japan: The Religion, Superstitions, and General History of the Hairy Aborigines of Japan*. London: Religious Tract Society, 1892.

____. *Ainu Life and Lore*. Tokyo: Kyobunkwan, 1927.

Bayley, Harold. *Archaic England: An Essay in Deciphering Prehistory from Megalithic*

Monuments, Earthworks, Customs, Coins, Place-Names, and Faerie Superstitions. London: Chapman and Hall, 1920.

Bazielichowna, Barbara. "Further Notes on Polish Dancers." *Folklore* 69 (1958).

Beaumont, Cyril W. *The History of Harlequin.* 1926. Reprint, New York: Benjamin Blom, 1967.

Beck, Jane C. "The White Lady of Great Britain and Ireland." *Folklore* 81 (1970).

Bendix, Regina. *Progress and Nostalgia: Silvesterklausen in Urnäsch, Switzerland.* Folklore and Mythology Studies no. 33 Berkeley and Los Angeles: University of California Press, 1985.

Benet, Sula. *Song, Dance and Customs of Peasant Poland.* London: Dennis Dobson, 1951.

Bernheimer, Richard. *Wild Men in the Middle Ages.* Cambridge: Harvard University Press, 1952.

Billson, Charles J. "The 'Jass' at Thun." *Folklore* 19 (1908).

Briggs, Kathryn M. "The Fairies and the Realms of the Dead." *Folklore* 81 (1970).

____. *The Fairies in Tradition and Literature.* London: Routledge and Kegan Paul, 1967.

____. *The Personnel of Fairyland.* Oxford: Alden, 1953.

Brody, Alan. *The English Mummers and Their Plays: Traces of Ancient Mystery.* Philadelphia: University of Pennsylvania Press, 1969.

Brown, James William. *Blood Dance.* New York: Harcourt Brace Jovanovich, 1993.

Brown, Philip. "Black Luck." *Folklore* 71 (1960).

Burke, Peter. *Popular Culture in Early Modern Europe.* Brookfield, Vermont: Ashgate, 1994.

Byron, Frank. "Masks and the Origin of Greek Drama." *Folklore* 27 (1916).

Calhoun, Mary. "Tracking Down Elves in Folklore." *Horn Book* 3 (1969).

Campbell, Joseph. *The Masks of God: Primitive Mythology.* New York: Viking, 1964.

Campbell, R. J. *The Story of Christmas.* Ferris, 1934.

Carr, Andrew T. "Pierrot Grenade." *Caribbean Quarterly* 4 (1955-56).

Carrington, Dorothy, and Grinsell, Leslie. "The Folklore of Some Archaeological Sites in Corsica." *Folklore* 93 (1982).

Cawte, Edwin Christopher. *Ritual Animal Disguise: A Historical and Geographical Study of Animal Disguise in the British Isles.* England: Brewer, 1978.

Chambers, E. K. *The English Folk Play.* 1933. Reprint, New York: Russell and Russell, 1964.

____. *The Mediaeval Stage.* Vol. 1. Oxford University Press, 1903.

Charlip, Remy, and Supree, Burton. *Harlequin and the Gift of Many Colors.* New York: Parents' Magazine Press, 1973.

Coffin, Tristam Potter. *The Illustrated Book of Christmas Folklore.* New York: Seabury, 1973.

Collinder, Björn. *The Lapps.* Princeton, New Jersey: Princeton University Press, 1949.

Count, Earl W. *4000 Years of Christmas.* New York: Schuman, 1948.

Craigie, W. A. *The Religion of Ancient Scandinavia.* London: Constable, 1914.

Crawford, William H. *God Jul!* New York: Oxford University Press, 1955.

Crowley, Daniel J. "The Traditional Masques of Carnival." *Caribbean Quarterly* 4 (1955-56).

Cumont, Franz. *The Mysteries of Mithra.* New York: Dover, 1956.

Cushman, L. W. *The Devil and the Vice in the English Dramatic Literature Before Shakespeare.* 1900. Reprint, London: Cass, 1970.

Dalton, C. F. "Kings Dying on Tuesday – Irish King Killing." *Folklore* 83 (1972).

_____. "The Ritual Killing of Irish Kings." *Folklore* 81 (1970).

Davies, Edward. *The Mythology and Rites of the British Druids Ascertained by National Documents; and Compared with the General Traditions and Customs of Heathenism, as Illustrated by the Most Eminent Antiquaries of Our Age.* London: Barfield, 1809.

Dean-Smith, Margaret. "The Life-Cycle Play or Folk Play: Some Conclusions Following the Examination of the Ordish Papers and Other Sources." *Folklore* 69 (1958).

DeRopp, Robert S. *Sex Energy.* New York: Delacorte, 1969.

De Voragine, Jacobus. *The Golden Legend.* 1483. Translated and adapted from Latin by Granger Ryan and Helmut Ripperger. New York: Longmans, Green, 1941.

De Vries, Jan. "Contributions to the Study of Othin Especially in His Relation to Agricultural Practices in Modern Popular Lore." *Folklore Fellows Communications* 94 (1931).

Dragomanov, M. P. *Notes on the Slavic Religio-Ethical Legends: The Dualistic Creation of the World.* Translated by Earl W. Count. Bloomington: Indiana University, 1961.

Duce, Frances. "Dissertation on the Ancient English Morris Dance." In *A Lytell Geste of Robin Hode.* London: Longman, Brown, Green and Longmans, 1847.

Duvignaud, Jean. "Festivals: A Sociological Approach." *Cultures* 3 (1976).

Dyer, T. F. *Folklore of Shakespeare.* New York: Dover, 1966.

Edwards, Gillian. *Hobgoblin and Sweet Puck: Fairy Names and Natures.* London: Bles, 1974.

Eichler, Lillian. *Customs of Mankind.* Garden City, New York: Garden City, 1924.

Ellis, Hilda Roderick. *The Road to Hel: A Study of the Dead in Old Norse Literature.* New York: Greenwood, 1968.

Elworthy, Frederick Thomas. *Horns of Honor and Other Studies in the By-Ways of Archaeology.* London: Murray, 1900.

Enäjärvi-Haavio, Elsa. "The Finnish Shrovetide." *Folklore Fellow Communications* 61 (1954).

The Epic of Gilgamesh. Translated and edited by N.K. Sander. London: Cox and Wyman, 1972.

Evans, John D.; Cunliffe, Barry; and Renfrew, Colin, eds. *Antiquity and Man: Essays in Honour of Glyn Daniel.* London: Thames and Hudson, 1981.

Forenbaher, Staso. "Radiocarbon and the Central European Early Bronze Age." *Antiquity* 67 (1993).

Frazer, Sir James George. *The Golden Bough.* New York: Macmillan, 1940.

French, Walter. *Mediaeval Civilization as Illustrated by the Fastnachtspiele of Hans Sachs.* Baltimore: Johns Hopkins, 1925.

Garry, Jane. "The Literary History of the English Morris Dance." *Folklore* 94 (1983).

Gaster, Theodor. *New Year: Its History, Customs and Superstitions.* New York: Abelard-Schuman, 1955.

Geddes, Arthur. "Scots Gaelic Tales of Herding Deer or Reindeer." *Folklore* 52 (1951).

Gibbon, H. N. "The Human-Fairy Marriage." *Folklore* 66 (1955).

Gmelch, Sharon Bohn. "Puckish Pleasures: Old Customs Survive at Irish Town Fair." *Kansas City Star,* 13 March 1988.

Goonatilleka, M. H. "Mime, Mask and Satire in Kolam of Ceylon." *Folklore* 81 (1970).

Grimm, Jacob. *Teutonic Mythology.* 4 vols. Translated from 4th ed. New York: Dover, 1966.

Gutch, John Mathew. "Dissertation Upon the Morris Dance and Maid Marian." In *A Lytell Geste of Robin Hode.* London: Longman, Brown, Green and Longmans, 1847.

Gyory, Jean. "The Folklore of Belgium: Feasts and Carnivals of a People." *Culture* 3 (1976).

Hall, Frederic T. *The Pedigree of the Devil.* London: Trübner, 1883.

Hallowell, A. Irving. "Bear Ceremonialism in the Northern Hemisphere." *American Anthropologist,* 1926.

Halpert, Herbert, and Story, G. M. *Christmas Mumming in Newfoundland.* Toronto: University of Toronto Press, 1969.

Háppe, P. "The Vice and the Folk-Drama." *Folklore* 75 (1964).

Harrison, Michael. *The Roots of Witchcraft.* Secaucus, New Jersey: Citadel, 1974.

_____. *The Story of Christmas: Its Growth and Development from the Earliest Times.* London: Odhams, n.d.

Heaney, Michael. "Kingston to Kenilworth: Early Plebian Morris." *Folklore* 93 (1989).

Helm, Alex. "In Comes, I St. George." *Folklore* 76 (1965).

Henderson, Yorke; Miller, Lenore; Gaden, Eileen; and Freed, Arnold. *Christmas Holiday Book.* New York: Parents' Magazine Press, 1972.

Hervey, Thomas K. *The Book of Christmas.* London: Warne, 1888.

Hilger, M. Inez. *Together with the Ainu: A Vanishing People.* Norman: University of Oklahoma Press, 1971.

Hill, Errol. *The Trinidad Carnival: Mandate for a National Theatre.* Austin: University of Texas Press, 1976.

"Historical Argument on the Origin of the Irish Gold Antiquities." *Ulster Journal of Archaeology* 8 (1860).

Hole, Christina. "Winter Bonfires." *Folklore* 71 (1960).

Hone, William, *Ancient Mysteries Described.* Croydon, England: New Temple, 1823.

_____. *The Every-Day Book, or a Guide to the Year.* London: Hunt and Clarke, 1827.

Hough, P. M. *Dutch Life in Town and Country.* New York: Putnam, 1901.

Irving, Washington. *Knickerbocker's History of New York.* Garden City, New York: Doubleday, Doran, 1930.

_____. *Old Christmas and Bracebridge Hall.* Boston and New York: Houghton Mifflin, 1919.

James, E. O. *Seasonal Feasts and Festivals.* New York: Barnes and Noble, 1961.

_____. *The Worship of the Sky God.* University of London: Athlone, 1963.

Janvier, Thomas A. *Christmas Kalends of Provence.* New York: Harper and Brothers, 1902.

Jones, Charles W. "Knickerbocker Santa Claus." *New York Historical Society Quarterly,* October 1954.

Judge, Roy. "May Day and Merrie England." *Folklore* 102 (1991).
Kainen, Ruth Cole. *America's Christmas Heritage.* Funk and Wagnalls, 1969.
Kendrick, T. D. *The Druids: A Study in Keltic Prehistory.* London: Methuen, 1927.
Kightly, Charles. *The Customs and Ceremonies of Britain.* London: Thames and Hudson, 1986.
Kindaiti, Kyosuke. *Ainu Life and Legends.* Japan: Board of Tourist Industry, Japanese Government Railways, 1941.
Knowlson, T. Sharper. *The Origins of Popular Superstitions and Customs.* London: Laurie, 1910. Reprint, Detroit: Gale Research, 1968.
Kott, Jan. *The Eating of the Gods: An Interpretation of Greek Tragedy.* New York: Random House, 1973.
Landland's Vision of Piers the Plowman. Translated by Kate M. Warren. New York: Macmillan, 1894.
Lawrence, Dorothea Dix. "The Mummers' Parade in Philadelphia, Pennsylvania, U.S.A." *Folklore* 66 (1955).
Leach, Robert. "Punch and Judy in Oral Tradition." *Folklore* 94 (1983).
Lewis-Williams, J. D., and Dowson, T. A. "On Vision and Power in the Neolithic: Evidence from the Decorated Monuments." *Current Anthropology* 34 (1993).
Macalister, R. A. S. *Ireland in Pre-Celtic Times.* Dublin and London: Maunsel and Roberts, 1921.
____. *Tara: A Pagan Sanctuary of Ancient Ireland.* London: Scribner, 1931.
MacAloon, John J., ed. *Rite, Drama, Festival, Spectacle: Rehearsals Toward a Theory of Cultural Performance.* Philadelphia: Institute for the Study of Human Issues, 1984.
MacBain, Alexander. *Celtic Mythology and Religion.* New York: Dutton, 1917.
MacCulloch, John Arnott. "Celtic Mythology." In *The Mythology of All Races.* Boston: Marshall Jones, 1918.
____. "Eddic Mythology." In *The Mythology of All Races.* Boston: Marshall Jones, 1918.
Machal, Jan. "Slavic Mythology." In *The Mythology of All Races.* Boston: Marshall Jones, 1918.
McKnight, George H. *St. Nicholas.* New York: Knickerbocker, 1917.
MacNamara, Nottidge Charles. *Origin and Character of the British People.* London: Elder, 1900.
"The Mad Pranks and Merry Jests of Robin Goodfellow." Printed in *Early English Poetry, Ballads and Popular Literature of the Middle Ages*, Vol. 2. London: Richards, 1841.
Madden, David. *Harlequin's Stick, Charlie's Cane: A Comparative Study of Commedia Del'Arte and Silent Slapstick Comedy.* Bowling Green, Ohio: Bowling Green University Press, 1975.
Maple, Eric. *The Domain of Devils.* New York: Barnes, 1966.
Meaney, A. L. "Woden in England: A Reconsideration of the Evidence." *Folklore* 77 (1966).
Miles, Clement A. *Christmas in Ritual and Tradition: Christian and Pagan.* 1912. Reprint, Detroit: Gale Research, 1968.
Miller, Katherine. *Saint George: A Christmas Mummers' Play.* Boston: Houghton Mifflin, 1967.

Monsarrat, Ann. "The Stone Age Temples of Malta." *Unesco Courier* 47 (January 1994).
Monter, William. *Ritual, Myth and Magic in Early Modern Europe.* Athens: Ohio University Press, 1983.
Morgan, Gareth. "Mummers and Momoeri." *Folklore* 100 (1989).
Motz, Lotte. "The Craftsman in the Mound." *Folklore* 88 (1977).
____. "Giants in Folklore and Mythology: A New Approach." *Folklore* 93 (1982).
Murray, Margaret A. *The God of the Witches.* New York: Oxford University Press, 1952.
____. *The Witch-cult in Western Europe.* Oxford: Clarendon, 1962.
Nagy, Joseph Falaky. "The Paradoxes of Robin Hood." *Folklore* 91(1980).
Nicoll, Allardyce. *The World of Harlequin: A Critical Study of the Commedia dell' Arte.* Cambridge University Press, 1963.
Paine, Albert Bigelow. *Thomas Nast: His Period and His Pictures.* New York: Blom, 1971.
Patterson, Lillie. *Christmas in Britain and Scandinavia.* Champaign, Illinois: Garrard, 1970.
Piggott. "'Vast Perennial Memorials': The First Antiquaries Look at Megaliths." In John D. Evans, et al., eds., *Antiquity and Man.* London: Thames and Hudson, 1981.
Procope, Bruce. "The Dragon Band or Devil Band." *Caribbean Quarterly* 4 (1955-56).
Proctor, Richard A. *Myths and Marvels of Astronomy.* London: Longmans, Green, 1889.
Rademacher, C. "Carnival." In *Encyclopaedia of Religion and Ethics*, Vol. 3. New York: Scribner, 1910.
Renfrew, Colin. "Ancient Europe Is Older Than We Thought." *National Geographic* 152 (November 1977).
____. *Approaches to Social Archaeology.* Edinburgh: Edinburgh University Press, 1984.
____. *Before Civilization: The Radiocarbon Revolution and Prehistoric Europe.* New York: Knopf, 1973.
____. "Carbon 14 and the Prehistory of Europe." *Scientific American* 224 (October 1971).
____. "What's New in Archaeology?" *Unesco Courier* 38 (July 1985).
Robertson, Margaret. "The Symbolism of Christmas Mummering in Newfoundland." *Folklore* 93 (1982).
Robinson, Herbert Spencer, and Wilson, Knox. *Myths and Legends of All Nations.* New York: Doubleday, 1960.
Rodgers, Edith Cooperrider. *Discussion of Holidays in the Later Middle Ages.* New York: Columbia University Press, 1940.
Rolleston, T. W. *Myths and Legends of the Celtic Race.* London: Harrap, 1917.
Ross, Keith L. *The Devil in 16th Century German Literature: The Teufelsbücher.* Berne: Lang Druck, 1972
Rudwin, Maximilian. *The Devil in Legend and Literature.* Chicago: Open Court, 1931.
____. *The Origin of German Carnival Comedy.* New York: Stechert, 1920.

Rugg-Gunn, Jane A. "Straw Bear." *Folklore* 42 (1931).
Rukhadze, Juliet, and Chitaya, Georgi. "Festivals and Tradition in the Georgian Soviet Socialist Republic." *Culture* 3 (1976).
Russ, Jennifer M. *German Festivals and Customs.* London: Wolff, 1982.
Russell, Jeffrey B. *Witchcraft in the Middle Ages.* Ithaca: Cornell University Press, 1972.
St. Hill, Thomas Nast. *Thomas Nast's Christmas Drawings for the Human Race.* New York: Harper and Row, 1971.
Saintine, X. B. *The Myths of the Rhine.* Rutland, Vermont: Tuttle, 1875.
Sansom, William. *A Book of Christmas.* New York: McGraw-Hill, 1968.
Senn, Harry. "Romanian Werewolves: Seasons, Ritual, Cycles." *Folklore* 93 (1982).
Severniak, Serafim. "Bulgarian Festivals, Old and New." *Culture* 3 (1976).
Shinichiro, Takakura, "The Ainu of Northern Japan: A Study in Conquest and Acculturation." Trans. by John A. Harrison. *Transactions of the American Philosophical Society* 50 (1960).
Shoemaker, Alfred. *Christmas in Pennsylvania: A Folk-Cultural Study.* Kutztown: Pennsylvania Folklore Society, 1959.
Simpson, Jacqueline. *European Mythology.* New York: Bedrick, 1987.
_____. "Some Scandinavian Sacrifices." *Folklore* 78 (1967).
Singleton, Esther. *Dutch New York.* 1909. Reprint, New York: Blom, 1968.
The Song of Roland. Trans. by Dorothy L. Sayers. London: Whitefriars, 1957.
Spence, Lewis. *The Mysteries of Britain.* Caxton Hill, Hertford, England: Austin, 1928.
Story, G. M. "Mumming and Janneying: Some Explanatory Notes." In *Christmas Mumming in Newfoundland.* University of Toronto Press, 1969.
Sumberg, Samuel L. *The Nuremberg Schembart Carnival.* Columbia University Germanic Studies no 22. New York: Columbia University Press, 1941.
Täuber, Conrad. "Fastnacht in the Black Forest." *Journal of American Folklore* 46 (1933).
Thompson, R. Lowe. *The History of the Devil: The Horned God of the West.* London: Kegan Paul, Trench, Trubner, 1929.
Thonger, Richard. *A Calendar of German Customs.* London: Wolff, 1966.
Tiddy, R. J. E. *The Mummers Plays.* Oxford: Clarendon, 1923.
Tille, Alexander. *Yule and Christmas: Their Place in the Germanic Year.* London: Nutt, 1899.
Tindall, Gillian. *A Handbook on Witches.* New York: Atheneum, 1969.
Tokofsky, Peter Ian. "The Rules of Fools: Carnival in Southwest Germany." Ph.D dissertation, University of Pennsylvania, 1992. Ann Arbor: UMI Dissertation Services.
Turi, Johan. *Turi's Book of Lapland.* Oosterhout N.B. The Netherlands: Anthropological Publications, 1966.
Turville-Petre, E. O. G. *Myth and Religion of the North: The Religion of Ancient Scandinavia.* New York: Holt, Rinehart and Winston, 1964.
Vorren, Ornulv, and Manker, Ernst. *Lapp Life and Customs.* London: Oxford University Press, 1962.
Wace, A. J. B. "North Greek Festivals and the Worship of Dionysos." *The Annual of the British School at Athens* 16 (1909-1910).

Bibliography

Walsh, William Shepard. *The Story of Santa Klaus: Told for Children of All Ages from Six to Sixty.* New York: Moffat, Yard and Company, 1909. Reprint, Detroit: Gale Research Company, 1970.

Warner, Lisa. "The Quack Doctor in the Russian Folk and Popular Theatre." *Folklore* 93 (1982).

____. "The Russian Folk Play 'Tsar Maximillian': An Examination of Some Possible Origins and Sources." *Folklore* 82 (1971).

Warren, Kate M., trans. *Langland's Vision of Piers the Plowman.* New York: Macmillan, 1894.

Weidkuhn, Peter. "Carnival in Basle: Playing History in Reverse." *Cultures* 3 (1976).

Welch, Charles E. "The Philadelphia Mummers Parade: A Study in History, Folklore, and Popular Tradition." Ph.D. dissertation, University of Pennsylvania, 1968.

Welsford, Enid. *The Court Masque: A Study in the Relationship Between Poetry and the Revels.* Cambridge University Press, 1927.

____. *The Fool: His Social and Literary History.* London: Faber and Faber, 1935.

West, Henry Litchfield. "Who Wrote ''Twas the Night Before Christmas'?" *Bookman* 52 (1920-21).

Widdowson, J. D. A., and Halpert, Herbert. "The Disguises of Newfoundland Mummers." *Christmas Mumming in Newfoundland.* University of Toronto Press, 1969.

Willeford, William. *The Fool and His Scepter: A Study in Clowns and Jesters and Their Audience.* London: Arnold, 1969.

Winnington-Ingram, Reginald P. *Euripides and Dionysus: An Interpretation of the Bacchae.* Amsterdam: Hakkert, 1969.

Withington, Robert. *English Pageantry: An Historical Outline.* 2 vols. Cambridge, Massachusetts: Harvard University Press, 1918.

Index